Aileen – A Pioneering Archaeologist

Aileen
A Pioneering Archaeologist

Aileen Fox

Gracewing
2 Southern Avenue
Leominster
Herefordshire HR6 0QF

ISBN 0 85244 523 7

Typesetting by
Shapebusy Ltd, Dunns, Cheriton Fitzpaine, Crediton, EX17 4JE

Additional Typesetting by
Action Publishing Technology Ltd, Gloucester, GL1 1SP

Printed in England by
Cromwell Press, Trowbridge, BA14 0XB

Contents

'To see life steadily and see it whole'
Matthew Arnold

Acknowledgements

The main body of the autobiography was written after my return to Exeter from New Zealand in 1983 and has recently been brought up to date. I would like to thank all those people who expressed their interest and encouraged me to publish it.

My special thanks to Audrey Erskine for her original assessment and favourable comments: to Sue Rouillard for producing the maps: to Judi Brill for skilfully turning my typescript into the format for this book: and to my son, George, for helpful criticism and advice and for patiently over-seeing the project.

I would also like to thank the *Western Mail & Echo* for their permission to use the photograph on page 10 of the plate section, and Exeter City Museums for their permission to use the second photograph on page 13 and both photographs on page 14 of the plate section.

Front cover: Aileen at work examining the newly-discovered section of Exeter's Roman wall at Southgate, South Street, Exeter in 1964, reproduced with the permission of the *Express & Echo*.

Back cover: Family group portrait by Alan Sorrell (cf. p. 109).

Foreword

I'm delighted to provide a foreword to Aileen Fox's book, though I feel my credentials for the task are slight. I first met Aileen in the summer of 1966 when she served as a highly perceptive and acute external examiner in archaeology at Nottingham University. I could not then know that thirteen years later I would take over the sub-department at Exeter which she had developed and peopled with such distinction in the face of a fair degree of opposition and even a measure of *odium academicum* over the previous twenty years. Happily, these obstacles were surmounted and archaeology at Exeter was able to weather the severe storms of the 1980s which swept away several university departments and weakened others. When Aileen returned to Exeter after a decade of astonishingly fruitful work in New Zealand, it was a particular pleasure to welcome her back and to do what was possible to further her work, which was to continue until her ninetieth year.

Aileen's book is many things. It is, of course, a personal memoir, but it is much more than that. It chronicles a fascinating and formative period of archaeology in Britain, from exigent, hand-to-mouth days in the 'twenties to the brief period of affluence in the 1960s and early 1970s and onward to the splintered and fractious days in which we now operate. Aileen's career thus coincided with the huge rise in archaeological activity between 1930 and 1970, and her own involvement naturally brought her into close contact with the great figures of that epoch: Wheeler, Piggott, Daniel, Richmond and a whole cadre of others. Of course, her highly successful marriage and academic partnership with Cyril Fox is set out here as never before. Her memoir also offers fascinating light on British social history in the middle to late decades of the twentieth century, as observed by one of the very few women who held senior posts in British universities at the time - a fact now too easily forgotten. Throughout the volume there shine Aileen Fox's passionate enthusiasm for the past and its place in the present, her social conscience and, above all, her innate humanity. In all this, her book will enlighten and enthral all who read it.

Malcolm Todd
Durham, April 2000

Chapter One

A London Childhood

1907 – 1918

I was born in London at 12 Kensington Square on 29 July 1907, the anniversary of my parents' wedding day and, by a strange coincidence, the birthday of Charles, my eldest son. My mother was a diminutive woman, and I was told it was a prolonged labour and a difficult birth. Whilst the doctor and maternity nurse were attending to the patient, the baby was revived only by a visiting Swiss midwife called Fristed, who had been detained on another case and so unable to attend my mother.

The house still stands at the south-east corner of the Square, then untouched by commercial buildings; it is a pleasant, small late seventeenth- and eighteenth-century brick construction with long sash windows and a doorway with a curved shell hood. I remember nothing of its interior since we left it before I was three, but I can remember running round the paths and on the grass plot in the garden of the Square to which we had a key.

My father, Walter Scott Henderson, was an able young solicitor, who had joined the firm of Stephenson Harwood in Lombard Street as an articled pupil in 1898 and became a partner in 1901, after completing his LLB externally at London University. As a child he had had an attack of poliomyelitis which left him with a wasted leg and one foot smaller than the other, but he never allowed this to prevent activity. He was the second son in a family of six, four boys and two girls, children of Dr Edward Henderson, a Lowland Scot. Walter was born in Shanghai in 1871, where my grandfather was surgeon at the General Hospital, the first Medical Officer of Health from 1869 until 1898, and a family doctor to the English colony. He had a house in Bubbling Well Road, at the west end of the English concession, which was described in 1900 as, 'a poplar-lined avenue, with handsome mansions with porticos and verandahs in the colonial style'.[1]

Shanghai in many respects was still a primitive place in the 1870s, with a lack of sanitation and a proper water supply, and the prevalence of infectious diseases including outbreaks of cholera, typhoid and smallpox. The settlement was growing rapidly and was still in the process of formation; the law courts, hospitals, prison, churches and the racecourse were all being built. It was hardly a place to bring up young children and the Hendersons, like many others, sent their children back to England for their education to avoid the risks of disease and the debilitating effects of the hot weather in southern China. My father went to Cheltenham, one of the smaller public schools, whereas his older brother, Edward, was at Charterhouse. I do not know why the boys were separated or who looked after them in the school holidays; my father never talked about his early days and I foolishly never asked him. All the boys did well in their professions. Edward went on to Cambridge and became a Fellow of the Royal College of Surgeons and an eye surgeon at the East London Hospital, Jack went into the army, a captain in the 27th Light Cavalry, and Charles, the youngest, known to us as 'Uncle Bear', joined the Indian Civil Service having taken a First in Greats at Oxford. Mary, the elder girl and my father's favourite sister, trained as a nurse at St Bartholomew's Hospital despite her parents' misgivings; she caught scarlet fever, at that time a serious disease, and died in 1908. The younger, Clara, remained at home looking after her parents in London; the Hendersons had left Shanghai in about 1901.

At the time of my parents' marriage in 1905 the Hendersons were living at 37 Onslow Gardens in South Kensington, moving to 49 Barkston Gardens in 1910, with a final move to Lexham Gardens after my grandfather's death in 1913. I well remember our Sunday afternoon visits to Granny Henderson and Aunt Clara: these were rather a trial. There was a parrot in a cage, a bad-tempered Pekinese in a basket, and much that 'you mustn't touch' in the drawing-room, and really nothing or nobody to play with. On occasions I was taken for a drive in Hyde Park; the carriage was probably hired since I don't remember any talk of horses, stables or coachman. I sat on the little seat, dressed in my best, facing Granny, Aunt Clara and my mother and unable to see much else; again, not much of an entertainment for an active child.

There was much more fun among my mother's relations, and indeed the McLean family was a dominant factor in our life. Like the Hendersons, there was a Shanghai connection: my grandfather, David McLean, had been the first manager in Shanghai of the newly-founded Hong Kong and Shanghai Bank, living in the colony from 1865 to 1873. He and the head accountant had rooms over the bank, which was in an old house on the Bund, to which a third storey was later added. Servants, heat and light were paid for by the bank. Although offered the post of Chief Manager in

Hong Kong in 1870, he preferred to remain in Shanghai, then rapidly developing as a business centre. He left in 1873 and became manager of the London branch of the bank, then housed in Lombard Street, which post he held until March 1889 but continued to serve on the Bank's London Committee. He was an able and successful businessman, interested in financing small concerns, buying shares on his own account as well as working for the bank. His most successful venture was backing a Mr Lamson, who had invented the Paragon overhead rail system widely used in shops. The shop assistant put the bill and the customer's money in a container shaped like a pepper grinder with a screwed-on lid, clipped this into a little hanging cage, pulled a cord and with a ping it travelled along the overhead wires to a central cash desk: the customer's change and receipt came back the same way. The system was eventually replaced by Lamson's pneumatic tubes which have only recently been superseded by the video screen and computer. This and other shrewd investments made the family fortunes which, skilfully tended by two successive generations of McLeans, have meant that I received a good education and have never had to worry about money. The McLean background ensured that, like all good Scots, I also knew that money had to be looked after, without extravagant spending.

David McLean married in June 1874 Elizabeth Manson, 'Lizzie', from an Aberdeenshire family of Old Meldrum; no doubt this was the reason for his leaving Shanghai the previous year. Her elder brother was Patrick, 'the father of tropical medicine' and the discoverer, with Ross, of the malarial mosquito. Patrick had worked in the Treaty Port of Amoy, South China, studying filariae worms as the cause of elephantiasis from 1871 onwards,[2] and this circumstance may have been the source of the family connection with Henderson in Shanghai. A consequence of marrying into an Aberdeenshire family was my grandfather's decision in 1884 to rent from the Forbes estate a small shooting lodge called Littlewood Park near Alford, with some farmland, grouse moors and three or four miles of fishing in the river Don. He was a keen sportsman and he and all the family, two boys, Alan and Colin, and two girls, Alice and Isabel, became very attached to the place. I was taken there with my mother Alice in 1907 when I was four weeks old, and we spent some two months there each summer as part of a family gathering of uncles, aunts and cousins, presided over by my grandmother after grandfather's death in 1908.

Whether McLean the bank manager was acquainted in the 1870s with Henderson the doctor in Shanghai, I do not know, though it seems likely. There is another possible reason for my parents' romance. Walter was articled to the firm of Stephenson Harwood 'a few years before 1900'. The founder of the firm, William Harwood, had practised in Shanghai from 1867 to 1875, at a time when both McLean and Henderson were there, before forming a partnership with H. G. Stephenson in London in 1877. 'He brought with him a large and important eastern connection, of which the Hong Kong and Shanghai Banking Corporation was one and which still exists to this day.'[3] It is therefore understandable that a solicitor son of Dr Henderson should choose to join this firm, and that in his professional capacity he should be acquainted with the bank's affairs and with David McLean, who had only recently retired as London manager amidst general acclaim.[4] Presumably Walter was invited to the McLean's home, Comrie, at Epping or to their flat at 5 Kensington Court where he met Alice. They were married in some style at St Mary Abbots Church in Kensington on 29 July 1905 with bells pealing, and their friends as ushers, 'distinguished by buttonholes of white heather'. There are photographs in gilt frames of the bride and her younger sister, Isabel, the chief bridesmaid, both in white gowns of incredible elaborateness, clasping their bouquets and looking very attractive. The Aberdeen newspaper recorded that there were over 300 presents, including gifts of large pieces of silver and Sheffield plate from the tenantry and the servants at Littlewood. After a honeymoon on the west coast of Scotland and a visit to Littlewood, they returned to London and the little house in Kensington Square. It was a happy lifelong marriage; my father supplied the brains and the initiative, my mother the social contacts and the artistic taste.

Soon after I was born, my mother engaged a nanny, 'to take the new baby from the month', as was customary in well-to-do middle class circles. I have no idea how she obtained the services of young Edith Adley, perhaps from Mrs Lines' Registry Office in Marylebone which she used frequently in later years. It was a fortunate choice, for Edith not only looked after me and my two sisters, but also nursed my parents in their old age in Surrey, until her death in their house at Walton on the Hill in 1964; my mother survived her for three years. It was a lifetime of dedicated service. Nanny refused ever to take a holiday or a day off, just an occasional Sunday evening to visit her relatives in south-east London. There had been one disastrous occasion when she had gone away for a week and a temporary nurse had been engaged to take her place, but I had cried and played up so much, I was told, that the experiment was never repeated; after that Nanny was always there. In later years it became rather oppressive to be enveloped in so much devoted attention. She had had no formal training in child care but had started as a nursery maid in London. Obviously she was intuitively suited to the life, simple, affectionate, soft-spoken, very kind but firm. There could be no argument about bedtime or putting away the toys. Indoors she wore a long grey woollen or poplin skirt, and a white blouse with a high-necked boned collar, all covered with a white apron. Outdoors there are photos of her wearing a long fitted jacket over a full skirt and the most incredible peaked black bonnet tied with ribbon under her chin. I remember also a series of black straw hats trimmed with ribbon rosettes which she wore in the summer.

Before I was three, we had moved from Kensington Square to Cottesmore Gardens nearby, where we lived from 1910 to 1919 in rented houses, as was customary, first in No. 18, where my sister Sheila was born, and then moving to No. 14 early in 1914 before my youngest sister, Mari, was born. Cottesmore Gardens was, and still is, one of several quiet streets branching off Victoria Road, within an easy walk of Kensington Gardens as well as the shops in Kensington High Street.

It was an attractive neighbourhood, with a preponderance of small stucco Victorian houses in the late classical style. In our street, the houses were built in terraced blocks, three or four storeys high, each with a flight of steps up to the front door, and a flight down to the back door in the basement. Each had its round coal-hole with a patterned iron slab cover in the pavement, through which the sacks from the horse-drawn cart were emptied into a cellar, with a loud rustling sound and a puff of black shiny coal dust. No. 18 was different in appearance from the other houses, being an architect's design in the modern style of Norman Shaw, with brick detailing round the lower windows and to the roof parapet.

It was a narrow house, with only two rooms on each floor, opening on to a spacious landing and stairs. The nurseries were on the third floor; the four servants slept in the attic bedrooms above, shut off by a gate to prevent children climbing the steep stair. There was a lift on the landing to haul up food from the basement kitchen and coal for the nursery fires. The lino-covered landing was a splendid place to run about on a wet day. The two windows in the day nursery looked out on the rows of back gardens and the tall spire of the church in Eldon Road. A rocking-horse stood between the windows, our doll's house was on the opposite wall beside a deep walk-in toy cupboard and at the far side was the table at which we took our meals and the open fireplace enclosed by a brass railed fireguard. There was a speaking tube in the wall, with a bell connected to the kitchen which Cook rang to say that the lift was on its way up with the hot lunch. I remember being put to dry my long auburn hair hanging in a damp fringe over my face and poking my small fingers through the hot diagonal mesh of the fireguard. Nanny washed my hair in the bath and curled it in rags each night, as well as brushing it; indeed, I never effectively brushed my hair myself until I went away to school at Tadworth in 1918.

My parents' bedroom and dressing-room was on the second floor below, a spare room and a billiard room on the first floor, and on the ground floor the dining-room facing the street and a drawing-room with a bow window opening on to a double flight of steps to the small back garden. I can still visualise the whole house and could place all the furniture in it. The garden was only a small patch of grass surrounded by a brick-edged path and a shrubbery and some tall lime trees at the end under which a patch of lily of the valley surprisingly thrived. Nevertheless there was space enough to play, to push my doll's pram or a wooden horse, and even for a birthday tea party in July when Cook made a large iced cake with a filling of fresh raspberries at my special request. We rarely went into the kitchen, which was approached by a dark backstairs from the pantry beside the dining-room, shut off by a green baize door. My mother went down each morning to give 'the orders', to arrange the menus, and to give out supplies from a locked store cupboard. I only went with her occasionally to thank Cook for making the birthday or party cake, or to stir the Christmas pudding and put in the little silver threepenny bits. I never saw cooking in action or learnt unconsciously how to set about preparing and dishing up a meal, which was a great handicap in later years. I still lack confidence in cooking anything except my own simple meals, even though my efforts usually turn out all right.

Although my father was then only a junior partner in Stephenson Harwood, the Hendersons kept four servants, a cook, a parlourmaid, a housemaid and a between-maid as well as Nanny. It was a well-ordered household and a well-ordered childhood with a regular routine. We were always expected to be clean, well-groomed and well-dressed. Nanny not only bathed us and brushed our hair, but made practically all our clothes, even to winter top coats, and party dresses. We were taken to Hayford's in Sloane Street for jerseys, gloves and gaiters and to Daniel Neal's in Kensington High Street for shoes. It was my misfortune to have a foot that turned in as I ran and the remedy for this was boots, brown leather boots which did up with buttons or laces. These took an eternity to fasten, so I was always the last leaving the cloakroom when it came to school days.

Unvaryingly, winter and summer, we went to Kensington Gardens, Nanny pushing a heavy two-seater pram up 'the hill', a gentle slope in reality, at the top of Victoria Road, then across the main road with the occasional open double-decker bus, taxis and horse-drawn carts, and into the gardens at the Broad Walk Gate, where the old lady sat who sold balloons and paper windmills. Usually we went along the Flower Walk and turned left to an open space bordered with an avenue of horse-chestnut trees known as 'The Plot'; here on warm days all the nannies congregated, bringing camp stools to sit on beside the prams, whilst the bigger children played nearby.

The nannies became acquainted as a reflection of their employers, after whom they were named, so Nanny Henderson and Nanny Burge, also from Cottesmore Gardens, sat and hob-nobbed, whilst Aileen and Sheila played with Nancy, Hugh and Tubby. We preferred 'pretend games', centred on special trees with fantastic roots, in which imaginary little people lived, to ball games like rounders or cricket which needed a grown-up to organise. Some children had scooters, but our mother did not approve of these, saying they were bad for posture and dangerous in the streets, which was a great disappointment. We had to cadge rides from other children, but these were never satisfying and only whetted the desire for more of those rapid flights, propelled by one foot. Similarly, we were not allowed to have iron hoops, which made a splendid noise when bowled with a metal hooked stick. The hook was designed to catch the hoop if it lurched over or went too fast. These were also said to be dangerous, and we had to be content with bentwood hoops which never ran well. On colder days we played on the elaborate stone pavement around the Albert Memorial, treading only on the squares of one particular colour, or running and balancing on the granite kerb, as well as a type of 'hide and seek' around the corners below the monumental groups of statuary symbolic of the four continents – Europe, Asia, Africa and America.

We went for longer walks in the winter, across to Lancaster Gate past the Achilles statue at its focal point of the radiating avenues, or down to the Serpentine to feed the ducks and to play 'dodge' around the statue of Peter Pan when the uniformed park keeper was not looking, as well as stroking the bronze rabbits at the base of the statue. Other days Nanny might take us up 'the hill' in the Broad Walk, to see the toy boats sailing in the Round Pond, or to run by ourselves round the pleached alley surrounding the sunken Dutch garden beside Kensington Palace, whilst she waited with the pram for us to emerge at the other end of the leafy tunnel.

Shopping was limited to the groups of small shops nearby in St Alban's Road and Gloucester Road. Our favourite was Turners on the corner, which was a post office and newsagent but had a sweet counter as well as selling children's comics and the cheap paperbacks of Stead's *Books for the Bairns*. That was where we spent our pocket money and collected our favourite monthly magazine called *Little Folks*, a rather pious semi-educational production, as well as the weekly *Rainbow* with its crude coloured pictures and the endless saga of Mrs Bruin, a mother bear who kept a school for Tiger Tim and other unruly animal boys. Nanny subscribed to *Weldon's*, a magazine with paper patterns for children's clothes, and drawings of all the latest fashions. Frequently we went to Sharp Gatts, a drapery and haberdashery in Gloucester Road with its windows solid with rows of items priced at 1s. 11¾d. – nearly ten pence, to give the illusion of cheapness. Nanny bought sewing cottons and some material there. The rolls of cloth were lifted down from the shelves behind the long wooden counters by the assistant, were carefully fingered and taken to the light to check the colour, and then, if approved, were measured out against a brass yard strip at the inner edge of the counter. A summer straw hat was once bought for me there: I remember being allowed to choose a wreath of tiny artificial flowers and feathery grass to trim it.

Occasionally in December an expedition was made by No. 46 bus to South Kensington to visit Porter's, which was a proper toy shop: it had a wonderful counter with small toys priced at a penny, twopence, threepence or sixpence, as well as big expensive toys such as dolls or woolly animals on the shelves above, which we eyed and made a wish that they would be ours at Christmas. We rarely went to the big shops in Kensington High Street – Barkers, Derry and Toms, Pontings – though our meat and groceries came from Barkers' food hall; I remember the delicious smells there, when I accompanied my mother giving her written orders for delivery. This must have been in the store rebuilt after the great fire on the night of 2 November 1912, when part of Barkers was burnt down. Nanny regaled me with horror stories of the wretched shop assistants trapped in their dormitories over the shop, and of their rescue by firemen on long ladders or by jumping to be caught in safety nets. When we went to see the sights the next day we could not get near, as Young Street was roped off above the post office, and was still full of fire engines. It left me with a horror of fire, much in evidence later on at a children's birthday party, where a flickery comic film was projected on to an inadequate fabric screen in a dark room, full of small children and accompanying nannies. To me the picture was absolutely real despite its obvious shortcomings. The culminating point of the story was an outbreak of fire, when the hero went to summon the fire brigade, and found the telephone was too hot to handle. Everyone roared with laughter when he tried to pick it up and dropped it, but I burst into tears and had to be removed from the room.

I was not very fond of parties in any case, though they were not always so traumatic: I disliked being washed again and dressed in my best thin frock in the middle of a chilly winter afternoon. We were wrapped in shawls or in our party capes lined with rabbit fur for the taxi ride accompanied by Nanny. Although we probably knew our hosts and their children, most of the guests were strangers, since children's parties were arranged by parents as a social duty. Not even the elaborate tea with jelly and cakes, conjuring tricks or presents from the Christmas tree were compensation for my shyness and boredom. I liked best the singing games with piano accompaniment, such as 'Oranges and Lemons', with a procession of children running round two grown-ups holding hands to form an arch, and catching a child at the end of each verse, who was asked in a whisper which she would be, orange or lemon? Sides were formed by children clinging to their chosen grown-up, and the game ended in a tug-of-war. 'Musical chairs' was also enjoyable, running around a set of little gilded chairs, brought in by the caterer, which were removed one by one when the music stopped and someone had failed to find a seat; the winner, usually a determined little boy, was the sole survivor.

Actually our parents impinged very little on our nursery existence.

Father left each morning for the City where we were told he was 'making pennies for our pocket money' – this he gave us on Saturday on a graduated scale of one penny to a silver sixpence for weekly spending. There was also the occasional largesse of a golden half-sovereign (ten shillings – fifty pence) from an uncle, which had to be hoarded as savings. Daddy left the house wearing a shiny black top hat, jacket and striped trousers, the uniform of a city gentleman in the pre-war era; he caught the tube at Gloucester Road and returned only when I was going to bed.

Sheila and I said good morning to Mother on our way downstairs for our walk to the park or to school, and rarely saw her again until after nursery tea, when we were spruced up and taken to the drawing-room until our six o'clock bedtime. There she would play the piano whilst we danced about, or sang nursery rhymes from the song-book with Kate Greenaway illustrations, joining in with her pretty, tuneful voice. She was certainly musical, but like all Edwardian ladies lived a life of indolence and was something of a hypochondriac in consequence. I never remember her doing anything except watering or arranging the flowers, which she did most beautifully to the end of her life. All the household tasks were left to the servants: I was told in the drawing-room at No. 14 to ring the bell for Lovell, the tall parlourmaid, to come and put some more coal on the fire, or to pull the curtains. Our nursery regime encouraged a similar state of helplessness with Nanny expected to do everything for us; oddly enough, I suspect that whilst acquiescing, it made me long for independence.

There was a certain amount of formal entertaining; there was an 'at home' day when the afternoon was set aside for callers, who left their cards and were offered tea, and whose call had to be returned in due course. Once a year my mother gave a musical party to which I went, when her friends and acquaintances were entertained by a singer such as the young Anemone Balfour or by a pianist such as our cousin, Lilias Mackinnon. There were dinner parties for my father's professional contacts, including his partner Robert Witt, and one splendid occasion when everyone came in fancy dress from Carroll's *Alice in Wonderland* or *Through the Looking Glass*. Mother was the White Queen in a white sateen dress with padded hoop bands, an exact copy of the illustration, which had been made by a dressmaker on the premises. I remember sitting on the stairs at No. 18 in my dressing gown with Nanny, watching them all process into the dining room.

The quietness of the London streets was remarkable; if a taxi was wanted, the parlourmaid went out on the steps and blew the curved horn whistle kept on the hall table. If there was no response, she would walk in her white apron to the end of Cottesmore Gardens, face up Victoria Road and blow again: soon a cab would appear from the rank. From the landing window, standing on the window-seat, I could gaze into the street and listen to the tinny sound of a barrel organ or occasionally a Salvation Army band, and throw down pennies for them to collect. There was also a regular visit from a muffin man, ringing a handbell and carrying muffins and crumpets wrapped in a cloth in a tray on his head. The between-maid might be sent out to buy some for tea, though only Nanny had one because they were said to be indigestible for children. Another caller was a knife-grinder whom I watched sharpening the kitchen knives and Nanny's cutting-out scissors on his grindstone turned by a treadle. On warm sunny days a woman walked up the street calling in a nasal cockney voice, 'Lavender, sweet lavender, who'll buy my blooming lavender? Sixteen branches for one penny, makes your clothes smell nice and sweet'. The silence of the streets was most in evidence when a thick yellow fog came down which prevented us from going out. It smelt awful and at times was so thick that it was impossible to see across the road. The street lights hardly penetrated for more than a few yards and traffic ceased. It was all rather frightening until the next day when the sun eventually appeared as an orange-red ball above the chimney pots.

Illness, though infrequent, was taken seriously: quarantine for infectious diseases, measles, whooping cough, mumps and chickenpox, was strictly enforced, for there were no vaccines except for smallpox. We could not go to school or play with other children for two or three weeks. If we caught the infection, we had to stay in bed, following Nanny's rule that no one could get dressed until their temperature had been normal for twenty-four hours. Because there was no central heating, a fire was lit in the night nursery; it flickered on the ceiling, instead of the usual steady flame of a night-light in its saucer of water. In case of any alarm, my mother would consult the great man, Sir Patrick Manson – Uncle Pat, who though a specialist in tropical medicine was prepared to pronounce on childish ailments.Thanks to Uncle Pat, I was spared the ordeal of the removal of tonsils and adenoids which many of my contemporaries had to undergo.

There were breaks in our London routine at weekends; my father acquired a car before 1914, a Sunbeam Talbot open tourer, and drove us down to Richmond Park or to Hampton Court. Sheila and I were provided with thick dark brown overcoats, fastening with large copper buttons embossed with elephants. I imagine these buttons had been sent as presents from relatives in India, perhaps by Uncle Jack Henderson who certainly had sent a tiger skin and stuffed head with teeth which became a splendid rug and ornamented the drawing-room landing at No. 14. In the car, our hats were tied on with fine motoring veils to guard against the dust and petrol fumes: I remember Sheila being told not to suck the gauze of hers. There was a windscreen, a folding contraption that opened and pulled forward to cover the back seat passengers, Mother, Nanny and the children. It had a waterproof skirt to cover our knees although these were already swathed in rugs. Even so, it seemed to be very blowy. A hired chauffeur sat in front with Father, to be at hand in case of a breakdown or the all-too-frequent punctures to repair.

My father was a keen golfer, proficient despite his wasted leg. He always had to have special boots and shoes made to order but he never made the least fuss about it and was a great walker. At Easter usually he took a short holiday and went to Sandwich for the golf, along with his City friend, Owen Bevan, a stockbroker from the firm of Pember & Boyle. They and their wives stayed at the big Guildford Hotel on the wind-swept sandy coast. Nanny and we two children were boarded with the baker, Mr and Mrs Larkin, in Sandwich itself, a small establishment near the church in a cul-de-sac at the back of the town ramparts. There I could watch the dough being mixed and kneaded in long wooden troughs, the loaves being shaped and then baked in an oven in the wall, and taken out when done on a long-handled wooden shovel. There wasn't a shop: the bread was loaded into a covered cart and driven away for delivery. The smell of new bread is strongly reminiscent of Sandwich for me; little did I think when riding in the baker's trap with Sheila for a treat in 1912, that I should be back there for my first contact with the world of archaeology in 1929.

It was possible to catch a ramshackle small bus to the Guildford Hotel and then spend a day at the seaside, where Mother and Mrs Bevan joined us on the beach, building sand-castles and digging holes for the tide to fill or collecting the pretty coloured shells, which if you were very lucky might include a cowrie. Other days, Nanny took us for walks around the ramparts, to feed the ducks in a small pond, or out along the country road towards Richborough to pick daisies in the meadows. I suppose that even at the tender age of six or seven, I acquired some idea of an encircled town fortification from Sandwich.

We drove to Kent in the car; once on the return we ran into a severe thunderstorm near Rochester which was absolutely terrifying: a sequence of darkness, lightning flashes and cracks and rolls of thunder. We had to take refuge in the cold front parlour of a small inn for what seemed like several hours until the torrential rain abated and we could drive back to London, half asleep. I have disliked thunderstorms ever since.

Our main summer holiday was of course the visit to our grandmother in Aberdeenshire. We left London at the end of July, returning in late September, though Father had to leave at the end of August to return to business. A whole day was devoted by Nanny to packing, ironing our better clothes to be swathed in tissue paper, and collecting our favourite toys, which were stored with boots and shoes at the bottom of a large brown trunk with a domed lid. There was also a 'hold-all', a canvas roll with many pockets fastened by straps, as well as a Japanese wickerwork basket in which our night-clothes and toiletries were packed for the train. My parents had a similar mountain of luggage which included gun cases, shooting sticks, fishing-rods as well as their hat boxes and trunks. There was never any shortage of porters at King's Cross, who pulled the heavy trolleys and loaded the pile into the luggage van. Then there was the excitement of finding the Scott Henderson name on the sleeping-cars and finally being installed by Nanny in our bunks; Sheila and I went 'head to tail'. The rhythm of the train, together with the sight of our clothes swaying from the pegs, soon put me to sleep.

Waking early in the morning, I would wriggle to the window and pull the blind sideways to see out. It was wonderful to see the sea, the rocky coast and the marshland around Montrose, and to hear the musical long-drawn-out call of the Scottish porters from the stations, 'Montro-o-se', or 'Sto-o-nehaven'. There were the stone field-walls, the dykes, so different from the English hedges, and the fresh cool air so different from the London summer heat. After breakfasting in state with our parents at Aberdeen Station Hotel, we caught the slow train to Alford, with its other musically-named stations – Tillyfourie and Monymusk. The branch line has now long been closed. The journey ended with a five-mile drive along the dusty main road up the Don valley, past well-remembered landmarks, the Bridge of Alford with its general store, open stretches of bright water in the river and the outline of the surrounding hills, the rounded summit of Lord Arthur, and the curving back of Caillievar.

Littlewood Park itself then seemed an enchanted place and it still retains its charm for me after more than seventy years. The house was originally built as a shooting box by the landowner, Lord Forbes, and was rented by my grandfather, David McLean, from 1884 onwards. The property was finally bought by my uncle, Alan McLean, in the 1920s and then totally rebuilt in an enlarged but not dissimilar form in the same place in 1929–30. It was used as an officers' hospital in the Second World War and today, despite the comfort of central heating and extra bathrooms, is rather too spacious for modern living.

The house of my childhood was a white twin-gabled affair set about halfway up a gentle valley between two low heather-covered hills, spurs from the higher Lord Arthur. It was surrounded by wide lawns sloping towards the river, broken by magnificent specimen trees, mostly beeches but also a great horse chestnut close to the house.

As a child, I don't suppose I was conscious of the beauty of the scene, the view southwards across the Don valley to the cultivated farmlands rising again to the undulating slopes of Caillievar, with the colours changing as the cloud shadows swept across the face of the hill. There was no formal garden beside the house; nearly a quarter of a mile away up the valley there was a walled garden stuffed with fruit and vegetables with a long herbaceous border and beds of flowers for cutting, rows of sweet peas, patches of mignonette, stocks, sweet williams, and love-in-a-mist. It then seemed an afternoon's expedition to get there, up a stony path, across the burn, over a grass field, and in through the garden gate: now it is a ten-minute walk.

The house was approached from the main road by the Long Avenue, along the sunny hillside from the Alford direction or by the somewhat sinister Short Avenue shaded by trees, from the Huntley direction. There was a ghost story of those in the house hearing the sound of a galloping horse coming up the Short Avenue when the original owner was on his deathbed at Castle Forbes.

My recollections of these summer holidays are inevitably conflated, since I went there every year from 1907 at the age of one month until 1917, and then again at frequent intervals during the 1920s. What stands out in my memory is the gaiety of a house full of relatives who came and went, uncles and aunts, and their friends, coming for the shooting and fishing. It was presided over by my grandmother, a venerable lady, who was much cosseted by her family and her maid, though I suspect there was nothing much wrong with her and like so many ladies of that period she rather enjoyed ill health.

Uncle Alan, her eldest son, was a solid, kilted figure, who managed very successfully all the family business affairs, quite jolly as an uncle and very good for presents at Christmas and birthdays. Uncle Colin was much more lively, full of jokes, and teasing his nieces. Although a good shot he was a keen naturalist and made me aware of the bird life around, the wagtails busy on the lawn or wild duck or a hawk in flight overhead. He also introduced me to fishing: first digging for pink wriggly worms in a compost heap, and putting them in moss in an old tobacco tin, then setting off up the tiny burn above the house and finding out the best places where the run of water slowed and was a little deeper, keeping very quiet after dropping in the baited hook, and then the tug and the excitement of landing a very small trout in my net on the bank. There is a photo of me, aged six, with a catch of seven or eight, standing on the front door step with all my gear looking very pleased with myself. Despite this promising start, I never took to the serious business of salmon or trout fishing in the river, lacking patience and getting too disheartened by my lack of success.

The third member of the family was Isabel – Aunt Bel – a singularly lovely person with long red-gold hair wound around her head, and a transparent complexion. Before she married Captain Eric Hervey she had contracted tuberculosis, for which the only remedy then was rest and fresh air, so she spent most of the days lying out in a revolving wooden summerhouse on the lawn at Littlewood. We were never allowed to kiss her for fear of infection, but were drawn to her to listen to stories or to run her errands which I feel sure she invented.

In Scotland I felt much freer than in London; although we were still in the charge of Nanny, it was much easier to associate with the grown-ups. There was a swing, and uncles to give you a push; there were huge trees to climb, and lots of places to explore on the heather-covered hillsides. A favourite place was an old quarry where granite had been dug when the Long Avenue was made. I remember Nanny sitting there on an old tree trunk with the pram whilst Sheila and I made gardens outlined in stones with fir-cones for trees, and stuck in heather, cranberry, scabious and hare-bells. We also played an elaborate game of 'princesses' each with her 'palace' under a convenient small birch or pine tree, and enacted a long serial story in daily instalments which I invented.

Walks with Nanny were mostly down the Avenues and so on to the main road. I remember the dust cloud from the daily bus, and also the stone-cutter sitting at the roadside wearing glasses and chipping at a heap of granite to reduce it to the right size for patching the pot-holes. This must have been in autumn because I visualise the shabby old man against a background of rose-hips on the briars growing on top of the field walls. We picked the hips into paper bags and then threaded them on black cotton to make long red bead necklaces and bracelets, very suitable as jewellery for the 'princesses'.

Some years there was no room in the house for children during the August shooting season, and we were boarded out with Nanny at Kirkton Farm, on the river, across the main road at the bottom of the Long Avenue. It was worked by the Thompson family: old Mrs Thompson and her daughter Mary, and two sons, Jimmie and Johnnie, both large grown men in their thirties. It was undoubtedly there that I became aware of the rhythms of the farming year, the variety of agricultural practices before mechanisation, and the close relationship between man and animals. All are highly relevant to the understanding of archaeological findings which a child brought up solely in an urban setting would have missed.

We lived in the farmhouse, a granite building with two bay windows, and a small garden in front with colourful flower borders screening the vegetable patches on either side. The farmyard was alongside, an open rectangle framed by the byre, stable, and barn and stores: in the centre there was a heap of muck steaming in the open air. There was a lightly-metalled track down to the river to water the beasts. The cattle were brought into the byre for hand milking, a herd of some ten to twenty brown cows, probably Ayrshires. There was one special cow called Betsy that only old Mrs Thompson could milk. Hens with a magnificent cock, ducks, geese and turkeys wandered about the place. Kirkton Christmas turkeys were famous, but they were still mostly juveniles in August, though there was one great cock who spread his tail and uttered his frightening 'hobble-gobble' cry: we gave him a wide berth. I was curious about the various sizes of eggs and wanted to sample them, so one week Mary Thompson started me with a bantam's egg for breakfast on Monday, proceeded to the usual hen's egg on Tuesday, followed by a duck's egg on Wednesday, a turkey's egg on Thursday and finally a goose's egg; the last was really too much for me and I could manage barely half of it when it came on Friday.

Most of the farm was worked by cart-horses; the hay was cut by a clattering mower with toothed blades, and the oats with a more up-to-date 'reaper and binder' which cut the stems to fall on to a moving belt, collected them, bound them into sheaves and tossed them out from a pronged rotating fork to the ground. The sheaves were then picked up by hand and tilted upright to make a 'stook' of six or eight. We sometimes used to take our tea into the 'stookie field'and have our picnic there. We played at houses too, crawling into the stooks. The hay, and later the corn sheaves, were carted by wagon and built into conical ricks which stood on a base of river cobbles on the south side of the farm buildings. These were thatched with rushes cut from the riverside and secured by a network of twisted rush ropes, pegged down with sharp forked wooden pegs. The ropes were made on the premises: in the barn, the rushes were carefully fed in through a hopper with a string secured to a hook, which was rotated by hand. The operator walked backwards for the length of the barn and then rolled up the coil into a loose ball about the size of a football. I used to walk alongside and sometimes was allowed briefly to make the handle turn. Ploughing took place after we had left in the early autumn, so I never saw the stubble disappear, but I remember a long conversation in broad Aberdeenshire dialect with Jimmie about crop rotation, which was spread over five years – a succession of oats or barley, followed by hay, turnips and then two years fallow.

Back in Kensington, I went to school at the age of over five. Nanny had endeavoured to teach me to read from a horrid little blue book, *Reading Without Tears*, with its tiny woodcuts as illustrations and monosyllabic sentences starting with, 'The cat sat on the mat'. I had no use for this, nor for the copybooks, bought at Turners, with the rows of 'pothooks' and 'hangers' which were designed to form a sloping copperplate hand. Fortunately my mother was persuaded to let me join the Froebel classes organised by Mrs Holland-Martin instead of having a governess. This formidable lady, wife of Robert Holland-Martin of Martin's Bank, had five sons; before they reached the age of eight when they could go to a prep school and thence to Eton, she collected the five- and six-year-olds from her friends and acquaintances in successive years and so made up a class for each son. Morning lessons were held in their large stuccoed house in

Elvaston Place, off Gloucester Road, or as numbers grew in the houses of friends nearby. The teachers were all trained at the Froebel Institute; the methods were informal and, in contrast to other schools, there were no punishments.

I started off in the house of Mrs Ernest Crawley in Queen's Gate, playing singing games, cutting out pictures, modelling in wax, with about half a dozen others, including Thurstan Holland-Martin. We had a percussion band in which it always seemed to be my turn to have the triangle, which made so little sound. A young golden-haired Miss Broome instructed us, but she did not stay for long. It was a fairly long walk for a five-year-old and there was a rota of nannies and nurserymaids who escorted us on the public motor bus in a group on our daily trip. Our class eventually moved to Wychwood House, No. 1 Cottesmore Gardens, the home of the Norman family, another banker, where the classes were run by Miss René Ironside, a highly skilled teacher. This was wonderfully convenient, since I could run down the road in full view from our house, in at their garden gate, and round the house to the large empty basement room at the back where we hung up our coats and hats and took part in physical activities and played in the mid-morning break when it was too wet for the garden.

I quickly learnt to read; I well remember the sudden realisation that I had read a whole page to myself about a thrush's song, without spelling out the words; it was like skating: suddenly you could go unaided and without falling over. The magical world of books was opening, which offered a share in exciting stories, different scenery and new people, the products of another person's imagination. Reading, then as now, was a perpetual pleasure. Writing was more of an effort: we had very big books with lines two inches apart in which we wrote with broad reed pens, pressing up and down to vary the thickness, and forming an italic script. The transition to an ordinary pen with a 'relief' nib came later. I still like my own handwriting, though it is not as attractive as my husband's, or my son George's. I never remember having any trouble with my sums.

Learning was made easy; there was a lot of drama and singing based on Cecil Sharpe's folk song book. 'The Raggle-Taggle Gypsies' or 'Strawberry Fair' were dramatised by allocating roles to different children, with everyone joining in the chorus. Tunes and words of songs like 'The Keeper' and 'The Boy Who Sold Broom' still echo in my mind, though I can't have heard them for over seventy years. We recited and acted out Longfellow's scenes of Hiawatha's childhood, which we also illustrated by making a tiny wigwam for old Nokomis out of scraps of chamois leather, surrounded by painted pine trees, and blue water. Three of us, reciting from Macaulay and armed with cardboard silver swords, kept the bridge over the Tiber with Horatius at the top of a flight of steps at one end of the classroom. We also made models as part of the history lessons:

I remember helping to make a Viking ship from brown paper, with a white sail painted with an apple as its device, and rows of round silvered shields fastened to the sides with brass paper clips. I even wrote a short poem about a Viking expedition, beginning with:

> Our Viking ship sails o'er the wave,
>   outward bound is she,
> Her captain is young Rolf the Brave,
>   outward bound is she.
> Women must weep and women must wail
>   when outward bound is she,
> For never ever more may they see their men,
>   outward bound is she.

The second line was a refrain but I have forgotten the rest of the three verses. We made a model of a Norman keep, with its drawbridge across the moat, and of a monastery with a green-painted cloister garth. We were taken on a visit to St Bartholomew the Great to see the Norman church, and to the Temple to see a crusader knight's tomb. These, together with M. and C. H. B. Quennell's books, *A History of Everyday Things in England*, a birthday present which I devoured, must have given me a foretaste of archaeology. I have always realised the need to translate a plan into another dimension, and to complete a reconstruction of an excavated site.

My mother felt it was important to supplement our schooling by French lessons, piano playing and dancing classes; these reflected her own attainments, since she and her sister Isabel had been 'finished' in Brussels, where she had learnt to speak French fluently. A curvaceous blonde, Mademoiselle Thuilliez, came twice a week to lunch at No. 14, where we aired a few sentences and Sheila and I were instructed in the billiard room overlooking the courtyard at the back of the house. We did 'dictée' and learnt to conjugate French verbs. We learnt our vocabulary by playing French Lotto, drawing little picture cards out of a bag, and having to name an assortment of everyday objects and finally having to construct a sentence about each one. I don't think either of us was very interested in the process.

For my piano lessons, Mother engaged Lilias Mackinnon, a distant cousin, a tall willowy intense young woman with her dark hair looped through a velvet hairband. Actually she was a fine pianist, a concert performer who had specialised in the works of the Russian Alexander Scriabin, who was considered very avant-garde. I was taken to hear her play at the Wigmore Hall, but naturally could not make much of it. I was an indifferent pupil with very little manual dexterity, and there was a big gap between my performance and what I wanted it to be. I remember struggling with a little piece of a Bach gavotte, in which my left and right hands refused to synchronise. However, she taught me the fundamentals, how to read music and to listen to it.

For dancing I was sent at an early age to Miss Vacani's classes held in the ballroom of the De Vere Hotel nearby and later moved to the grander Empress Rooms in Kensington High Street. This was partly a social occasion with snob parents and nannies vying with each other in the achievements of their young. Miss Vacani, known as 'Madame', was a petite blonde woman wearing elegant satin dresses in various pastel shades, firmly draped across her bosom in the fashionable style. She had a commanding manner and a penetrating voice. The class was lined up in well-spaced rows and started with the 'five positions' followed by the 'graceful arm exercises'. 'First position, heels together; second, right foot in line with the shoulder; third, in the middle of the foot; fourth, in front; fifth, toe and heel together.' It was most important to point the toes. There was an interlude for singing games, including 'Poor Mary Sits A-Weeping', for which children brought their own dolly, the subject of Mary's lament, rather than the lover of the original ballad. The class then continued with instruction in the waltz, the polka and the gallop and concluded with a march past and a curtsy or bow in front of Madame. All the little girls came in their best party dresses with flat bronze shoes secured by elastic cross-over straps. I wore an accordion-pleated dress in an old gold tussore silk with a lace collar, which must have looked rather fetching with my auburn curly hair. I was rather self-conscious about it, realising that it was very different from the pink and white frillies of the others. Unlike my talented youngest sister Mari, destined to become a professional dancer and a choreographer, I was not an outstanding performer.

I much preferred the Grecian dancing, as it was called, or the Dalcroze Eurythmics, which had a brief vogue in London about 1914–16. The classes were held in the empty first-floor drawing-room of a large house in Lexham Gardens owned by two Misses Brown, who lived upstairs. We wore short Grecian tunics and danced with bare feet. Nanny strongly disapproved of the green tunics she had to make, shapeless sleeveless garments which had elastic round the middle and did up with a set of snap-fasteners, 'poppers', along the shoulder and upper arm. One Miss Brown played the piano, the other took the class, and there was a thin unhappy-looking teenager called Angela, wearing a strawberry-pink tunic, who performed as demonstrator. We learnt to move in strict time to the music, and to interpret the notes: one step for a crotchet, two for a minim, three for a semibreve, to run for quavers and faster for semiquavers. We beat time with set arm movements to a variety of rhythms from the piano. There were times for free dancing on a theme like 'a falling leaf', or making up a story as we went along. It was all a trifle serious and I had to concentrate, but I learned in a practical way of the connection between music and movement, and had an inkling of the links of music and mathematics. A feeling for music is not a necessary part of an archaeologist's mental equipment, but it has made for much personal satisfaction as an adult and I am very glad that it formed part of my early education.

Surprisingly the Great War made very little difference to our lives. I well remember the outbreak in August 1914. The parents were at Littlewood for the shooting and we had been boarded out with Nanny in a little villa at the Bridge of Alford run as a guesthouse by a prim and proper Miss Underwood. No doubt I had caught something of the excitement from general conversation, but the climax was when a Highland regiment came marching down the main road from Strathdon, kilts swinging, pipes playing, on their way to entrain at Alford. We leaned over the low garden wall, enraptured. The shooting party soon disbanded, and my mother and other ladies were occupied picking over piles of sphagnum moss gathered from the moorland bogs by the keepers, and spread out to dry. It was then packed into sacks and sent off to make swabs for hospital supplies; I wonder if it was ever used and if so, how it was sterilised.

Back in London, everything continued as usual. My father with his shrunken foot was not fit to serve, and somehow the McLean uncles, Alan and Colin, and Isabel's husband, Eric Hervey, escaped the carnage, though Colin was slightly wounded. No doubt the grown-ups hid their stress and anxiety from the children. I remember vividly the first Zeppelin raids; we were in Kensington Gardens as usual one summer morning with the nannies assembled in a group under the trees, when we heard the drone of planes, the bursts of gunfire, and saw the tiny silver cigar-shaped airship high in the sky. Everyone scattered and ran, Nanny pushing Mari in the pram, Sheila and I trotting beside. By the time we had got out of the park it was all over, but we went straight home nevertheless. I saved up my pocket money to buy a souvenir, a brooch mounted with a little metal bar said to have been part of a Zeppelin, which I cherished for a long time and wore on my overcoat.

The other dramatic event was the Silvertown explosion in east London, when a munitions factory caught fire and exploded. We heard the rumble and the bang and could see from the nursery windows the glow in the sky miles away down the river. Otherwise my recollection is of dreary maize puddings substituting for rice, and the nasty taste of margarine. Finally in March 1917 I remember coming downstairs first for breakfast in the dining-room, picking up the newspaper and reading the big headlines to my father who had joined me, 'The Czar of Russia has Abdicated', and enquiring what the strange word meant.

Although the war had made so little difference to our lives, changes were about to take place. By 1917 our parents were worried about the children's health and safety in London. I was ten years old that year and coming to the end of the permitted stay at René's classes. I suspect that my father, now a busy senior partner in the firm of Stephenson Harwood, already felt he wished to escape from city life once the war had ended. His interest in golf and his circle of golfing friends was increasing, and led him to rent a small furnished house at Walton Heath in Surrey, near the famous golf course some twenty miles south of London. There we spent the school holidays and the occasional weekend, and there was to be our permanent Surrey home from 1919 onwards, until my mother's death in 1966.

The move from London marked the end of my childhood. All in all, it had been a happy one. I had felt secure in the nursery and the family routine. The lack of a mother's personal care and demonstrations of affection had been adequately compensated for by Nanny's loving attentions. Although I had no special friends, I had two sisters to play with: Sheila whom I dominated, and Mari, the baby six years younger, whom I petted. It had been easy living in Kensington where the park with its grass and trees and the Serpentine had been a substitute for the countryside. There had been relatives within easy walking distance, Granny Henderson in Lexham Gardens, Granny McLean in her flat in Thorney Court and her widowed sister Mrs Blaikie-Smith, our wrinkled Aunt Nell, in Gloucester Road. There were visits from mother's friends, who became aunts by adoption, for no child ever called a grown-up by his or her Christian name in those days. Society and the environment had been such that a child could absorb and master; I knew where we belonged. My basic schooling had gone well; I had learnt with enjoyment. The Froebel system, practised in a modified form at René's, had stimulated my powers of observation, my creative activity and self-motivation. I had lived in harmonious surroundings, perhaps over-protected by affluence. I never saw poverty and was untouched by trouble or anxiety; it was a good foundation for the future.

Chapter Two

Growing up in Surrey
and at Downe House School

1919 – 1926

The move to Surrey and the establishment of a permanent home at Walton on the Hill was a gradual process, starting with the purchase in 1919 of the hitherto rented villa at the junction of Heath Drive and Chequers Lane, with the preposterous name of The Grange. More land was quickly bought to double the size of the garden and eventually in 1920–1 to extend it along Chequers Lane to the next residential road, Hurst Drive, about four acres in all. At the same time the house was altered and added to, central heating installed, a gardener's cottage built as well as a large garage with a flat for a chauffeur above it. I tremble to think of the cost in modern terms, but this was nothing out of the way then at Walton. The pity is that architecturally the original house was so poor, built of brick and roughcast with mock Tudor timber uprights in the gables, brown tiled roof, and small pane leaded casement windows, fronted by a red tile floored verandah. A new wing was added in the same style with a large oak-panelled billiard room and three bedrooms and bathroom over. The three servants still slept in the attics but were provided with a 'servants' hall' facing north over the enlarged kitchen and scullery. My sister Mari and I agree that though we lived there for a long time, we never really became attached to the place, though obviously our parents were, in their different ways, as were my own children later on.

The development of the garden became the main centre of interest. The first extension into the rough grass of a neglected field enabled my father to plant an orchard, mainly apples but a few plums and pears, and to keep bees. In this way I learnt the names and characteristics of a sequence of dessert apples – Irish Peach, James Grieve, Worcester Pearmain, Allington Pippin, Elliston Orange, Blenheim Orange – and how and when to prune and store them. I also helped Father with the bees and their vagaries; I wore a black net veil over my hat and used a 'smoker' filled with rolls of brown corrugated paper, whilst we examined the brood frames. We pursued and captured the occasional swarm in a conical straw skep. We extracted the honey, which was deliciously flavoured from the heather on the nearby Walton Heath. Father also waged war on wasps' nests; as soon as one was discovered cyanide tablets were bought from the chemist on signing the poisons' register. These were dissolved in boiling water at dusk, and the mixture was poured into the tiny tunnel approach. It was possible next day to dig out the papery grey nest, full of dead wasps and grubs, which I found most intriguing.

For the second enlargement of the garden, a professional landscape gardener, Alfred Luff of Wimbledon, was employed. The main feature was a double herbaceous border backed by yew hedges, on either side of a broad sunken grass path ending in a circle with a sundial. This cut across the orchard and provided the central axis of the new layout. Beyond it there was a tennis court where my father and sisters and their friends played, screened by groups of birch trees, and by plantations of azaleas and Japanese maples which produced wonderful displays of colour in early summer and in autumn. At one side of the tennis court there was a circular rose-garden with a tall maple tree in the centre and, at the far end, a rock garden built of Westmorland limestone, and a peat-filled bog garden for growing special wet-loving things. My mother's interest was in colour and in cut flowers; she was also anxious not to be 'overlooked' and insisted on large Lombardy poplars and Douglas fir trees being planted on the Hurst Drive boundary, much to my father's disgust. He was interested in growing a variety of shrubs needing special care including species rhododendrons; these were planted in the shrubbery beside the perimeter fence. There was also a large vegetable and soft fruit garden, shut off by a privet hedge, and the whole thing required two full-time gardeners and a garden boy to keep it up, working under the direction of my father. At first it looked rather stark, but once the trees, shrubs and plants got their roots down into the rich yellow clay with flints which here overlies the chalk of the North Downs, they grew apace. By the 1930s it was a lovely mature garden, full of diversity and interest. After my father's death in 1945, and with the difficulties of obtaining labour, it became sadly overgrown, but still remained a joy for my mother. Now it has been broken up and the house divided.

There was a lot of attractive open country around Walton. First, the heath itself which extended for two miles from the edge of the built-up zone up to the wooded crest of the North Downs and its open south-facing escarpment on Colley Hill. From here there were superb views across the chequered low-lying Weald to the distant line of the South Downs, with Chanctonbury Ring visible on a clear day. The long finger of Leith Hill and the line of the Hog's Back beyond Guildford made up the western horizon. Most of the heath was taken up with the two eighteen-hole golf courses which were the main attraction for my father, but otherwise it was unspoilt heathland, covered with bell and ling heathers, feathery purple-stemmed molina grass, some gorse, bracken, and small birch and thorn trees, all kept down by grazing of the commoners' animals. It was seamed with footpaths and bridleways on which we rode on our bicycles, furiously bumping over the ruts and through the puddles. There were good long walks along the top of the chalk ridge and on the Pilgrims' Way through the ancient yew woods at the foot of Box Hill. In one place near Pebblecombe Hill we discovered that the chalk flowers were particularly good. In the close-cropped turf, there was an abundance of bee orchids *(Ophrys apifera)* with subtle mauve and velvety brown petals, and many deep pink cones of the pyramidal orchid *(Anacamptis pyramidalis)*, as well as the sweet-scented pale mauve spires of the scented orchid *(Gymnadenia conopsea)*. At the right time there were enough wild straw-berries to be worth picking to take home for our tea. In the nearby wood a few tall white butterfly orchids *(Platanthera chlorantha)* could be found along with the common twayblade *(Listera ovata)*.

In the opposite direction there was Headley Woods, a beautiful tract of undulating country between Walton village and Headley church, full of primroses and bluebells in the spring beneath the hazel coppice, oak and beech trees, and always good for a walk. I remember one Good Friday sitting in the warm April sunshine on a grassy bank overlooking the little open valley in the midst of the wood, feeling utterly peaceful and remote. Alas! This is no longer possible, for London's orbital road, the M25, has been cut through it. Farther afield there was Headley Common, all open heathland, though like Walton Heath, now sadly overgrown since it is no longer grazed. In a thicket on its northern fringe, there was a clump of wild dusky pink martagon lilies which was kept secret. It was possible to follow the Roman road, Stane Street, across Mickleham Downs, where the raised *agger* (raised part of the road) survived, towards Juniper Hall and the river Mole, or in the other direction towards Epsom Downs and thence to walk back to Walton.

I had learnt of Roman roads and of the Pilgrims' Way by reading Hillaire Belloc's *The Open Road*, at Father's suggestion. It was on walks with him in Surrey that I learnt to read the one-inch Ordnance Survey maps, how to correlate the contour lines with the visible relief and how to use a compass to check direction. These were useful accomplishments for an archaeologist, when it came to locating sites and relating them to their environment. I developed an inward consciousness of the north point, which was only upset when in later life I went to the Antipodes, where the world seemed upside down and I frequently confused the points of the compass. Surrey winters were cold and Walton was relatively high, 500 to 600 feet, so there was regularly skating on the village pond and tobogganing down the nearby north slope of Motts Hill. We had one large Canadian flat type of toboggan on which three or four children could sit, and a small Swiss toboggan for one or two which went very fast but was more controllable. If the two-seater Morris car was available for transport, we went off to Box Hill, with its much longer slopes which were thrilling. Certainly we did not lack exercise or fresh air.

London, too, was close at hand, fifty minutes by train from Tadworth, and about the same on narrow suburban roads by car. My father had kept on some of his business clients, which necessitated journeys by train to the City: I remember the row of red box files in the little sitting room labelled, 'H. van Cutsem, deceased', which struck me as a little odd, that the dead could have need of a lawyer. Later on, there were other rows of green ones, when he had become deeply involved in local government, first with the local rural district council, and then with the Surrey County Council, of which he became an alderman, as well as chairman of the Mental Health and of the Records and Ancient Monuments Committees. My mother felt that London was the only place for shopping, certainly for clothes, so the chauffeur frequently brought the large Humber car to the front door, and off we all went, often including Nanny who despised the country life, bound for Harvey Nichols, Woollands or other Knightsbridge shops. The Harrods van paid a weekly call, bringing the library books and other goods that had been ordered by telephone.

As I remember it, the parents' life was very sociable. Every year there was a Derby Day party for relatives and friends; a wagon was hired from the village blacksmith and very early on a June morning it was driven over to Epsom Downs and placed on the rails in an enclosure facing Tattenham Corner. This acted as our grandstand; the chauffeur followed with my mother in the car, bringing a super picnic lunch and the drinks; the rest of us walked the two and a half miles through the wooded lanes from Walton and up and over the downs, avoiding the traffic now converging from London. It was always an animated scene with bookies shouting odds and taking money, and gypsy women offering to tell your fortune. I did once 'cross one old lady's palm with a silver sixpence', only to be told, among other vague remarks, 'You like your bed of a morning, dearie', which then was only too true. The races were all over in a flash, with the drum of hooves and splashes of colour from the jockeys' silks as they rounded the famous corner, urged on by the excitement of the crowd. Despite studying the racing columns in the newspapers, and picking out some fancy names of the horses as good omens, I never collected much in the way of winnings from my customary stake of half a crown ($12\frac{1}{2}$ p), which then was a perfectly acceptable amount.

In the early twenties Walton Heath and its golf club was a place of some importance. James Braid was its professional, a tall Scotsman with a strong accent, a famous international champion at the time. Lloyd George, the Prime Minister, could sometimes be seen playing on the course when he came to spend weekends at Chussex, a small house nearby designed by Edwin Lutyens, with a characteristic tall central chimney block. I was faintly aware from the grown-ups' conversation of some scandal attached to Lloyd George's ménage, which did not include his wife. Father had an interesting set of golfing friends: Sir Howard Frank, a jovial, gangling figure from the big London estate agents, Knight, Frank & Rutley; Lord Riddell, the thin-faced wealthy proprietor of the *News of the World*; Edward Hudson, a connoisseur and founder of *Country Life* magazine; Herbert Mappin, an astute but retiring little man from the silversmiths' firm of Mappin & Webb, and Owen Bevan, a stockbroker in the firm of Pember & Boyle. They forgathered for games of bridge as well as golf, usually at the Dormy House, another small Lutyens house where the Londoners stayed, but sometimes at our house. It was then that I realised the interest and variety of male conversation, so much more stimulating than the female equivalent, centred on domesticity. Much of the discussion concerning politics, finance and economics went over the head of an immature teenager, but I listened and learned. It was perhaps a sort of preparation for the male-dominated academic society in which I eventually found my place in life.

Edward Hudson, 'Huddy', was a great favourite; he was an affable little man, grey-haired, with a deceptively fussy manner but with great artistic sensibilities. He was a patron and friend of Lutyens who had built him the fine house, Deanery Garden, at Sonning in 1901 and restored Lindisfarne Castle on Holy Isle, where Father sometimes went to stay. I remember lunching with him at his lovely town house in Queen Anne's Gate, Westminster, full of the finest eighteenth-century furniture. He was, at this time, deeply attached to Madame Suggia, the great cellist. When she was with him at Walton, she sometimes came to practise before a concert in our large oak-panelled room and filled the place with rich sounds. She was an amazing-looking imperious woman, immortalised in Augustus John's portrait with her flowing red draperies, now in the Tate Gallery. Obviously she exploited Edward Hudson as her 'sugar daddy'.

I went to school at Chinthurst, a small private establishment at Tadworth. There was no question of attending the state Council School in Walton, then regarded as only suitable for the working class and filled with noisy and dirty children, according to Nanny. Chinthurst was run by the formidable Miss Thwaites, and took some thirty girls, some of them boarders, between the ages of eight and fifteen. We were divided into three classes, mostly taught by Miss Thwaites with an assistant, the mild

Miss Titmus, and another teacher for the youngest ones. Miss Thwaites was a Dickensian figure, shabbily dressed, thin, erect, with a sallow complexion, a pointed nose, dark eyes and a penetrating voice. She was a good teacher though severe and had little patience with the mediocre or lazy child. I started there as a weekly boarder in October 1918, and so remained during the family's move from London to The Grange in the spring of 1919. Thereafter I bicycled daily, with Sheila aged nine, the mile and a half through Walton village and across the common; traffic was minimal and no one was in the least concerned for our safety.

The teaching was a change from what I had had at René's; it was much more disciplined and less imaginative. It relied on textbooks for the various subjects, containing parcels of facts and few illustrations; these we had to read at home and come prepared to answer questions in class, whether it was on French verbs or the reign of Queen Anne. Scripture consisted of learning by heart passages from the Old and New Testaments and reciting them verse by verse, whilst English lessons consisted of grammar, dictation, précis writing and composition. There was also a poetry book, Woodward's *Selection of English Poetry*, from which we had to memorise a poem, regardless of its context. I quickly acquired the art, and in this way first enjoyed Wordsworth's *Daffodils*, bits of Coleridge's *Ancient Mariner*, Keats's *Nightingale* and Shelley's *Skylark*, and Wolfe's *Burial of Sir John Moore*. It all sounds rather old-fashioned but it demanded concentration and was an effective training for eye and ear, which I enjoyed. I found it relatively easy to master facts, to learn rules, and apply them, whether it was in arithmetic or language; my main failure was in drawing, where I never succeeded in mastering perspective or shading. Rather surprisingly, Miss Thwaites gave us lessons in physiology, so from an early age I became familiar with the human skeleton, the names and positions of the bones and the principal organs and their functions, though of course the sexual organs were omitted. This was useful information for a future archaeologist; when it came to uncovering inhumation burials, I knew what to expect.

My schooling was supplemented by extensive reading at home. I read incessantly, disappearing with a book and a rug into a sheltered corner in the garden whenever possible. I acquired as Christmas or birthday presents the fat dark-blue volumes of children's history books by H. E. Marshall, *Our Island Story*, and others covering Scotland, the British Empire, and most importantly, English Literature. I was fascinated by *King Arthur's Knights*, a rendering down of tales from Malory's *Morte d'Arthur* and the *Mabinogion*, and by a series concerned with ancient religions, *The Myths of Greece and Rome*, *of Ancient Egypt*, and *of the Norsemen*. I delighted in Kipling's *Puck of Pook's Hill*, as well as semi-historical fiction by Stanley Weyman, or Baroness Orczy's *Scarlet Pimpernel* series. All were grist to my mill, developing and ordering my interest in the past, stimulating my imagination and the growing emotions of an adolescent.

Another outlet was play-acting. At Chinthurst 'elocution' was an optional extra, taken in the afternoons and consisting mostly of play readings, in which we learnt to be audible, to speak slowly and clearly, and with the right emphasis. In the summer, there was an entertainment for parents and friends in the garden, where a nut hedge formed the background and a screen for the young actresses. I remember taking part in an abbreviated version of Milton's *Comus* as Sabrina, wearing a flowing robe of green chiffon and garlanded with water-lilies. Millicent Hawkins, daughter of Antony Hope the novelist, was a graceful-moving Comus, and Joan Haslip, a future writer of historical fiction, was 'The Lady'. It says much for our teaching that we mastered Milton's blank verse and no one forgot her lines. At a later stage I took the leading role as Katherine in scenes from *The Taming of the Shrew*, opposite to my best friend, Pamela Lovibond, as a swaggering Petruchio: we both enjoyed the ferocious interchanges of words and the accompanying horseplay. I failed, however, to secure either the part of Prospero or Miranda in scenes from *The Tempest*, and had to be content with Stephano, the drunken butler, much to my annoyance: but any part in the play was better than none at all.

At Downe House, my boarding school at Cold Ash near Newbury, from 1921–5, there was also a tradition of producing a Shakespeare play. My first appearance was rather traumatic. I had been given the role of understudy for Olivia in *Twelfth Night* and so attended the rehearsals and learnt the part. About a week before the performance Olivia went sick with a sore throat; I ardently hoped she would not recover, but of course she did. I had a few glorious days when I performed centre stage, before returning to obscurity. Subsequently I played Lysander in *A Midsummer Night's Dream*, and a romantic Jessica in *The Merchant of Venice*. Interest in the theatre was encouraged by the headmistress, Miss Olive Willis; she read aloud to girls in the evenings, and in this way I became acquainted with the plays of Ibsen and Shaw, and with Greek tragedy in Gilbert Murray's verse translations of Euripides. Whenever practical, school parties were taken to the theatre. The Ben Greet Company came to Newbury, playing on a bare stage in the Corn Market. I sat on the edge of my hard chair tense with terror during Duncan's murder by Macbeth, and whilst waiting for the appearance of Banquo's ghost. The performances must have been crude, like the Elizabethan originals, but equally effective. We also went to London to see Sybil Thorndike in *Saint Joan*, an unforgettable performance of Shaw's masterpiece, enhanced by the splendid colourful costumes and scenery designed by Charles Ricketts. Sybil's playing of Joan carried complete conviction, with her deep voice, slightly accented, bringing out the commonsense and combativeness of the girl in the early scenes. Knowing the inevitable end, I fully experienced the pity and terror of tragedy in the trial scene, mitigated by the lowering of tension in the Epilogue.

Acting and the theatre then remained an abiding interest, so much so that for a long time I thought to make it my career. I liked the excitement of a performance, and dressing up, as well as my ability to project a personality other than my own, to convey emotion and to be in touch with an audience. Some of these things did not come amiss to a university lecturer in the distant future.

Downe House was then a small rather unconventional boarding school of about a hundred girls. It had started at Charles Darwin's old home in Kent, hence the name, but moved to Cold Ash in the summer of 1921, when I went there. The house had been built as a retreat for an Order of Silence, on a hilltop surrounded by pinewoods. There was an extensive cloister, part converted to a temporary chapel, and a small stone amphitheatre which we used for the plays. Classrooms were in a detached house previously used by the Superintendent of the Order. We wore a curious uniform which I detested; a shapeless A-line green serge djibbah, with 'D. H.' embroidered in purple on an inset in the V-neck, worn over a white flannel blouse, and a clumsy overcoat of thick purple Irish tweed, crowned by a purple velour hat. In the summer we abandoned the djibbahs in favour of pleated cotton gym tunics of any plain colour we fancied, which looked very gay on girls dotted about the cloister garth.

The school was dominated by Miss Olive Willis, whom I found a bit oppressive with her efforts to mould the girls' characters at end-of-term interviews and by the sermons she preached in chapel. Nevertheless I was grateful to her for introducing me to a wide range of English literature and to the classics in translation. I remember in my last year, getting up to read Plato's *Republic* in the sixth-form common room before breakfast. Her partner was the down-to-earth Miss Heather, the administrator, who taught elementary mathematics as far as the end of the textbooks, so I was never tested as to whether I could have progressed farther. History was well taught by a supercilious Miss Eliott who made sarcastic comments on our essays and made me aware of the need to read more than one book in preparation. For a short time I was taught some elementary science in a makeshift laboratory by a young Audrey Richards, who became a well-known Cambridge anthropologist. I remember her enveloped in a mass of chalk dust as she wrote the formulae on the blackboard, and running her messy fingers through her curly red hair.

I was bright for my age (14+) and responded well to the stimulus of more advanced work, so in September I was placed in a higher form than my contemporaries. Unfortunately this meant I was held back the following year and had the boredom of repeating what I had already mastered. I sailed through School Certificate in 1923 with six credits, but intellectual achievements were not greatly valued in those days; excellence in sport was far more important. I was no good at any ball games, since due to a mild astigmatism I was unable to focus correctly and so make contact with a fast-moving object. No one ever told me the reason; it was just put down to stupidity. Equally, rapid growth and increasing weight in adolescence made gymnastics a trial. I could not balance, swing along the bar or vault over the horse with any certainty, let alone elegance. The gym mistress was rather a tartar, so I gave up trying. Fortunately girls were allowed to go for country walks in small groups on afternoons when they were not playing games. In this way I explored the Cold Ash woodlands, and the cultivated lands towards Hampstead Norris. I found it easy to slip away from my companions if they were disinclined for a long walk and it never occurred to me that I might come to any harm. No doubt such freedom for schoolgirls is now considered impossible. Another pleasant feature was that during the summer we were allowed to sleep out of doors on camp beds in the cloister enclosure or under the nearby pine trees. There were the sounds of nightjars and cockchafers, the scent of the pine needles and of course the moon and the stars and the fresh night air to be enjoyed.

I was rather a loner at school, where I made no lasting friends. I remained permanently attached to Pamela Lovibond of Chinthurst days and we spent a lot of time together in the holidays. Pam was an attractive vivacious person, highly intelligent and a great talker. She was of striking and unusual appearance, with a broad brow, prematurely lined, above grey-green eyes, in a pointed oval face, emphasised by the current fashion for a centre parting in her dark wavy hair. Even then she was rather a coquette, hard to pin down, and frequently late in coming to a meal at The Grange in contrast to the Hendersons' punctuality. I found her fascinating and was never happier than in her company. I can't think what we talked about for hours on end in each other's houses, where we played dance records on a wind-up gramophone, or furious card games of racing demon, and old maid on the floor with my sisters.

Pam was the cause of my first visit to Devon in 1921, when she had had a bout of typhoid fever due to eating contaminated oysters, and was sent down to Salcombe to recuperate with her uncle and aunt, Mr and Mrs Sharp. I was invited to join her for part of the Easter holidays and so found myself on a train from Paddington, with instructions to change at South Brent for a little local train to Kingsbridge. The line has long been closed. There I was met by Pam and Uncle Henry Sharp in his boat, in which we chugged down the long tidal estuary to land at their house on South Pool creek. All this was completely new to me, the spectacular cliffs, the rolling countryside with wooded combes and remote farms surrounded by flowery orchards of cider apples. The house was very isolated; if we wanted to go shopping in Salcombe we either took the boat if the tide was right, or else bicycled a couple of miles down the narrow lanes to the ferry from East Portlemouth. Aunt Helen Sharp, who lived to be 101, was very easy-going: it was all very different from life at The Grange. Pam and I walked and bicycled to explore the seacoast around Prawle Point; we made a long expedition to Start Point, nearly getting lost in the maze of deep-set Devon lanes. We went for picnics in Uncle Henry's ancient car, in which I had my first experience of Dartmoor, so very different from the hills of Aberdeenshire. Altogether it was a wonderful holiday in which I am sure my attachment to Devon has its roots.

I had no boyfriends; indeed at that time it was not expected that schoolgirls needed them. The dominant influence in my adolescence was undoubtedly my father. I valued his judgement, I shared in his interests and we were very companionable. We went together to hear Roger Fry's lectures to the National Art Collections Fund on Italian painting and on the French Impressionists at the Queen's Hall in London, and on walks to Surrey villages where he explained the styles of church architecture and the features of old houses. I accompanied him on visits to William Robinson, who was crippled and in a wheelchair, to see his lovely Gravetye Manor garden at East Grinstead, as well as to Wisley Gardens, home of the Royal Horticultural Society. In contrast, I thought little of my mother and rebelled, often quite violently, when made to conform to her ideas of conventional behaviour. I was often rude, difficult and disobliging. I can now recognise that it was a form of jealousy, not uncommon in teenagers deeply attached to a parent of the opposite sex.

My first trip abroad with my father was to Norway in 1923, when I was just sixteen. He had been invited to share a fishing on the Lærdal river by an old friend, Charles Mackintosh, a partner in his firm of London solicitors, Stephenson Harwood. His wife, Mary, was coming to run the house and since my mother declined to travel, they suggested I should go instead. A long time ago, I had been a child bridesmaid at the Mackintoshs' wedding in Kensington, wearing a cream satin dress embroidered with rose-buds and edged with brown swansdown, of which my mother disapproved: for the Norwegian expedition I invested in a Burberry waterproof jacket and trousers and some heavy boots with felt soles, advised for keeping one's footing on smooth wet rocks. We sailed from Harwich to Oslo, when I made the discovery that even on a fine day with only a gentle swell in the North Sea I was seasick. On our return from Bergen to Newcastle with a rough crossing, the result was catastrophic. I could barely stagger up the steps from the boat on landing. In Oslo, I saw the splendid Viking ships from Oseberg and Gokstadt, with their rich contents so well displayed in the National Museum. I think it was the first time that I realised how museum exhibits could be the means of illuminating the past. Our journey was completed in a slow train across the bleak mountains of central Norway to Gol and by the postbus to Selton. The little white timber lodge was perched above the foaming Lærdal river, here flowing in a deep valley before joining the head of the Sogne fiord about five miles downstream. Even in high summer, it was rather claustrophobic. Salmon fishing was the order of the day, though not for me, but I went along with Father to help land the fish; a photo shows a record catch of nine fish in two days. Mary Macintosh proved to be an unimaginative housekeeper and when the salmon supply failed, we lived off a large tin of small Norwegian sardines – brisling – canned in tomato sauce, much to my father's disgust, for he was something of a gourmet.

It was possible to explore the valley by means of the daily postbus. Downstream was the village of Lærdal Sören on the fiord, where I was astonished to see someone cutting the grass which grew on the turf roof of a stone cottage to feed to the animals; it brought home the stringency of the peasant economy. Upstream there was Husum, a village with one of the finest Norwegian *stavekirke*, a wooden church with tiers of steeply pitched shingle roofs, miraculously surviving from the twelfth century, the exterior weathered to shades of reddish brown and the shingles to a silvery grey. We made one successful attempt to get out of the valley by an arduous three-hour walk on a track up the rocky hillsides and through the pinewoods which emerged on the *fjeld*, a moorland plateau of 2000 feet. Our guide took us to a *saeter*, one of a group of small stone houses used for summer dairying. It had a turf roof held down by stone slabs at the edges; the windowless interior was dark and smoky from a smouldering peat fire in the centre of the earth floor. Three or four women lived there for a few months in the summer, milking the cows and goats driven up from the homesteads in the valley, and making cheese and butter. They were visited from time to time by their menfolk, who brought up their supplies. I am glad to have seen this living example of transhumance; I retained a mental image of this primitive dwelling and pastoral way of life for reference in my later studies of prehistory.

The Norwegian flora was limited and rather disappointing, apart from one silver-edged rosette pyramidal saxifrage, *(Saxifraga cotyledon)* which inhabited the shady rock crevices and produced a long arching spray of white flowers. Surprisingly, the few plants we brought back flourished in our Surrey rock garden and were much admired. More and more my father became interested in alpine plants, stimulated by reading William Robinson's *Alpine Flower Gardens* and Reginald Farrer's *Among the Hills* (1911). He decided that he wanted to see the flowers in their mountain surroundings and to collect plants which could be grown at home. In those days no country except Switzerland raised any objection to the removal of native plants. All that was necessary was a permit from the Ministry of

Agriculture and Fisheries to bring them into England, which was easily obtained. We found this official document very useful in allaying the fears of the frontier police.

Following closely in the footsteps of Reginald Farrer, our chosen destination was the Hôtel de la Poste in Lanslebourg, on the French side of the Mont Cenis pass to northern Italy, and easily accessible by an overnight train to Modane and then by bus. Lanslebourg was a picturesque Savoyan village with narrow streets of old houses with overhanging eaves, and gardens running down to a stream spanned by the elegant arch of an ancient stone bridge. When I went back there in 1980 with George, my youngest son, I was very concerned that I could not recognise the place, and felt my memory must have played me false. There was now a broad main street flanked by drab tall houses and hotels, down which heavy traffic to and from the Mont Cenis pass roared incessantly. A Bailey bridge had replaced the stone arch. The changes, we discovered, were the consequences of the war; the Savoyards had been active in the Resistance movement: when the German occupying troops left, they had burnt the place and several other villages, which were later totally reconstructed. However, the flowers had not changed; we still found the dainty pink bird's-eye primrose *(Primula farinosa)* beside the stream, and the creamy wintersweet *(Pyrola uniflora)* in the pinewoods exactly where Farrer had described them in 1910 and where Father and I had joyfully recognised them in 1924.

The flora of Mont Cenis, a zone of primary siliceous granitic rocks, is rich and varied. The relationship between altitude and the varieties and character of the plants is obvious. At 4,000–4,500 feet, before the hayfields around Lanslebourg are cut in early July, there is a mass of colour provided by blue and purple vetches and rampions, yellow rattle, pink campion and rest-harrow, white marguerites, and the occasional spires of pale mauve and deep purple orchids. After a two-hour climb, the true alpine meadows are reached above the tree line at 6,000 feet, with their patches of brilliant blue star gentians, *Gentiana verna* and *G. bavarica,* and the solid trumpets of *G. acaulis.* There are pink pincushions of moss campion, *Silene acaulis,* mats of blue *globularia,* a spread of mauve, white and yellow pansies, *Viola calcarata* and clumps of taller white and pale yellow anemones, *Pulsatilla alpina, P. apifolia* and *P. alba,* in the grass, to name but a few. On the rocky outcrops, there are trails of purple saxifrage *(Saxifraga oppositifolia)* and creamy mountain avens *(Dryas octopetala),* with rosettes of encrusted white saxifrages and pink *Sempervivum* in the crevices. Higher still, in the wet loose screes at the foot of the granitic rocks above the pass, there are the white cups of *Ranunculus glacialis,* the lilac clusters of Alpine pennycress, *Thlaspi rotundifolium,* as well as the rare local *Viola cenisia* and cushions of pink *Androsace alpina.* Although

Father and I were complete novices, we could not fail to find many of these and to be delighted at the vivid colours and abundance of the flowers.

We were soon joined at the hotel by two professionals, Colonel Gavin Jones and his wife, Marjorie. They had just started a nursery garden at Letchworth and had come to collect specimens for propagation. With their help, we quickly learnt to identify the common plants and where to look for rarities. We had come armed with pointed steel 'fern' trowels and a supply of collapsible cardboard boxes, plastic labels and a wicker hamper. I learnt how to work gradually round a plant to avoid damaging the roots and to deepen the hole before trying to lift it, just as I later was able to teach my students to do when excavating a fragile object of metal or bone; patience and perseverance are necessary in both cases. I always looked after the specimens we collected, wrapping them in moss and damp newspaper and seeing that each had its dated label firmly affixed. I made notes of their habitat and compiled a daily list. The collection was stored in the hotel cellar and packed in the hamper for the journey home. This was a good preparation for museum work in later life, which needs the same sort of attention to detail in recording, and in the care of specimens.

Two incidents stand out in my memories of that trip. The Gavin Joneses and ourselves were especially anxious to see the rare alpine blue *Eritrichium nanum*, which we learnt grew on the sensitive Italian frontier in the direction of the Petit Mont Cenis. We had to get special permission from the military and, having stayed overnight at the modest inn on the col, set out early next morning to find we had an escort of two bored French soldiers. It was quite a long walk on the military track up to the small lakes at the foot of the pass but we were rewarded by finding the neat cushions of the *Eritrichium* studded with brilliant blue flowers growing on the rocks at the roadside. We duly photographed them, under the supervision of the soldiers; unfortunately colour film was not available in 1924.

The other was a rather comic if shameful event. After the Gavin Joneses left, another pair of established nurserymen arrived, Clarence Elliott of Stevenage and Walter Ingerswen from Croydon. They were both rather arrogant and intolerant of us amateurs. We set off on our usual day trip to the col of Mont Cenis; Father took the bus tickets, and since it was our last day, he tipped the driver quite lavishly. In the afternoon we decided we would rather walk down to Lanslebourg, where we found Elliott in a state of frenzy because the bus had not arrived on time, and in consequence they would miss their sleeper reservations on the Paris Express. The bus eventually appeared, the driver having waited for us with the best intentions. We thought it prudent to disappear to avoid any recriminations.

Our Alpine expedition had been a success and the Gavin Joneses became our firm friends. It was agreed he should remake our Surrey rock-garden using larger stones so that it resembled a natural limestone outcrop, instead of something like a Dundee cake, with stones stuck in without any relation to their original bedding or stratification. Pockets of scree, filled with either limestone or granite chippings, were constructed to accommodate special treasures that needed good drainage; these were covered each winter by glass. Gavin was a pioneer in this work and in the following year won a gold medal at the Chelsea Flower Show for his construction of a rock-garden. His wife organised the planting, modelled on alpines in their natural habitat rather than the massed bedding-out of other competitors. We made a second expedition with them in 1925, this time to the Dolomites in the Italian Tyrol to see the rather different flora on the limestone, as well as the remarkable Alpine scenery. It was one of those cold late summers and when we started on the Pordoi pass at 6,000 feet, the crocuses and soldanellas were only just coming up through the patches of snow in the high pasture. We had to move down to find specimens of the rare *Phyteuma comosum* in flower, a rampion with curious rosettes of dark-tipped cream tubular flowers with protruding stamens that have given it the name of the Devil's Claw. Ensconced in a rocky crevice with its circle of serrated leaves, the plant had an architectural quality that is apparent even in the black and white photos we took. Other delights were the yellow lady's slipper orchid, *Cypripedium calceolus,* flowering freely in scrub below the Rolle pass, the sweet-scented *Daphne striata* and many varieties of alpine primula, the yellow *Primula auricula*, the purple *Primula hirsuta* and the rare pink *Primula tyrolensis* as well as the almost stemless *Primula minima* studding the grass slope with its tiny pink stars. Like the English primrose and cowslip, there is something special about alpine primulas.

After the Gavin Joneses had left, Father and I made an expedition with a guide into the heights of the Rosengarten range, sleeping at an Alpine Club hut at the head of the Vaiolet valley. It was a tremendous experience to be right up at the base of those fantastic tower-like formations, which we had so often seen in profile from the lower ground. In the reflected light of the setting sun, the jagged outlines of the peaks looked pink, turning red or even purple as we watched from the verandah of the hut. The next day we crossed below the Grasleiten pass, still covered by snow; here Father found his balance was difficult, and was glad of the help of the guide, but I bounced along the narrow path above the drop without a qualm. We circled down in the afternoon to finish up at a simple *pension* in the woods, where good German tourists were taking an easy holiday stroll. It was a different world from the austere rocky landscape we had left and I was conscious of regret on leaving the heights. I had no desire to climb the rock faces but I fully understood their attraction for mountaineers, having seen them at close quarters.

These Alpine expeditions loom large in my memories because they provided an enduring source of pleasure. Although no botanist, I had no difficulty in extending my limited knowledge of the Alpine flora to that of the Mediterranean, to the wild flowers of the English and Scottish countryside, and to some degree to what I later saw in New Zealand. Throughout my life the recognition of wild flowers has been an important part of holiday pleasure. The efforts we made to transfer some of the alpines and to get them to grow in the Surrey garden and to survive the English climate aroused my interest in gardening, which I subsequently applied to all the small gardens attached to my future homes in Cardiff, Exeter and Topsham. I am still keen to try to establish unlikely shrubs and plants and derive pleasure from an occasional success. Until very recently, I retained from my Alpine experience a sense of physical pleasure in hill walking and confidence in my powers of endurance, whether in the Roman *campagna* or during archaeological field work in the uplands of South Wales, on Dartmoor, or in Hawke's Bay, New Zealand. In the Alps I had become aware of the vegetation changes due to altitude and to the nature of the rocks and soil; in my later archaeological field work I could recognise the effects of these same elements in human settlement.

I have rather run ahead of events in describing this flower hunting. Back in 1923 I had to think of what to do next, after my School Certificate success. Gradually it became clear to me that I wanted to go to a university and to read English Literature. There were two obstacles to this; first, although I had matriculated I had no Latin, then a prerequisite for Oxford and Cambridge, and secondly my parents, who would be required to pay the fees, did not like the idea. Father said he did not want me to become a 'bluestocking', whilst Mother had set her heart on my early marriage to a suitable nice young man, preferably a Scot. It was thought odd in those days for daughters of the well-to-do middle class to want to go to a university, whereas it was taken for granted that the sons would, though often in search of athletic rather than academic distinction. Gradually my parents gave way in the face of my determination, but I had to submit to some teasing from my relatives at Littlewood.

It was a friend of my mother's who indicated to me the way round the Latin, by suggesting I should try for Cambridge; she knew from her sons' experience that the Latin required for the preliminary 'Little Go' examination was minimal, and convinced me that I could do it. I had taken Italian at Downe House as my second foreign language, which I have never regretted, so I had a useful basic vocabulary. With the help of extra tuition, in less than a year I had learnt enough to construe simple sentences of the type required, and to translate passages from the set book, using a dictionary. This was part of Book XII of Virgil's *Aeneid,* but I found the conflicts of Aeneas and Turnus, taken out of context, incredibly tedious. I think my schoolgirl's dislike of Latin was due to this masculine preoccupation with warfare as much as to the complexity of an inflected language. The examination took place in Cambridge in November and I stayed with Professor and Mrs Langley in their big Victorian house in Madingley Road, since their daughter Alison from my school was also taking some papers. On arrival there was time to explore the colleges on the Backs where the elms were golden and to go to look at Newnham College garden through the elaborate ironwork gates, wondering if eventually I would be admitted. Greatly attracted by the beauty of the Cambridge scene, I felt confident I had made the right choice and an inward assurance that I would succeed. The next day a cold damp fog descended, and after the examination was successfully over, it became so thick that the Langleys insisted we stayed an extra day before we went back to school.

The next hurdle was the Newnham entrance examination which was highly competitive and for which I would need special coaching. My parents agreed to my leaving Downe House at Easter 1925, where I was then a Senior (prefect) in the Upper Sixth Form, and to my boarding in South Kensington with a very respectable lady who took in 'nice girls' as paying guests. I went to English lectures at Bedford College, where I listened to the redoubtable Professor Caroline Spurgeon on Shakespeare's metaphysical imagery, and wrote weekly essays for a young tutor, Miss Joan Barber, an Oxford post-graduate student who lived in Queen's Park, Hampstead. I learnt that I was nothing like as good as I had thought I was, that my purple patches were trite, and that I needed to master my facts and to think out the construction of my essays in advance. Nevertheless, in 1926 I got through the papers, went to Newnham for interviews and was accepted. I found that the principal, Miss Strachey, was almost as diffident at the interview as I was, and I felt that I had to make some of the running.

I had agreed with my mother that if I passed, I would join her in a London Season before I went up to Cambridge in October. This involved choosing a lot of new clothes, including a dress of apricot-coloured silk embroidered in silver, with a flame-coloured sash and train, for my presentation at Buckingham Palace. As all dresses in the 1920s, it was short, just below the knee, and I have a photo of myself holding a sheaf of gladioli and with the compulsory white feathers in my hair, looking very serious. It was all quite ridiculous, and I cannot pretend that I enjoyed any of it – the Royal Garden Party, Ascot races, Henley, or the various dances I went to in London and Surrey, accompanied by equally bored and polite young men in tailcoats who could talk about nothing else than the various makes of motor cars whilst we foxtrotted. Much more fun were the informal gramophone dances at Littlewood in August and September, which featured eightsome and foursome reels as well as the strenuous and exhausting romp of 'Strip the Willow'.

There had been a change of management at Littlewood, which my grandmother had made over to her eldest son, my uncle, Alan McLean. He had lately married a Welsh girl, Blodwen, a daughter of a Welsh Nonconformist minister, the Reverend Isaiah Jones: they had met whilst they were both in the army at the end of the war. Together with several small Joneses and Colin McLean's two daughters, my sisters and I had been bridesmaids at their grand wedding at St Mary Abbots, Kensington, in 1921. We wore frilly dresses of lilac taffeta and poke bonnets trimmed with flowers. Blodwen had a kind heart and a lot of good intentions, but she was a real social climber. The character of the summer house parties changed accordingly, to my mother's disgust. For a stay at Littlewood, I now needed smart tweeds and at least three evening dresses as well as one with sleeves to be worn for Sunday supper, when the servants, who included a butler, had time off. The change in life style was symbolised by Blodwen's lavish provision of Turkish cigarettes, specially ordered from Harrods, each with a purple ribbon tip, typical of the 1920s.

I still enjoyed the days out on the hill or by the river. I went with my father or one of the uncles in the butts when the grouse were driven over; I shared in the tension as the coveys approached, flying low over the heather ahead of the line of beaters. As the birds came into range, silhouetted against the skyline, the firing began; my job was to count and mark where they fell to my father's gun. I was not worried, as I now would be, by the slaughter, but picked up the warm dead birds or took them from the retriever dogs without a qualm. Aunt Blodwen and most of the ladies joined the shooting party for lunch on the moor, a more elaborate hot meal from thermos containers having replaced sandwiches.

Certainly the house parties were fun, with a mixture of relatives, young cousins and familiar friends. There were big dinner parties for which the whole day might be taken up with picking and arranging flowers; there were visits to neighbouring house parties equally given over to shooting and fishing, either for a tennis afternoon or for a riverside barbecue with potatoes roasted in the ashes of a bonfire. There was an annual visit to the Aboyne Highland Games on Deeside, and to the flower show and the church fête at Alford. There was, of course, no television or even radio: for evening entertainment most people settled for bridge, sometimes mah-jong or Monopoly; occasionally there was some singing of popular songs from *No, No Nanette*, as well as informal dancing to a gramophone. Sometimes the Hendersons were house guests, sometimes my parents rented a small lodge nearby. It was an agreeable, idle life, but I found it unsatisfying in comparison with my purposeful existence in London and later in Cambridge.

As a teenager I was conscious that I had not yet found my social niche. At school and in the family circle, I was at a disadvantage by being considered 'clever', and I did not play tennis, which was a real social handicap. I was sexually unawakened, as were most of my contemporaries, and my knowledge of romantic passion was derived only from extensive reading of novels, plays and poetry. It is amazing how much went over my head.

Chapter Three

Cambridge and After
Beginning in Archaeology

1926 – 1930

I went up to Cambridge in October 1926 with high hopes and great expectations. I had been allotted one of the larger ground floor rooms in Peile Hall at Newnham, with big windows facing on to the garden with a row of old thorn trees. The cost was £52 a term, which included all college fees as well as board and lodging: only university examination fees were extra. The room was sparsely furnished, and was heated by a coal fire for which a daily scuttle of coal was provided. There was an iron bedstead on which the bedclothes were rolled up in the daytime and placed beneath a fitted cover, to simulate a sofa. Clothes were hung behind a curtain in one corner and a washstand was discreetly hidden behind a screen in another. There was an oak bureau with a wheelback chair in the window at which I worked, bookshelves and a wickerwork armchair by the fireplace. I quickly supplemented these with an antique walnut chest of drawers, a reproduction eighteenth-century wall mirror at a cost of £10, and a cane-topped long stool which was also used as a coffee table, together with some extra cushions and Japanese prints from home, and some new brown rep curtains. I then felt ready for entertaining as well as working.

Newnham College buildings at that time consisted of the gatehouse with a porter, and the Principal's lodging above, four separate halls and the library, linked by covered corridors. All were fine examples of Edwardian baroque, designed by Basil Champney, built of red brick with many scalloped gables and with lavish decoration of moulded terracotta reliefs.

The buildings ranged round three sides of a garden court with playing fields beyond on the fourth side. Each hall accommodated some sixty students, with a Tutor-in-Charge, a working don, who was expected to keep an eye on our morals and behaviour. Peile Hall was agreeably and efficiently run by Mrs Helen Palmer, who was also Director of Studies for Architecture, for which her qualifications were minimal: grey-haired and

dignified, she seemed elderly to me, though probably only in her late for-
ties. Young Jocelyn Toynbee, a classicist newly arrived from Oxford, was
the other Fellow-in-Residence, they were joined for evening meals in Peile
by Enid Butler, specialist in German and Director of Studies in Modern
Languages, and her friend Isobel Horner, the librarian. I encountered them
when it came to be my turn to sit with four or five others for a week at
High Table for dinner. The Principal, the tall, elegant Philippa Strachey
might also be present, confronting her lifelike portrait by Henry Lamb on
the opposite wall. The food was abominable, having been cooked in a central kitchen some hours before and brought round in a heated trolley, but
the conversation could be excellent. Enid Butler laughed and sparkled,
Miss Strachey, 'Streak', was witty and sarcastic, Jocelyn informative. I listened to academic women at their best, commenting on topics of the day.
This is no longer possible; with the adoption of a central cafeteria for all
undergraduates, the opportunities for a formal meal are limited and the
college fellows are segregated at High Table in the Great Hall, as in the
men's colleges. The catering has improved, but at the cost of easy informal contacts between staff and students.

In 1926 the college rules were strict; everyone had to be in by 11 p.m.,
checked at the Porter's Lodge before the gates were closed. A late night
pass was obtainable from a tutor if one went to a ball. Some girls managed
to climb over the spiked fence of the playing fields, with male assistance,
and took advantage of my ground floor window. Men were allowed in students' rooms only between 3 p.m. and 6 p.m., provided another girl was
present. This was a great advance on the previous regulations, which had
stipulated that a married woman should act as chaperone, both at
Newnham and at men's colleges to which a Newnhamite had been invited.
Nowadays young men come in to meals at the cafeteria and can be
encountered in the corridors and in the garden at all times of the day.
Unlike Girton, Newnham has remained a women's college, though it now
has a few men among the Fellows. Having taught for many years in
provincial universities at Cardiff and Exeter, I have become habituated to
a mixture of the sexes among students and academic staff, and I doubt if I
would have been contented in an all-female institution.

I came up to read English, so my Director of Studies was Miss Steele-
Smith, an old lady on the verge of retirement who had lost touch with
recent developments; her only advice to me was not to attend too many
lectures. Her replacement was the diminutive Dr Enid Welsford, who was
much more effectual. It was an exciting time as the English Tripos had
recently been reconstituted, and we were the first to work under the new
regulations for the two parts. It was no longer necessary to study Anglo-
Saxon and *Beowulf* or old Norse: one could embark straight away on
English literature, life and thought from Chaucer onwards. The onus was

on the student to select from this wide field the works and writers to study in depth, to evaluate them and to relate them to the historical background; an understanding of literary criticism was also required. Guidance came from the lecture courses provided by the faculty and from supervisors provided by the college, who read and marked our essays, no more than two or three times a term. We were very much left to our own devices.

The lecturers were mostly young men enthusiastically committed to the development of the new school after the break with linguistics, with the emphasis now on the understanding of poetry. I remember outstanding lectures by F. L. Lucas in King's on Meredith's sonnet sequence, *Modern Love* : by E. M. W. Tillyard on Milton, and by F. R. Leavis. There was H. S. Bennett's course on medieval literature and life which provided a firm historical sequence. For sheer inspiration there were lectures by the eccentric Mansfield Forbes, 'Manny', given to a handful of students in Clare. The titles of the lectures, often irrelevant, varied from year to year but featured the Romantic poets, particularly Wordsworth and William Blake. One could never tell what to expect; it could be a prolonged consideration of a poem by Gerard Manley Hopkins or by the more recent Edward Thomas, but it could also be a discussion of new Swedish architecture, or of Pictish carved stones, or of Clare's Memorial Court by Giles Gilbert Scott, with which Manny was deeply concerned. It was from him that I learnt of Trystan Edward's work on town planning and Geoffrey Scott's *Architecture of Humanism* (1926), which rationalised my feelings for and developed my understanding of Georgian architecture. I well remember Manny coming a little late into the small lecture room on the ground floor in Clare, wearing a disreputable gown over shabby flannel trousers, his round-rimmed spectacles sometimes held together with string, and after an uncertain start, intoning a Wordsworth sonnet or almost singing William Blake's 'Tis the Voice of the Bard'. His voice dropped to a whisper for the last lines of Edward Thomas' 'Melancholy':

> And, soft as dulcimers, sounds of near water falling,
> And, softer, and remote as if in history,
> Rumours of what had touched my friends, my foes, or me.

Oddly enough, Manny was a would-be archaeologist with an abiding interest in Celtic antiquities and mythology. He had been with my husband in 1923 assisting with Tom Lethbridge and Jack, Lord Cawdor, both then undergraduates, at the excavation of a large Bronze Age barrow at Barton Mills, Mildenhall. He was singularly ineffectual: my husband, Cyril, later told me how a large workman among the onlookers had snatched away Manny's overloaded barrow and emptied it, unable to bear the sight of his struggles. I saw him again soon after my marriage when we lunched with him in Finella, the large early Victorian house in Queen's Road that he had altered and redecorated with a young architect, Raymond McGrath, in a fine fantasy of contemporary art. Little did I think as we sat in the domed dining room beneath the Pictish symbols engraved on the glass overhead, with Manny dishing out alternate slices of lamb and beef to his guests, how often I would return to Finella. Manny died suddenly in 1935; the house was divided, the garden with the great cedar tree was shared, and my sister Mari, the dancer, with her husband Peter Bicknell, the architect, lived in the eastern half from 1946 until 1980. There she brought up a family of four, as well as starting the children's dancing classes that were to develop into the Cambridge Ballet Workshop. It would have seemed very odd had it then been possible to look forwards as well as backwards in time.

Another attraction was I. A. Richards' course in practical criticism, at which we were given a set of anonymous poems to interpret, criticise and evaluate. These varied from a sonnet of John Donne to one of the *Rough Rhymes of a Padre* by G. H. Studdert Kennedy. It was a real challenge to extract the meaning, to sort out the gold from the dross and to justify one's likes and dislikes. I was fascinated by the difficulties of fully understanding Gerard Manley Hopkins's 'Spring and Fall', with its unusual rhythms, but like many others fell into the trap of admiring the purple patches in a second-rate poem by Edna St Vincent Millay. In the ensuing lecture, Richards would comment on our misunderstandings, analyse the reasons for our mistakes and finally reveal the authors of the poems. Later he published the results of the experiment in *Practical Criticism: A Study of Literary Judgement* (1929).

For my generation there was the feeling that great literature was still being produced and was not just a thing of the past. T. S. Eliot's *Collected Poems*, including 'The Waste Land' had recently appeared for us to puzzle over, and there was a sense of more to come. D. H. Lawrence's novel, *The Plumed Serpent*, Virginia Woolf's *To the Lighthouse*, Aldous Huxley's *Point Counter Point* were published during my Cambridge years, 1926–9, and were bought instantly to add to their previous works on my shelves. I heard E. M. Forster give the Clark Lecture in Trinity College on *Aspects of the Novel* in 1926 and Virginia Woolf her topical feminist lecture, *A Room of One's Own*, in Newnham in 1928. Unlike today, we felt certain of the lasting value of contemporary literary work.

I gained a great deal from my three years' reading English Literature, besides an upper second degree. There was the enjoyment of participating in the imaginary world of great writers to which it is possible to return by rereading today. I increased my enjoyment of the sound of words in the mind's ear, and in the accompanying speech rhythms. I learnt the importance of understanding exact meanings in poetry as well as prose. I perceived the past as an ordered sequence, in which writers were related to their background and to their contemporaries. In these ways, Cambridge trained my mind, my imagination and my historical sense and developed my powers of writing; all these were to be deployed when my interests changed to archaeology.

My life at Cambridge was transformed when I made a lasting friend of Sophia Fry. I cannot remember the occasion we first met and discovered our affinity, but she too was in Peile and reading English so there was plenty of opportunity. Sophie was a little older than most undergraduates, the youngest daughter of Sir John Fry, Bt., a Quaker businessman with a fine classical early nineteenth-century house in Great Ayton, Yorkshire. She was an attractive little person, though plain with fine mousy hair, and a great talker. She was much more intellectual than I was, gaining first class in Part Two of the Tripos. She was philosophically inclined, whereas I once assured my supervisor when asked why I did not attend Basil Willey's rather abstract lectures on eighteenth-century writers, 'You see, Miss Welsford, I don't like Thought.' We found we had many interests in common. We both liked walking, and, with the aid of our bicycles, enjoyed exploring the Cambridge countryside, the fens and its villages. Sophie introduced me to bird-watching, sharing an ancient pair of binoculars; it was a great day when we saw a stone curlew on the Breckland near Barton Mills, and a gadwall with her ducklings on a stream nearby. Together we went to hear the Lener Ensemble play all the Beethoven quartets in sequence, and Margaret Field-Hyde sing in Purcell's operas *The Fairy Queen* and *King Arthur*. We patronised consistently the newly-opened Festival Theatre, where we saw in three successive weeks a marvellous performance of Aeschylus' trilogy, the *Oresteia*, as well as other classic dramas by Synge, Shaw, Chekhov, Eugene O'Neill and Ibsen. We even got permission to hire a car to go to Oxford to see *King Lear* performed by the Oxford University Drama Society one summer day after examinations were over. I shut my eyes whilst Gloucester's were put out. It was a traumatic experience. For entertainment at a lower level, we went to the university rugger matches at the Grange Road ground near Newnham, and occasionally sat around at Fenners to watch cricket on a warm summer's day, which Sophie enjoyed more than I did. I acted with the Newnham Dramatic Society in Sheridan's *The Critic* produced by Barbara Nixon, and with the Cambridge Mummers as one of the Three Marys in their first production.

Two of the three winters in Cambridge were severe, and for several weeks of the Lent term we enjoyed skating on the frozen flooded Grantchester Meadows. The Cam froze in 1929 and my future brother-in-law, Peter Bicknell, with his cousin Jock Lovibond, were the first to skate from Cambridge to Ely since the great frost in the eighteen-nineties. Less agreeable were the cold morning bicycle rides down Sidgewick Avenue in time for H. S. Bennett's nine o'clock lecture. On Sundays there was the chance of a formal afternoon tea with a number of dons who kept open house, including my old friends, the Langleys, Professor Burkitt at West Road, the Carters at the Botanic Gardens, and even with the Master of Trinity, J. J. Thompson, to whom Sophie had an introduction. There was always good conversation to be had as well as cake. It was a full and varied life.

It was Sophie who introduced me to the Burkitts; her elder sister, Peggy, had married Miles, the eminent prehistorian, the only son of the Regius Professor of Divinity, and they lived in Holly Cottage alongside the Newnham playing fields before moving to the larger Merton House in Grantchester in 1929. Miles was an oddity both in appearance and in character; he was of pale complexion, with a high forehead to a large head on top of an awkwardly long body, and a high-pitched voice. Essentially unconventional, he flaunted incongruously an Old Etonian tie. As a child he had been considered 'delicate' and when I knew him, suffered from nervous palpitations of the heart and was very demanding. Peggy, a calm and stable character, pampered him too much. He was, by all accounts, a good teacher of the rather arid discipline of Paleolithic archaeology and very proud of his pupils who included Grahame Clark and Louis Leakey. The subject did not attract me, and though we became good friends, Miles and I frequently crossed swords.

However, I owe my introduction to practical field archaeology in 1928 to the Burkitts. The previous year, Father and I had been on the last of our flower-hunting expeditions, travelling to San Dalmazzo di Tenda in the Maritime Alps, in pursuit of the rare *Primula allionii*, which grew in the crevices of the limestone rocks. After a week, we found we had exhausted the local flora and, hearing that there were prehistoric rock engravings as well as Alpine flowers in the higher Casterino valley, set off on a three-hour walk, with our baggage on a mule, accompanied by a guide. We put up in a very modest inn, and after our evening meal were agreeably surprised by an invitation, conveyed by a manservant, to visit Mr and Mrs Berry at their Casa Fontanalba on the opposite hillside. James Berry was a nephew of the late Clarence Bicknell, a talented amateur botanist and artist, who had lived in Bordighera and had built an attractive little house in order to study the rock carvings as well as the flora.[1] Mr Berry knew exactly where to find them on the rocky slopes when he took us up the Val Fontanalba the next day. We were both much impressed, and so was Miles Burkitt when I told him what we had seen. When the Berrys came to England that winter it was arranged that they would lend Casa Fontanalba to us and the Burkitts for a month the following summer, complete with their servants, Giuseppe, and his wife, Matilde, to run the house and cook for us. We had Clarence Bicknell's illustrated book *Prehistoric Rock Engravings* (1913), as well as Giuseppe to be our guide.

Peggy and I spent long hours lying on the smooth, glaciated rocks above Fontanalba warmed by the July sunshine, making rubbings, with Miles and my father looking on. No English archaeologist had visited this remote area other than Bicknell. The subjects were mainly agricultural: horned oxen, rendered schematically sometimes pulling a primitive plough *(ard)* and followed by a ploughman; there were also curious rectangles that Bicknell thought might represent fields and perhaps settlements. Very similar but more elaborate imagery has now been recorded in the Val Camonica, in northern Italy.[2] We made an arduous day-long expedition with mules to the Lago delle Meraviglie, now Lac des Merveilles since the region was restored to France. It was an awesome barren landscape at the foot of Monte Bego (2,873 metres). There we recorded the important engravings of daggers and halberds which were the best evidence for an early Bronze Age date for the series. In the evenings, after a delicious Italian meal, Peggy and I blew fixative on to our large sheets of rubbings and we discussed with Miles the significance of the symbols. It was noticeable that most afternoons dark clouds gathered over Monte Bego, usually culminating in a small thunderstorm, and Miles's deduction that the mountain had been a cult centre, with symbolic offerings of stock, land and weapons carved on the rocks around it, still seems plausible.[3] I found the whole thing most absorbing; unconsciously I was learning the techniques of systematic archaeological recording, and about the influence of the environment on human activities, though I had no intention of pursuing the subject further. So far as I was concerned it had been a very good holiday.

I went back to Cambridge for my final year, still uncertain of my future. I had an idea, because I liked books and had catalogued my collection, that I might become a librarian. In the meanwhile there was Part Two of the Tripos to work for, and an optional long essay to submit – a so-called thesis on the Elizabethan dramatists, Marlowe and Ford. At Easter, Sophie and I felt we needed a break, and had a wonderful ten days in Paris, crossing by night ferry and staying in a cheap hotel on the Left Bank. We behaved as regular tourists; we strolled by the Seine in the spring sunshine, and along the great boulevards, so different from London's intimate townscape; we visited the Louvre but found the Impressionists' pictures in the Tuileries more absorbing. We went out to Versailles, where I found it difficult to appreciate the grandiose style of Louis XIV, which went against the belief in functionalism current in the 1920s. We walked, it seemed for miles, in the gardens and park admiring the geometric layout and the extensive vistas. Returning rather exhausted, we sat down for lunch at a café-restaurant, but when the waiter presented us with an expensive menu, all we could afford was a tomato salad followed by a fried whiting, that most dreary and bony of fish. The best day of all was in Chartres; I knew in advance about the glories of the glass in the great cathedral, but no one had prepared me for the splendours of the twelfth-century sculpture. Those tall slender figures of kings, queens and saints with their elegant draperies in the classical tradition flanking the portals, gave me a new insight into the Middle Ages.

After the final examination was over I was unhappy and unsettled, but had to consider how to fill in the summer. The family was going to holiday on Lake Garda in Italy and to play tennis, which did not appeal to me. I was firmly told that the painters would be in possession of The Grange and the servants would be on holiday. Suddenly it occurred to me that I would like to go on an excavation; when staying with Sophie in Yorkshire we had visited the ruins of the Cistercian abbey of Rievaulx, where I had spoken to someone who was digging and recovering potsherds. I thought it might be an agreeable way of spending August. I went for practical advice to Jocelyn Toynbee, the friendly young classics don in Peile, who admitted she had no information about medieval abbeys but she did know Mr Bushe-Fox, an inspector of Ancient Monuments in the Office of Works, who ran an excavation at the Roman site of Richborough Castle in Kent. After some correspondence with him, I arranged to go there for four weeks, the minimum stay for a beginner. My mother drove with me to Sandwich, where she approved of my taking lodgings with two other workers in a small house at the modest charge of 35s. (£1.75) a week for dinner, bed and breakfast and a packed lunch.

Richborough proved to be an attractive place, a little eminence of about 100 feet surrounded by reclaimed marshland of the silted-up Wantsum channel which separated it from Thanet. The river Stour flowed past its eastern edge towards Sandwich and beyond that the flat land extended to the dunes on the coast some two miles away. Industrial buildings have since intruded into the landscape and spoilt its isolation. In Roman times Richborough was practically an island with a harbour accessible by sea from a tidal estuary. Excavations from 1922 to 1938 demonstrated that it had a long and complex history, starting as an invasion base for the Emperor Claudius's army in AD 43. The great surviving walls of concreted flint rubble, with a stone facing and red tile bonding courses, outlined the final phase of the Roman occupation, when Richborough was part of a chain of forts built in the late third and fourth centuries against the Saxon raiders along the south-east coast.

When I arrived on my bicycle after an early morning ride of one and a half miles from Sandwich, I found I was joining a dedicated and close-knit team, some of whom had been there for five or six seasons. Practically all the manual work was done by paid workmen at 30s. (£1.50) a week, armed with picks and shovels, working under site supervisors. The headquarters were two army Nissen huts of the First World War; at the end of one hut there was a small room in which old Mr Thomas May was installed to draw the pottery. He was a fine draughtsman and a venerable bearded figure corresponding to my idea of King Lear, particularly since he had his little granddaughter as a Cordelia to look after him. The main room had long trestle tables in the centre for examining the pottery; coins and small bronzes were cleaned, identified and catalogued at the benches at the sides. The intention was to have all significant deposits examined and inventoried at the end of each week rather than delaying until the close of the excavation. This system had many advantages for a learner like myself, who could hang around whilst the Director, Bushe-Fox, pronounced on the sherds, listed the significant pieces and tentatively dated the deposit. In the same way I learnt to identify the numbered types of glossy red Samian ware, under the guidance of Dr Davies Pryce. He was an old darling, a retired general practitioner who, with Felix Oswald, registrar of Nottingham University, had written the standard work on Samian ware, *An Introduction to the Study of Terra Sigillata*. It was always referred to as 'O and P'.

I started out in the charge of Mrs Holland Walker, carefully brushing small bronzes with a toothbrush. I used to go round the site with her each afternoon to collect the small finds from the workmen, who were paid on a regular tariff: for example a penny or tuppence for a bronze coin according to size, sixpence for a silver one or for a bronze brooch. The system, current in the Middle East, was supposed to prevent workmen from concealing and selling what they had found. We had to ascertain from the site supervisor the exact find-spot and layer of each object, which we then labelled and recorded in our catalogue, later to be cross-referenced into the pottery inventory.

Soon I was promoted to mending pottery with Durofix glue in a sand tray in which the repairs were embedded. I remember laboriously putting together a shiny black 'poppy-head' beaker with panels of raised dots, only to be dismayed by the sarcastic comments of the assistant director, Professor Donald Atkinson. He broke up the crooked pot and showed me how to put it together again, starting at the base. Atkinson was Professor of Ancient History at Manchester and had excavated the Forum at Wroxeter and the Roman town of Caister near Norwich. He was a pale-faced little man, a true academic with a dry wit and an intimidating manner, but he never minded answering the most elementary questions. It was through him that I began to understand the structure of Roman military and civil government and thus to relate the Richborough sequence to its historical context. Bushe-Fox, the Director, was not at all academic, more of a countryman than a classicist; his interests, by virtue of his job at the Office of Works, now English Heritage, extended to earthworks of all periods. He had dug Roman houses at Wroxeter but also at the Iron Age site of Hengistbury Head and the Belgic cemetery at Swarling, Kent. Less of a showman than Mortimer Wheeler, he was a pioneer in archaeological method in the 1920s, with a strict attention to the niceties of stratification. He was also a good photographer using a plate camera and a tripod. I remember him striding round the site oblivious of the photographer's red and black cloth draped over his bald pink head.

Eventually I was allowed to work outside; my first job was to supervise the emptying of one of the numerous deep pits dug originally as wells in the hard Thanet sand, and then filled up with Roman rubbish. My task was to recover the sherds and other objects from the soil brought up by bucket and pulley by the workmen from 6 to 20 feet below. I had to record the depths at regular intervals, mark them on the labels of the stout brown paper bags and note any changes in the filling. Subsequently the associated contents would be examined and dated.

I was then promoted to examine a gravel road near the postern gate of the Saxon Shore Fort. I had to separate any finds embedded in the road surface from those deep in the metalling and recover others from the soil beneath, an elementary lesson in stratification. My two skilled workmen worked very delicately with their picks and I scratched about with my pointed trowel. We were fortunate in getting some late third-century coins from the metalling, which dated the road construction.

By now I was thoroughly involved in the work and rapidly becoming Bushe-Fox's chosen assistant. I agreed to stay on until the end of the season in late September, and I helped to pack up everything needed for drawing or for further research. We drove back to London in his big Armstrong-Siddeley car laden with boxes which were deposited at the Society of Antiquaries in Burlington House, where Bushe-Fox had a workroom. He then made the suggestion that not only should I return as Site Supervisor to Richborough for the 1930 season, but that I should arrange a selection of the finds in the small museum being built on the site. In the meantime, I ought to improve my knowledge of Roman civilisation, and at Donald Atkinson's suggestion I was advised to spend the next six months in Italy at the British School at Rome. It was an exciting prospect. I quickly decided that I did not want to become a librarian but an archaeologist, and before October had ended I found myself on my way in the Rome express from Calais in a sleeper paid for by my parents – they had no qualms in letting me go.

The British School at Rome was a prestigious foundation based in London, which offered valuable scholarships to young artists, architects, archaeologists and historians, in order that they might benefit from first-hand contacts with Italian art, architecture and the Mediterranean civilisation. It was housed in a classical-style building in the Valle Giulia, designed by Sir Edwin Lutyens in 1911, originally as a British pavilion for an exhibition of Fine Arts but not in use by the school until 1916. The principal rooms behind the imposing facade were a large library, a lofty dining room and lounge. At the back there was a modest little courtyard, *il cortile*, with cypress trees and a fountain, surrounded by north-facing studios for the artists, small bed-sitting-rooms for the archaeologists on the upper two floors, and a flat for the director.

In 1929–30 the school was in the doldrums, following the retirement of its director, Bernard Ashmole, who had succeeded Thomas Ashby, the great topographer of ancient Rome, in 1925. There were difficulties in filling the accommodation and consequently, though academically ill-qualified, I was accepted as a visiting postgraduate. The new director was A. Hamilton-Smith, just retired from looking after Greek vases for many years in the British Museum, and in search of a quiet life along with his elderly wife and unmarried daughter. He was completely out of touch with archaeology and seemed to have little interest in the curious mixture of young artists, architects and archaeologists in residence. On the administrative side, the efficient running of the school depended on the Italian factotum, Signor Bruno.

I found there were four classical archaeologists in residence, all from Oxford; two rather dull young men working on the towns of Pompeii and Ostia, and two quite brilliant women, Isobel Munroe and Diana Lucas, who were studying the Tartessian and Etruscan civilisations respectively. Whereas I envied them their knowledge of ancient history, they seemed to be impressed by my elementary archaeological expertise. Diana was secretly engaged to Michael Zvegintzov, a Wykehamist, son of a White Russian refugee; their marriage would necessitate her conversion to the Orthodox Church from her parents' atheism. I was a sympathetic listener to many conversations beginning, 'Supposing one was married to a Russian,' and eventually she happily was.

Isobel, who spoke fluent Italian, was already a well-known figure in sophisticated Roman academic society. She was a very intense person, one of the daughters of the Rector of Lincoln College, Oxford, and was to have a rather tragic life. She married Charles Henderson, an enthusiastic and equally talented Cornish historian, who died suddenly of a fever in Rome in 1933 within two months of their wedding. Cyril and I met them whilst all four of us were on our honeymoons in Santiago de Compostela, and we had an ecstatic evening together. We all hoped for many more such encounters, for we found we had much in common. Isobel did her best to put me wise to the elements of Roman history: I remember sitting in a small country station waiting-room south of Rome on a day when pouring rain had prevented us going on with our planned walk over the hills, whilst she explained to me the principles of the Emperor Augustus's policy and reforms. She gave me Hugh Last's great tome in a nutshell. After two hours, the slow train arrived to take us back to Rome.

I also made friends among the artists, with Timmy Brown, the soft-spoken fair-bearded sculptor who worked in terracotta and in clay, hoping to have his models cast in bronze. Like many others he did not succeed as a creative artist, and had to fall back on teaching in a London art school. Alan Sorrell, who had won the Prix de Rome for mural painting, awarded on the strength of his work in the Southend Town Hall, was a difficult young man, with a slight stammer, diffident yet determined. All the time I was there, he worked on a large canvas with the rustic figures of a young man and a girl sitting in an Essex cornfield, painted in the manner of Stanley Spencer. Like the other artists, he affected to dislike the Roman scene and to despise the Forum and other monuments, yet it became clear from his later work of reconstruction that he had subconsciously absorbed the Roman idiom. In the distant future, we were to be collaborators in producing a best-selling children's book describing and illustrating Roman Britain,[4] and he was to do some splendid archaeological reconstructions for the National Museum of Wales, and for the Ministry of Works. His painting of the Fox family, grouped in the study of our Cardiff home in 1947, ornamented my sitting-room at Topsham.

Another lesser artist was Kenneth Green who was much more sociable than Sorrell. He was my companion in a midnight walk along the Via Appia. This happened after a cheerful student *pizza* party at which we were dared to do it. We caught the last bus, and then were faced with an eerie five-mile walk along the ancient paved road between the rows of stone tombs of the early Romans. The night was dark and cold; by the time we got back to the school, it was 2 a.m. I decided what I most needed was a hot bath. Unfortunately the sound of running water woke the director in the flat below and the next day I had to answer for it. When he enquired where I had been to get back so late, I haughtily replied, 'I was on the Via Appia'. Somewhat taken aback, he said no more, and presumably thought it was all right for an archaeologist.

I did, however, do some work whilst at the school. I had selected the Mithraic monuments as my subject on my application form, probably with Kipling's, 'A Song to Mithras', in *Puck of Pook's Hill* in mind, but once I had visited the Mithraeum below the early Romanesque church of San Clemente, and those at the ancient port town of Ostia, I realised the material was rather thin. Bushe-Fox's parting words had been, 'Whatever else you do, dear girl, look at and study the Roman monuments'. Here the problem was the abundance, not the scarcity of the material. Lacking guidance from the director, I decided to begin with the earliest and to work steadily through. I started with the Servian Wall and the Etruscans and by the end of my time I had got as far as Hadrian and the second century. I taught myself to recognise the different types of stone masonry and the characteristic mortars. It was said of an American scholar, Miss van Diemen, that she distinguished the mortars by biting them, but I never went as far as that.

This project took me all round Rome and its seven hills and into the museums and made it possible to combine business with pleasure, as so often with the pursuit of archaeology. It was easy, for instance, to work conscientiously through the Roman sculpture in the long galleries in the Vatican Museum and then to luxuriate in the richly-painted Borgia papal apartments, decorated by Pinturicchio, or in the rooms with the marvellous Raphael frescos. I well remember the contrast of working in the cold of the museums with the sunshine out of doors. Though it rained a lot in November, there were many days of blue skies and clear light throughout the Roman winter, which sharpened the architectural detail of individual buildings and enhanced the panorama of the great spreading city seen from the Janiculum and other heights. There was the attraction of the formal vistas in the Borghese Gardens through which I walked most days into the city from the Valle Giulia, and with the spring there came the purple flowering of the Judas trees and the wisteria on the Palatine to enhance the ruins of the imperial palaces. There were, of course, drawbacks for a young woman walking around Rome on her own, stopping at street corners and gazing at buildings. I remember being accosted by an idle young Italian and being obliged to take refuge in the church of Santa Sabina on the Aventine where I sank to my knees, ostensibly in prayer, and so remained until he ultimately gave up his teasing pursuit and went away.

As a result of my wanderings, my mental horizons were widened. I began to appreciate baroque churches and to identify the works of Bernini and Borromini, hitherto unknown names. I learnt of Michelangelo's achievements as an architect and poet as well as a sculptor and painter of the Sistine Chapel. I became aware of the secular Roman origins of the basilican church plan and of the transformation of Roman floor mosaics into the magnificent wall and ceiling decoration in the early Christian churches. I perceived the connections of the Italian Renaissance style with its classical antecedents and with the later English developments of the sixteenth to eighteenth centuries.

There were other foreign schools in Rome, the German, the French and Swedish, for example, and from time to time we met for an evening of *conversazione* and refreshments. When it was our turn to be host, I was asked to contribute by exhibiting the school's replica of a massive silver platter found in the river Tyne in England and known as 'The Corbridge Lanx'. It was a fourth century AD piece with an incised scene of the Temple of Apollo with Diana, Minerva, and his mother, Leto, in attendance.[5] It was an elaborate work and a good test for detailing an accurate description for a would-be archaeologist.

At the weekends, there were the pleasures of the Roman countryside to be explored, usually in the company of Joan Curtis-Green, later Mrs

Yeo, a daughter of the well-known architect of the Dorchester Hotel and other London buildings. She worked as secretary to the formidable Mrs Strong, then the authority on Roman sculpture. I was occasionally invited to one of her cosmopolitan parties, a gathering at which notables from Italian society and from the Archaeological Schools were present.

On Sundays Joan and I would take a tram or local train to the Alban Hills to visit the little Roman theatre above Frascati or the newly-excavated imperial pleasure boats in Lake Nemi. We went to Palestrina or into the Campagna north of Rome with its landscape still much as depicted by English artists in the eighteenth and early nineteenth century. Teams of the heavy white oxen yoked for ploughing were still to be seen, and mules were the common method of transport; both are now supplanted by the tractor. We covered incredible distances, stopping only to buy bread, cheese, olives and oranges for our lunch; agreeably tired, we concluded with a decent evening meal and plenty of wine in one of the cheap restaurants by the Termini station back in Rome.

One memorable trip was a visit to the Etruscan tombs at Cerveteri and Tarquinia. Diana Lucas joined us, and Sophie Fry, who had come out to Rome for an Easter holiday, to my great delight. At Cerveteri there were big round grassy mounds, girdled by a moulded stone revetment, which covered the large underground rock-cut chamber tombs. These had contained the fine terracotta sarcophagi now in the Valle Giulia and the British Museum; these portray in the round a loving couple reclining together on their cushioned couch, smiling, quiet and attentive. Continuing our journey northwards, we spent an uncomfortable night in the only hotel in Tarquinia, a primitive place, and in the morning we set off with the official custodian of the painted tombs. He seemed amused at the quartet of learned ladies and ironically addressed us as *'Professoressa'*. The necropolis extended for over a mile along the upper slopes of a flowery hillside not unlike a chalk downland; a parallel ridge beyond a shallow dry valley, green with spring corn, had been the place of the living. The tombs were underground, small rectangular structures cut in the soft creamy-yellow limestone. The walls and ceilings were painted throughout with scenes of feasting, dancing, flute-playing, horse-riding, bird-catching and fishing, most gay, some solemn. At the gable end, facing the door, a pair of leopards, or lionesses or sea-horses *(hippocampi)* confronted each other above the frieze of garlanded reclining couples at the feast. The colours had perished in places, but in my mind's eye I can recall the blues, greens, red and umber on a cream ground. My remaining impression is of the contrast between the dark tombs and the sunny landscape outside, but also of the links between the colourful painted scenes within and the flowery hillside.

The time soon came when I had to leave the British School, and I travelled back in May via Asissi, Perugia and Arezzo, ending with a week of sightseeing in Florence. At Arezzo I worked away in the small cold museum, studying the output of the early red tableware that reached southeast Britain in small quantities before the Roman conquest. As Davies Pryce once said to me, 'Arretine ware can be recognised from its pinkish-red colour and its sympathetic glaze', in contrast to the orange-red and lustrous glaze of the later Samian ware, mass-produced in South Gaul and exported freely to Britain in the first and second centuries AD. By handling a fair quantity of sherds at their place of manufacture and by seeing the shapes and decoration of complete pots, I learnt to recognise small fragments likely to be found on an excavation in England. I never became a pottery specialist, but from the wide range of material at Richborough and from later studies in English and German museums, I acquired a good knowledge of the common provincial wares of the Roman period, their sources, methods of production and their dates. This was essential for any future research excavation.

Sometimes it may seem that archaeologists attach too much importance to broken potsherds, which are mainly the residue from the common activities of eating, drinking, cooking and storing. It is because the waste is so common, the wares are so varied and the products change so frequently, that it provides the best means of working out the sequential history of a site. When I came to work in New Zealand, where the Maoris never made any pottery, I realised how difficult it was to build a chronology without it.

On my return to England the next task was the organisation of the new museum at Richborough. I was very conscious of my lack of experience; in those days there was no Museums' Association Diploma or other training scheme. With the exception of the national museums, a curator with a university degree was a rarity; all had learnt by experience on the job and were very poorly paid. Bushe-Fox accordingly arranged for me to spend a week at the British Museum, where under the guidance of F. N. Pryce and Roger Hinks, I studied the display of objects to illustrate Greek and Roman life in the Department of Classical Antiquities as well as their storage system. I then went on to the Department of British and Medieval Antiquities, where the rather desiccated Keeper, Reginald Smith, handed me over to his more sympathetic young assistants, Tom Kendrick and Christopher Hawkes. I gained an insight into the cataloguing, numbering and marking of objects and to the writing of labels, which were succinct and informative. The arrangement of Romano-British pottery and bronze brooches in order to display their variety and chronology was discussed, though without reference to their appeal to the general public. My last day was spent with Dr Plenderleith in the conservation laboratory, and he initiated me into the mysteries of cleaning decaying bronzes with a solution of sodium sesquicarbonate, and other simple processes. I came away with the strong feeling that these things were best left to experts. As a museum training, my five days were obviously quite inadequate; nevertheless it did give me some basic ideas about what to do when I was confronted at Richborough with rows of empty display cases and a stack of wooden packing cases. I had supervised the two men from Pickfords when they packed up the finds in the cellars of the Society of Antiquaries in Burlington House, and nothing was broken in transit. Since then, I have always enjoyed the challenge of packing fragile awkward objects firmly in a small space.

Slowly the museum display took shape. Modelled on the British Museum display, small objects were arranged in the glass-topped sloping desk cases to illustrate aspects of Roman military and civil life, and the storage drawers below were filled with a series of sherds for students to handle. I received my first monthly pay-cheque of £28, and promptly bought a second-hand pair of Zeiss field-glasses for £7. I could then watch a rare bird, the grey shrike, which sat on the telegraph wires as I bicycled past each day from Sandwich.

When the main casework was finished, I felt that a guidebook was needed to expand the information provided by the labels; so I set to and wrote it, and presented the typescript to Bushe-Fox, now the Chief Inspector of Ancient Monuments at the Office of Works. There was already his official *Guide to Richborough Castle*, though of course it did not cover the finds in the new museum. I ought not to have been surprised when he declined to publish my efforts on the grounds that the Stationery Office would not issue more than one guide for a site. A compromise was reached by the provision of cyclostyled copies available free of charge for use in the museum, but I was very disappointed. I already had a missionary zeal for archaeological education and wanted to convey to interested spectators what archaeologists could see in the bits and pieces recovered from the excavations.

When the excavations began again in August, I found myself the site supervisor for Area XVI, responsible for uncovering a set of early timber buildings belonging to the first-century military supply base.[6] It was a complicated site, crossed by the ditches of the Claudian invasion camp which had been filled in and subsequently built over; it was seamed with later rubbish pits and partly covered by the remains of temporary huts, probably for workmen engaged in building a great central marble-cased monumental arch in AD 80–100. The huts had burnt down, leaving a thick red layer to be removed. I had been told this was the remains of wattle and daub constructions but I hadn't a clue what was meant; I associated wattles with cocks and hens, not osiers, and daub with paint, not clay. The workmen and I dug away, doing a lot of damage to the fragile remains, until we came across an unmistakable wall face, with stamped daub *in situ*.[7] The director was not pleased with the havoc I had wrought but the incident illustrates the danger of assuming that archaeological jargon and technical terms are understood by beginners.

At the lowest level the foundation trenches of the wooden military buildings showed up clearly as dark bands in the natural yellow sand after two skilled workmen had sharpened their shovels and scraped the level surface of the Thanet sand. I followed with my trowel to locate and peg the soft spots marking the postholes, which were subsequently cleared out. The plan showed a row of storehouses behind a portico along a gravel road. Opposite these were similar remains of timber granaries with raised floors supported on close-set rows of posts; these were investigated by Gerard Clauson, an eminent civil servant, who came regularly to Richborough with his young family for his holiday. There were many discussions with Bushe-Fox and Donald Atkinson about the interpretations of our findings. We were pioneering a new technique using area clearance instead of trenching, and scraping instead of digging. Our discoveries illuminated a whole new phase of Roman military activity in first-century Britain.

Unfortunately the Richborough results were not fully published for another twenty years, by which time they had been largely superseded by Ian Richmond's work at the Fendoch auxiliary fort in Scotland, and at Hod Hill, showing the predecessors of the later familiar stone buildings of the second century.

I enjoyed my second season at Richborough with new responsibilities and an accepted place in the workers' hierarchy. There was always varied and congenial company, as well as a steady stream of distinguished visitors to the site. In this way I became familiar with the faces and personalities of the archaeological establishment. Sir Charles Peers, shortly to become the President of the Society of Antiquaries, came from the Office of Works, and two new recruits to his staff of Inspectors, Bryan O'Neil, a lifelong friend in the making, and the fat indolent Roger Simms. There was Reginald Smith from the British Museum, conventionally and most unsuitably dressed for the country, in contrast to the young Ralegh Radford in khaki shorts and a blue open-necked shirt. Ralegh had worked on the site in 1926–8, and always shut his eyes when delivering an opinion on an obscure point in his high-pitched voice. Thurlow Leeds, long-haired and affable, the leading Anglo-Saxon expert, came from the Ashmolean Museum at Oxford. He drove me to Colchester to see Christopher Hawkes and Nowell Myres at work on the Sheepen site, the Belgic Camulodunum. Christopher, with whom I became great friends, paid a return visit to Richborough, where I showed him the museum. I rather think Cyril Fox came one day on holiday from Cardiff but if so, I paid him little attention.

Mortimer (Rik) Wheeler and his wife, Tess, were notable absentees, for they were busy digging at the Roman city of Verulamium, St Albans, and its antecedent Belgic settlements at Prae Wood and Wheathampstead. There was a fair amount of rivalry and ill-feeling between Wheeler and Bushe-Fox; I was warned that Rik jumped to conclusions too rapidly, and no doubt he thought Bushe-Fox was far too slow. The new Wheeler excavations were better organised and publicised than the long-established Richborough undertaking, and provided technical training in recording and interpretation far in advance of elsewhere. The Wheelers attracted a number of able assistants including Leslie Scott (Mrs Murray-Thriepland), Kathleen Kenyon, Thalassa Cruso (Mrs Hencken) and Kitty Richardson. How much was due to Rik's personal magnetism, how much to archaeology, it is difficult to judge. I doubt if St Albans would have suited me, though I might have been better equipped professionally as a result.

Chapter Four

Back in London
Love and Marriage

1930 – 1933

Returning to London in October, I realised that I now felt committed to a career in British archaeology, though I knew I still lacked much detailed knowledge and any experience of planning a site or of section drawing. As a long-term aim, I was uncertain whether I wanted to become a freelance director of an excavation, or to be a museum curator. In the meantime, there was work to be done in London that winter for the Richborough report, and I needed a place to live. Eventually I was able to move into No. 11 Trafalgar Square in Chelsea, where Sophie, now a lecturer in English studies for Cambridge extra-mural department, was living. She shared the accommodation with a mutual friend, Priscilla Boys-Smith, who worked in the Home Office and whom I replaced in the flat.

No. 11 was a small dingy terrace house of early nineteenth-century date; it was due to be pulled down and, like those already built on the other side of the Square, to be replaced with modern town houses with bright green tiled roofs, and later to be renamed as Chelsea Square. People never failed to be surprised when I gave my address as Trafalgar Square, thinking I was living close to Nelson's Column. The landlady, who was employed by the construction company, had her office on the ground floor, and Sophie and I each had a bed-sitting room facing the Square garden on the first and second floor respectively, with a kitchen and bathroom at the back. The bathroom was large enough for an occasional visitor on a camp bed. We both had our own furniture from Cambridge days, supplemented in my case by a divan bed and padded armchair bought at Peter Jones in Sloane Square. We had a cleaning lady twice a week, and did our shopping at Sainsbury's and the small shops in the King's Road. It was the first time I had any experience of catering or cooking, and I thoroughly enjoyed the new independence. As our charlady was once heard to exclaim, when I bought a guinea fowl to roast for dinner, 'They live high at Trafalgar Square'.

Other friends were nearby; Pamela Lovibond, surprisingly now working as a receptionist and library assistant in the all-male stronghold of the Athenaeum Club, lodged in Poulton Square, and Peter Bicknell, working for Grey Wornum and Louis de Soissons, the architects, was in Oakley Crescent. Chelsea was then quiet, cheap and respectable, and though many artists lived there, it was not in the least trendy. At weekends I usually went home to Walton. My parents paid my share of the modest rent and gave me an allowance of £250 a year on which I very happily subsisted. I had no need of a paid job.

My workplace was at the Society of Antiquaries in Burlington House, which was easy for me to reach by bus or underground from South Kensington. The ancient and prestigious society, founded effectively in 1717 and with a royal charter of 1751, had moved there from Somerset House in the Strand in 1874, in company with the Royal Society and other kindred organisations. The new Victorian buildings, designed by Banks and Barry in the classical style, flanked a courtyard in front of the eighteenth-century Burlington House, which had been altered previously and leased to the Royal Academy. As one walked through the elaborate ironwork gates from Piccadilly, the noise of traffic died away and, were it not for a few parked cars, the atmosphere was like that of a university quadrangle. At the Antiquaries, Bushe-Fox's workroom was on the second floor and had formerly been a bedroom in the house of the Secretary, who, in the person of St John Hope, had lived on the premises until 1910. I scuttled up the backstairs and lit the antique gas fire which gave out fumes, and set to work. I often gazed out of the window at the well-proportioned facade of the Royal Society opposite, identical to our own. Built of Portland stone, the engaged columns and window pediments in high relief had weathered silver-grey and stood out in contrast to surfaces blackened by London soot. There were pigeons incessantly strutting and cooing on the ledges and around the statue of Sir Joshua Reynolds in the courtyard. I was never wholly at ease at the Antiquaries until I became a Fellow in 1944. It was then still very much a man's preserve and youth was also frowned on. Women had been specifically excluded from meetings until 1918, and had only been grudgingly admitted as Fellows after the passing of the Sex Disqualification Act of 1920. Tessa Wheeler, a woman of outstanding charm and ability, was among the first to be elected in 1927.[1]

My work for Bushe-Fox was to help in getting the Third Richborough Report on the 1926–27 excavations to the Oxford University printers and in seeing it through the press, and to make a start on the Fourth Report covering the 1928–30 seasons. I learnt a lot about making corrections on the long strips of galley proofs, which could be altered, and on the page proofs, which could not. I saw how to make up plates and to mount line drawings for reduction. I checked cross-references from the text against the numbered plans and other illustrations, and vice versa. I learnt the need for incessant vigilance; it was so easy to think that words familiar from previous readings were correctly reproduced. It was all very useful experience, which ensured that when writing articles in the future I understood the stages of book production and the sort of work required from an author.

For the Fourth Report, Bushe-Fox decided that I should write the section dealing with 'Small Objects in metal, bone, etc.', previously undertaken by the learned young Ralegh Radford. This involved making a card-index, writing an accurate description of each item, and then searching for similar dated finds from other published sites. It was a struggle to find the right words for a technical description, to condense without omitting significant detail, and to provide an appropriate generalisation for each type. In the process I acquired some of the ingredients of scholarship, though it was seventeen years before my work was published by the Society. Whilst hunting for analogies in the books and periodicals in the Society's magnificent library, I gained a useful knowledge of Romano-British and continental sites, both military and civil, greatly assisted by R. G. Collingwood's synthesis, *The Archaeology of Roman Britain*, newly published in 1930.

Once or twice a week Bushe-Fox came over at the end of the afternoon from his office in Whitehall, checked on what I had done, and suggested new lines to be followed up. I tried to simplify the turgid prose of his draft text, but with little success. He was incredibly cautious in coming to a firm conclusion, and consequently the important discoveries made at Richborough failed to make an effect. It was left to Barry Cunliffe over thirty years later to produce a coherent historical account of this complex site in the Fifth Richborough Report of 1968.

After work we usually went out for an evening meal at the Trocadero Restaurant at the bottom of Shaftesbury Avenue. If there was an evening meeting, we returned to Burlington House where my name was added to the list in the visitors' book of 'those who beg leave to attend the Society's meeting', signed for by Bushe-Fox. It was a very formal occasion with preliminary rituals that had been handed down from the eighteenth century. The President and other officers were seated on ebony high-backed chairs on a dais at one end of the room, with the society's mace and the President's antique cocked hat of 1800 laid on the table in front of them. Fellows and their guests sat on red leather-covered mahogany benches across the room, divided by a central gangway. Newly elected Fellows, 'who had signed the obligations required by the Statutes', were summoned to the table and were admitted by the President holding the mace, with a bow and a handshake. The visitors' book was presented by the uniformed porter and guests were approved. Gifts of books to the library were read out and the society's thanks were formally recorded. There is an old story of a former President who inverted the formula and ordered that, 'thanks be received and the books be returned to the donors', which must have enlivened the proceedings. The President and the officers then moved away, a screen was lowered for the projector and the lecture began. At its conclusion, the President called on several Fellows by name for their comments, afterwards adding, 'Will any other Fellow address us?'. A high-powered and often critical discussion then ensued until at 9.30 p.m. the President closed the proceedings and added the familiar welcome announcement, 'Tea and coffee in the next room'. We all moved across the hall to the Council Chamber opposite. It is still an honour to give a paper to the Society and still rather an intimidating occasion.

It was from such meetings I learnt of important new discoveries, such as the enamelled hanging bowl from a Saxon burial at Winchester, and of the results of excavations in progress, including the Curwens' work in Iron Age hill-forts in Sussex, and Dorothy Liddell's excavations at Hembury in Devon, as well as the more exotic work of Leonard Woolley at Ur and Arthur Evans at Knossos. Each year there was an evening for the Society's sponsored excavations at Colchester (Camulodunum) by Christopher Hawkes, at St Albans (Verulamium) by the Wheelers, and at Richborough by Bushe-Fox, all of whom attracted big audiences. The amount of archaeological research and its publication was limited, and it was not difficult to keep up to date, adding gradually to one's store of knowledge. The first number of *Antiquity*, edited by O. G. S. Crawford, had appeared in March 1927, and from 1930 onwards I read it from cover to cover.

I found myself increasingly drawn to the British Iron Age, comprehension of which was only just taking shape as the evidence from the new excavations accumulated. I had long been interested in the hill-forts and appreciative of Celtic metalwork. I recognised that an understanding of Celtic culture was fundamental to the study of Roman Britain and of value in its own right. I was much influenced by Christopher Hawkes, then working on a new cultural synthesis to be published in an article on hill-forts in *Antiquity* (1931). I received an offprint inscribed in his distinctive bold handwriting, followed by another of his substantial surveys, written with Gerald Dunning, of 'The Belgae of Gaul and Britain' in the *Archaeological Journal*. It was apparent that the continental Hallstatt – La Tène chronology no longer fitted the British scene; he proposed a more flexible three-part A, B, C, system applicable to people, periods and artefacts, and this became generally accepted. It was exciting to be in at the birth of a new era in Iron Age studies when so much excavation was taking place and to see how new discoveries could be fitted into this framework.

Of course there were also many pleasures from living in London in the 1930s. Sophie and I made up parties of friends for the Russian Ballet, queuing for the inexpensive gallery seats at Covent Garden to see the exquisite trio of Diaghilev's dancers, Danilova, Doubrovska and Tchernicheva. There was the mounting excitement when the queue began to move and our anxiety grew as to whether we would all get in, culminating in the climb up the steep narrow stairs to our seats. I recollect the conductor, Sir Thomas Beecham, leading forward the young Constant Lambert after the first performance of *Rio Grande* in 1932, which we thought was very strange music. I also managed to see Hilda Sokolova in Stravinsky's *Sacre du Printemps,* in a special Sunday performance to the Society; it was unforgettable, with its stirring rhythms and dramatic tension building up to the scene of pagan sacrifice. It is strange that the ballet has not been revived, though the music remains a concert piece. We went often to the Old Vic for Shakespearian and Restoration plays: I specially remember Edith Evans as Rosalind in *As You Like It* and as Millamant in Congreve's *The Way of the World*, making every word tell with her wonderful enunciation.

Then there were the archaeological parties given by Christopher Hawkes in his flat in Gloucester Terrace, Bayswater, and by Tom and Marjorie Kendrick in their little house in Douro Place, Kensington. At Christopher's the young would-be archaeologists met and talked shop, comparing notes on our limited excavation experience. It was there I first met Stuart Piggott, who seemed a very young man to be the expert on the British Neolithic period. Occasionally we played the current game of 'Murder'; having drawn lots for the murderer, the lights were turned off and we moved around, waiting for the victim's scream, when we froze in position. The lights were restored and questions were asked until the murderer was identified. It was a good method of breaking the ice; we were very unsophisticated in the early thirties. Tom Kendrick's parties were more formal and well-behaved, with delicious food and drink, and often included a distinguished foreign visitor to the British Museum.

It became apparent that I needed to be able to read German if I wanted to progress in Roman provincial studies. The German frontier, the Limes, had been studied by the Romanisch–Germanischen Kommission since the days of the Kaiser, and they recently had published *Germania Romana, Ein Bilder-Atlas*, an illustrated comprehensive survey, comparable to Collingwood's *Archaeology of Roman Britain*. A visit to the Rhineland was clearly indicated and Bushe-Fox encouraged the idea, so I set about making the arrangements. First I had some lessons by the direct method at the Berlitz School of Languages in Oxford Street. I was confronted by a young German tutor, who proclaimed distinctly and slowly, '*Das ist der bleistift. Was ist das?'*, holding out his pencil. I looked blank, even when he repeated his remarks; finally the penny dropped and I managed to string a few words together in reply. In a couple of months' time, I had acquired some self-confidence and a small vocabulary from repeating the day-to-day activities of the mythical Herr and Frau Berlitz. When I arrived in Cologne in March 1931 after a night journey, I could ask for breakfast and the way to the museum, and was not completely tongue-tied.

Through an Anglo-German agency in London, I had found a couple in Wiesbaden willing to take a student paying guest. Herr Doctor Orb was a psychoanalyst, a rotund little man, who was visited daily by a succession of the bewildered; his wife was rather gaunt despite being a very good cook. Both were very kind to a solitary English girl. They found a little old lady to give me German lessons; she was obviously much in need, a victim of the post-war inflation. I sat in her one small room heated by a paraffin stove, on which she also cooked. The Orb ménage was very conventional: in the evenings a neighbour from the flat above came in, and he and the Doctor played Beethoven violin sonatas by way of entertainment; afterwards we were regaled with coffee and sweet cakes, sometimes with a blackcurrant *schnapps*. On Sundays we went for a short walk beside the Rhine, or on a boat trip, finishing up at a riverside restaurant for a prodigious *mittagessen* and glasses of the local white wine. I never became accustomed to the amount of food and drink I was expected to consume. Other days we went through the pinewoods on the Taunus hills to see a waterfall, which was pronounced to be *'sehr schön'*, or *'wunderbar'*, though to me it was nothing remarkable. Sometimes we met a band of young people, sketchily dressed, singing and playing as they went along the well-marked paths; these were the 'wandering birds', *Wandervogeln*, the forerunners of our hippies. Hitler and his goings-on in Munich were a topic of conversation, but Dr Orb did not take him seriously. The word 'Nazi' was practically unknown in 1931. Wiesbaden was then a small provincial town but it did have an opera house. There I saw my first performances of Wagner, *Tristan und Isolde* and *Die Meistersinger*, and despite the obvious physical limitations of the overweight singers, I was swept away by the music. This was before I had seen in Stuttgart a performance of Mozart's *Figaro,* which was pure enchantment.

Wiesbaden proved to be a good centre for my archaeological studies; it had a small museum and library with an important collection of objects from Hofheim, a nearby Claudian auxiliary fort. The large Central Museum at Mainz with a wealth of comparative Roman and prehistoric material and the Archaeological Institute at Frankfurt were only a short train-ride away, and the Saalburg, with its reconstructed Roman frontier fort and rather out-dated museum, could be reached on a day trip. I joined the local archaeological society, the *Nassauische Verein*, on their excursions to other Roman forts and signal towers on the Limes, the frontier constructed along the crest of the Taunus range. This gave me a good understanding of the changing methods of Roman frontier defence, which subsequently I could compare with the military work in northern Britain, especially Hadrian's Wall. It was odd to be the sole foreigner crammed into a bus with some twenty large German archaeologists and their wives. As instructed, I brought a packet of sandwiches etc., for a modest lunch, but hardly had we driven for half an hour when there was a rustle of paper: my companions started eating, and continued to do so at frequent intervals during the entire day, to say nothing of stopping for a beer.

Once I was able to manage some conversation, I became good friends with Hans Klumbach, an assistant curator at the Central Museum in Mainz, who was very helpful in suggesting what I should do and showing me the reserve collection. On one occasion he invited me to go dancing with him in Wiesbaden. I put on my evening dress, a low-necked black taffeta with a full skirt embroidered with blue bows, only to find to my embarrassment that everyone else in the basement café was in blouses and skirts. I felt terribly conspicuous, though I don't think Hans minded. We kept in touch for many years after we both had married; we exchanged offprints, and I wrote to him when he was still a French prisoner of war in 1945. We met up again at a Limes (Roman Frontier) Congress in Newcastle in 1959, and I stayed with him in Mainz and met his family on the way to the next congress in Arnoldsheim, Bad Homburg in 1964, by which time he was a university professor. I never had any difficulty in making friends with German archaeologists and I greatly admired their competence. I escaped the animosity and prejudice of the previous generation, dating from the First World War; for example, my mother always referred to the Germans as '*les sales Boches*' – 'the dirty Huns'.

In April I was invited to join a regional gathering of archaeologists from south-west Germany for a conference at Stuttgart. It was there that I first became fully aware of the wealth of the early Celtic civilisation in Central Europe from the sixth century BC onwards, as revealed in the local chieftains' graves, displayed in the Castle, *Alte Schloss*, Museum. The elegant bronze wine flagons, imported from north Italy, the incised patterned and coloured pottery, and above all the fine gold-work and bronzes decorated in the emergent flowing Celtic style as at Klein Aspergle, made a lasting impression. Long after, when much more had been discovered and published, I determined to share my enthusiasm with the archaeology students at Exeter University, and taught 'The Celts' as a special subject from 1968–72.

From Stuttgart, we had two full days of excursions, driving over the rolling country of the Schwäbische Alb, beside the upper Danube, here only a small river. We saw several of the great hill-forts which housed these people and their chiefs, including the Heuneburg, where excavations by Wolfgang Kimig in the 1950s and 1960s would reveal the mudbrick walls and bastions on a stone foundation beneath the massive grassy ramparts. These provided another link with the Greek civilisation of the Mediterranean in the sixth century BC, as significant as the discovery of pieces of Attic black-figure vases in the occupation layers. Nearby there was the gigantic tree-covered burial mound of Hoh Michele, over fifty feet high, not then explored. It proved to cover a couple buried in a plank-built chamber, laid on a wagon, he with his bow, she with her finery.

Gerhardt Bersu, director of the Archaeological Institute at Frankfurt, was of the party and showed us round his excavations of the Goldberg: he was, like Ian Richmond, a master of vivid exposition. He had uncovered a series of rectangular timber houses within the large hill-fort and located the chieftain's dwelling in a separate enclosure.[2] He explained to me in his fluent but accented English the significance of the roof construction, rolling his Rs and gesticulating with his fingers, 'In the house centre, two postholes means ridge-pole, one posthole, wigwam'. We now know there are more elaborate methods of roofing a round house, as Bersu was himself to demonstrate at his excavations at Little Woodbury, Wiltshire, in 1939, but he brought home to me the need to translate the holes in the ground into a three-dimensional structure. Long after, when I was excavating the Dartmoor granite round houses at Dean Moor in 1954, I overheard my students remark to each other, as they scraped interminably in the stony subsoil in search of postholes, 'She says we can't stop till we have got enough to keep the roof on'.

My return journey to England in May took me to Bonn, then only a small university town, and to Trier on the Moselle to study the monuments and the rich museum collections. It was a pleasant train journey up the idyllic winding Moselle valley, looking out of the window for the likely places where the villas of the wealthy Romans had been built, as celebrated by the late Latin poet Ausonius in the fourth century. At Trier I was deeply impressed by the scale of the surviving monuments: the magnificent Porta Nigra, standing four storeys high; the Basilica, probably an audience chamber in the imperial palace, surviving as a church; the Baths, and the amphitheatre, all reflecting the importance of the Gallic provincial and imperial capital in the third and fourth centuries.

Siegfried Loeschke, the museum curator, kindly took me to see the Igel column in the countryside overlooking the river. This was the tombstone of the Secundinii family, who were rich cloth merchants: it was elaborately carved with scenes of their business and their domestic life. It was the Whitsun holiday and Loeschke had brought his wife and two little girls with flaxen plaits, carrying a picnic in their rucksacks. Having taken me, the foreigner, to the site, he firmly instructed me to study the monument and they continued on their walk; I greatly envied them, but dutifully complied. Other fine tombstones and reliefs from Neumagen in the museum created a fascinating picture of daily life in the province, family meals, the lady seated in her basket chair with the mirror held up by her attendants, the schoolmaster with his pupils, tenants coming to pay rents, the transport of merchandise by river and road. I was able to make use of their imagery when it came to providing Alan Sorrell with authentic details to illustrate our children's book *Roman Britain*, published by Lutterworth Press in 1964.

The year 1931 was not a good one for me; I had only been back in England for a few weeks when I was suddenly taken ill and was operated on in Surrey for appendicitis. I endured the suffocating horrors of the only general anaesthetics then in use, chloroform and ether, and my apprehensive mother said that excavation was out of the question for at least eight weeks. I filled in the time with a West Country tour, visiting museums and Iron Age sites, including Glastonbury, Maiden Castle and Hembury hillfort. The parents had just acquired a new large Humber car which had to be run in at thirty miles an hour. They were only too glad to relieve the tedium by allowing me to take the car and the liveried chauffeur for my three-hundred-mile trip. It was the only time I have ever arrived at a site in a limousine.

I went back briefly to Richborough for the end of the excavations and to help pack up. Bushe-Fox was on the sick list after the shocking experience of being buried by the collapse of a trench at Colchester (Camulodunum). He was bending down to inspect a section with Christopher Hawkes when the treacherous gravel soil gave way and the full weight came upon his shoulder, which was badly broken. Christopher mercifully escaped unhurt, but Bushe-Fox never really fully recovered. That winter I had to manage the Richborough material on my own, occasionally taking proof and draft manuscript to his sick bed in Hampstead.

During the past year I had seen a good deal of Christopher and found his company very stimulating and agreeable. It was a new experience to be sharing intellectual interests and archaeological pursuits. The attraction was mutual. He had a great flow of speech punctuated by humorous comments and characteristic pauses: I found I enjoyed his teasing. Slowly I awakened sexually. I remember one day, after walking by the Serpentine happily brooding on our possible future together, I came across a bed of dahlias in the autumn sunshine near Lancaster Gate; suddenly they seemed to glow with an unearthly light, and I stood and gazed till the vision faded. The experience must have been self-induced by a flood of adrenalin, acting like a drug. I have occasionally been similarly carried away after gazing at a sunset. But 'the course of true love never did run smooth', and before long it was kindly intimated, with a parting kiss, that there was someone else; Jacquetta's star was in the ascendant.

As a diversion, I decided to help my father to produce a list of 'Antiquities of Surrey'. After his retirement, he had become involved with local government and was then a member, later an Alderman, of Surrey County Council, and Chairman of the Records and Ancient Monuments Committee. The original list of important sites and buildings which had been produced by the committee in 1912 was sketchy, and he had determined on a thorough revision. With the aid of a keen architect, C. D. Hawley, he visited and photographed many small houses in the vernacular style, mostly half-timbered, to which I added the barrows, hill-forts and other earthworks surviving on the extensive Surrey heathlands. The published list, though lacking statutory authority, was soon in general use by the planners in County Hall at Kingston, where the full records were filed, and was very much in advance of its time as a conservation project by a local authority.

To reward my efforts, Father decided to take me and my two sisters the following April (1932) on a Hellenic cruise organised by Sir Henry Lunn's Travel Agency, later Swan's Tours. We went by train to Milan, embarked at Venice the next day in a shabby Yugoslav boat and followed the well-worn route down the Adriatic to Crete, then to Athens and up through the Dardanelles to Troy and Constantinople, returning via Delos, Nauplion for Mycenae and Tiryns, and finally Corfu and Dubrovnik.

Two occasions stick in my mind. I was determined to see the walls of Byzantium, which were not on our itinerary in Constantinople. Father was confined to his cabin with a minor upset, brought on, he said, by the indifferent cooking on the boat, so having got the number of a tram and a written identification of our goal from the official tour guide, we three sisters set off. We found without difficulty the magnificent great walls with their succession of towers, all very neglected and grazed by sheep and goats. The afternoon went by very quickly, and by the time we got back to the city centre we could hear our boat hooting at the quay. In a panic we took the quickest way and ran downhill through the crowded bazaar, our long hair flying, much to the amusement of the Turks. We were the last to arrive before the gangway was raised.

The second encounter was of a different sort; it was during the visit to Mycenae and Tiryns that I first became aware of the qualities of Cyril Fox. He was on board with his wife, Olive, a rather arty type who spent most of her time sketching and in the company of two elderly gentlemen, Dr Louis Cobbett and Dr W. Palmer from Cambridge, whom we girls in our ribald way had written off as 'old funnies'. Somehow Cyril and I seemed to explore the same features away from the group: the postern gate at Mycenae, and the casement galleries within the city walls at Tiryns, where he explained to me the methods of corbel vaulting and of cyclopean wall building. I found it very exciting to make contact with and to learn from this good-looking and inspiring man.

I next saw him in action at the First International Congress of Prehistoric and Protohistoric Sciences at King's College in London the following August, when he gave one of four keynote evening addresses, entitled 'The Personality of Britain'. It was a memorable occasion; the audience realised it was listening to new ideas, eloquently expressed, which were fundamental to an understanding of human settlement in Britain at all periods. Cyril discussed and illustrated the position of the island in relation to the European mainland, and to the eastern and western seaways which governed the course of invasion and trade; the effects of geological structure which divided the island into a Lowland and Highland Zone, and of the changes in soils, altitude and vegetation which encouraged or inhibited settlement. These were some of the novel concepts which were to become part of archaeological thinking for the next forty years. At the time it was more than most of us could absorb, though I left the lecture hall feeling my mind had been stretched.

I had spent the earlier part of the summer in Devon, digging with Miss Liddell at Hembury hill-fort near Honiton. I had gone there because I knew she did all her own site recording, and I realised I must learn how to set out and plan cuttings, and how to draw sections. At Richborough this work was done by a professional surveyor sent from the Office of Works in London, and I realised it was inadequate when it appeared in the published reports.

Dorothy Liddell was a strange woman, middle-aged and grey-haired, permanently saddened by the loss of her only brother and of her fiancé in the First World War. She had learnt her archaeology from her brother-in-law Alex Keiller, a rich and wayward member of the Dundee marmalade family who was working at Windmill Hill, the Neolithic causeway camp near Avebury. She was, I think, uncertain of herself as a director of an excavation. She relied greatly on the support of her experienced working foreman, W. E. Young, who came with her from Avebury. At Hembury the work was carried out by six paid labourers, and by a succession of keen amateurs from the newly-founded Devon Archaeological Society, which sponsored the excavations. My fellow student was Mary Nicol, later Mrs Leakey of Olduvai Gorge fame in Tanzania. We were in lodgings in Honiton. Miss Liddell, as we always called her, never 'Dorothy', had a private sitting-room to which we were not invited, and also a tent on the site to which she withdrew to eat her sandwiches – fish paste on Fridays because she was a Roman Catholic. It was a great contrast to the convivial atmosphere at Richborough. I resolved that when I came to direct an excavation, I would never behave like that to my helpers.

Hembury was a magnificent Iron Age hill-fort on the end of a Greensand spur, at that time heathland, and clear of the trees and bracken that now swamp its triple lines of defence and the interior. The work that year concentrated on the deeply-inturned west entrance and I learnt much about the detection and clearance of large postholes in the stony and sticky yellow subsoil, so different from the Kentish sands. These held the massive revetment for the long entrance passage, and also revealed the position of the main gate and a timber bridge across the ends of the inner rampart. There was also the novelty of encountering slot trenches with close-set postholes in them separated by stone packing, so well-defined that it was possible to replace timber uprights in them and to make a reconstruction of a free-standing palisade.[3] Later work in 1983 by Malcolm Todd has now identified it as the front revetment of the original box rampart. I also learnt to recognise charred grain found in hearths and cooking holes belonging to the previous Neolithic occupation, as well as the differences between small pieces of Iron Age and Neolithic handmade pottery.

As students our main tasks were to count and to bag the masses of Neolithic flint and chert flakes, and to collect and label soil samples and charcoal fragments, which at Richborough were disregarded. These all went with the more spectacular finds of stone implements and pottery to be stored at the Exeter Museum. With the development of radio-carbon analysis in the 1960s I remembered the stratified charcoals from Hembury, and unearthed enough from the museum cellars to submit to the British Museum. These enabled the Neolithic occupation to be dated to the late fourth millennium BC, 3480–3000 BC, one of the earliest then known of the period.[4]

I found that the work at Hembury was technically of a high standard so far as the strict setting out of cuttings and the cleaning of features was concerned, but I was shocked to find that the soil was removed in arbitrary depths of nine to twelve inches regardless of stratification. This was the method used by Keiller at the Windmill Hill Neolithic causewayed camp, and it made a nonsense of a ditch filling, for example, and of the recorded position of finds. Nevertheless I decided to accept Miss Liddell's invitation to go with Mary Nicol to her next excavation for the Hampshire Field Club at Meon Hill in September. I wanted to see how to start an excavation from scratch and to gain experience of digging on the southern chalk, the basic material of many famous archaeological sites.

We stayed in Stockbridge, an attractive Hampshire village with a wide central market street and a clear chalk stream, the river Test, famous for its trout fishing, running below the bridge at the far end of the village. One Sunday I managed to get to see the splendid Lutyens white house, Marsh Court, lower down the valley, built of blocks of solid Lower Chalk and with lovely carved detail inside.

The Meon Hill site was in a large arable field on the hillside beyond the river. It proved to be an agricultural settlement of the early Iron Age, initially defined by a palisade, and later enclosed by a circular bank and ditch which had revealed the site on aerial photographs. It produced quite a lot of attractive decorated pottery, coated with a red slip, known as haematite ware, and also coarse ware jars with finger-tip impressions, both characteristic of the fifth to the third centuries BC in the Wessex region. Much of our time was taken up by cleaning the skeletons of some wretched Anglo-Saxons who appeared to have been killed and buried on the hill soon after the Norman Conquest. One had a coin of William Rufus beside him. I learnt a good deal about human anatomy as a result. When finally the underlying chalk was exposed, it was full of irregularities: there were worn hollows, pits of all sorts and sizes, scattered postholes, hearths, baked clay, burnt stones and charcoal in bewildering confusion. Miss Liddell could make little of it, though laboriously contouring and planning the site.[5] It was not until Gerhardt Bersu – the same eminent German archaeologist I had encountered on the Goldberg – had dug a comparable site at Little Woodbury in Wiltshire at the invitation of the Prehistoric Society in 1938, that the features could be satisfactorily explained. The pits were for grain storage, the hearths and associated baked clay ovens were for corn drying, some of the postholes were supports for drying racks, and the worn hollows and terracing were working places, where the people sat at harvest time, preparing the grain for storage.[6]

I regarded the Meon Hill excavation as the end of my practical apprenticeship; although largely self-taught, I felt I now had enough basic knowledge of archaeological techniques and material to direct the excavation of a small Iron Age or Roman site in England, and to produce an adequate report. I was conscious of my weakness in surveying, and in accurate setting out and section drawing, but I felt that these would improve with practice and could be supplemented by professional assistance. Little did I guess that it would be five years before I was digging again, and then as a married woman with a small son, on a hillside 1,350 feet up above a Welsh mining village, investigating the primitive long-houses at Dinas Nodda, Gelligaer.

The dramatic change in my circumstances started in August in the interval between Hembury and Meon Hill, as I sat in my London hairdresser in Beauchamp Place under the dryer. Glancing at the evening paper I saw a paragraph recording the death by drowning of the wife of Dr Cyril Fox, director of the National Museum of Wales. She had been on holiday at Llangennith in the Gower Peninsula with their two little girls whilst he was away in mid-Wales on field work. I was profoundly disturbed by the news, remembering our recent encounters in Greece. When I returned to Walton for the weekend, after much hesitation, I screwed up my courage and wrote a letter of condolence as best I could, ending 'it seems all wrong that this should happen to you'. After a long delay, I received a warm acknowledgement on black-edged notepaper in Cyril's distinctive bold handwriting, followed by a presentation copy of *The Personality of Britain*, similarly inscribed.

At this stage, I drew back, telling myself it would be foolish to involve myself further with a man twice my age who had the responsibility for two young daughters, however attractive mentally and physically he might be. I wrote a cool response. However, an invitation to meet at the Antiquaries, where I was again working on the Richborough small finds in October, and where Cyril came for monthly committee meetings, was difficult to refuse. We lunched together several times at Stewart's, a modest restaurant long since gone from the corner of Bond Street and Piccadilly, and after-wards walked down to St James's Park to admire the ducks. It was all very easy and agreeable. He told me how good the Wheelers had been to him, insisting that he stayed with them at St Albans, and that he and Rik had hired horses to ride from Verulamium across the Hertfordshire countryside to see the great Belgic earthworks at Beech Bottom and at Wheathampstead, which the excavations had identified as the *oppidum* of Cassivellaunus, the Belgic king and opponent of Julius Caesar. Though Cyril had left Cambridge for Cardiff before I came up to Newnham in 1926, I heard from the Burkitts of his achievements on the East Anglian dykes, and was familiar with his book, *The Archaeology of the Cambridge Region,* with its magnificent series of coloured period maps. Now I learnt a little of the Fox family background, less affluent than mine; his old father was a retired bank manager, living at Bursledon on the Hamble, and a keen Hampshire antiquary.

I heard much about his present job at Cardiff and of the glories of the National Museum of Wales, which he insisted that I should come to see for myself. Accordingly I made the excuse to my parents that I needed to visit the museum in connection with the Richborough work, and went down to Cardiff by a Saturday morning train at the end of November. Cyril met me in his small Austin Ten and took me straight away to the museum in its splendid open setting in Cathays Park. It was a monumental building designed by the London architects, Smith and Brewer, with the entrance fronted by Doric columns and a flight of granite steps. Beneath a central dome which diffused a warm light there was a marble-lined great hall, with twin flights of stairs at either end leading to the balcony and the first-floor galleries. It created a notable well-balanced space that was to give me pleasure for many years to come. At that time the BBC broad-cast morning concerts from the balcony, and on entering, the sound was overwhelming. After a brief conducted tour of the galleries and new Welsh folk rooms, I settled down conscientiously to study the Roman material from Caerleon and Caerwent in the archaeology department.

We stayed the weekend with Cyril's old friends, Joe and Barbara Blundell, at Nottage Court, a fine sixteenth-century manor house near Porthcawl. On Sunday we were sent off with a picnic lunch to explore the sand-hills at Merthyr Mawr Warren, where the Blundells had found the remains of an Iron Age settlement, and picked up pieces of crucibles and an uncommon bronze La Tène brooch. The sand dunes were immense, a hundred feet high and spreading inland; a film company had even used them as a substitute for the Sahara when making a movie of *Beau Geste*. With an effort we located the archaeological site, blown clear at the base of the shifting sand, but revealing only burnt stones, shells and charcoal. We ate our sandwiches happily in the wintry sunshine beside the Ogmore river, near the ruins of Candleston Castle. It was clear that we enjoyed each other's company, sharing in field work in the open air, though I was conscious throughout the visit of being 'on approval'. Equally, I was weighing up the prospect of living in South Wales, and was glad to find that Cardiff was not the black industrial city I had imagined, and that there was good country in the Vale of Glamorgan nearby.

Christmas then intervened, when the claims of our respective families took priority: a sad occasion, no doubt, for the Fox girls back from a new boarding convent school at East Grinstead. In January Cyril suggested a visit to Hampton Court, one of my favourite places. Together we went through the state apartments, where I had previously concentrated on the pictures and furniture. Now Cyril turned my attention to architectural detail, to the proportion of the Wren windows, the glazing bars, the panelling and the characteristic curves of the bolection mouldings of the fireplaces; I found it all enthralling. We strolled about the formal gardens where the first snowdrops were appearing before returning, sitting close together on the top of a bus. Nothing was said, but a visit to Kew Gardens was fixed for the next month. I was aware that my resistance had been overcome and that I was being swept along by a tide of strong feelings. When Cyril came in February to collect me from Trafalgar Square, bringing a bunch of sweet-scented pheasant's-eye narcissus, he threw his arms around me and the matter was settled, almost without words. We did go to Kew, but that day even the flowers in the Alpine House failed to distract me.

Later we both realised there was much to do. I told my parents, who were naturally rather taken aback, but my mother succumbed to Cyril's charm from his first visit, whilst my father, who approved my choice, was amazed that a museum director should receive a salary of only £1,100 a year. We agreed that I should meet his daughters at Easter, and that our wedding and my move to Cardiff should take place before their summer holidays. Obviously it had to be a quiet family occasion, coming so soon after the tragic event; this pleased me, but my mother was greatly disappointed, for she would have enjoyed a lavish wedding party. The event was fixed for 6 July, after Cyril had attended the Museums Association meeting at Norwich, and since I was resident in Trafalgar Square, we could be married in the attractive old Chelsea parish church on the Thames embankment.

In the meanwhile there was the choice of an engagement ring. Cyril took me to see H. G. Murphy, a first-class jeweller and silversmith who taught at the London County Council School of Arts and Crafts. I had no idea of the beauty of semi-precious stones and had no hesitation in accepting a translucent blue-green chrysoprase, to be set in gold and, at Cyril's suggestion, flanked by spirals; whether these were of Celtic or of Mycenean inspiration he never told me. I felt a little self-conscious at first wearing so large and beautiful an object from which I am now inseparable. The ring has been much admired and I have told many enquirers that chrysoprase is an uncommon stone found in Russia and in Australia, and was known to St John as the material of one of the gates of Heaven, in his Book of Revelation.

Before the public announcement of our engagement, I met the girls with Cyril for a day at the London Zoo followed by a long weekend in Cambridge, staying with the Lethbridges at Middlefield, then called Mount Blow, their spacious Lutyens house near Shelford. I had bought myself an elegant dark emerald-green suit with a boldly-patterned linen blouse, and hoped to make a good impression. The girls were a nice-looking pair: Felicity was thirteen, Penelope, then known as Tiny, was ten. It was difficult to judge their reaction or my own. I think we were all ready to be friendly, though I knew I could never be a substitute Mum, and would have to walk warily.

It must always be a difficult situation to become a young stepmother; it was aggravated in my case by some resentment at the speed of Cyril's remarriage from the Congreve-Pridgeon family, with whom Felicity and Penelope spent part of every school holidays at Steyning in Sussex. I cannot claim to have made a great success of this new relationship, but neither was it a conspicuous failure.

We never had a row, though I was sorely tempted to let fly when they made a terrible racket in the back of the car during my first trip across central Wales to Aberystwyth; had they been my own children I would have had no hesitation in ticking them off. I always tried to encourage them in their school work, helped them with buying nice clothes, and provided the creature comforts they needed in the holidays. I packed and unpacked a long succession of school trunks. The tension was eased after the birth of our first son, Charles, in 1934, and on the whole we grew to be a happy family.

We spent Whitsun together at Overbury Manor in Worcestershire, staying with the Holland-Martins. Robert was a director of Martin's Bank and treasurer of the Society of Antiquaries, and well-acquainted with Cyril, who had stayed there before. His wife was the same Mrs Holland-Martin who had been responsible for my early London schooling with René Ironside; we were both surprised by the coincidence. They lived in some style in a splendid stone house at the foot of Bredon Hill, with extensive well-kept gardens, culminating in a group of magnificent plane trees at the end of the lawn. It was hot that May, and we had most meals on the terrace. I remember Mrs Holland-Martin, a formidable domestic tyrant, telling off Rob for putting his knife into the marmalade at breakfast, and, in the fading light after dinner, she took him hunting snails in the flower border and drowned them in a pail of hot water. Cyril and I walked to the top of Bredon Hill to inspect the Iron Age hill-fort with two lines of ramparts and inturned entrances. It was excavated by Thalassa Hencken a few years later, and established as a work of several periods.[7] All around the woods below were breaking into their bright May greenery with drifts of bluebells beneath, and there were extensive views from the summit eastward across the blossoming Vale of Evesham to the Cotswolds and westward to the indented outline of the Malvern Hills. It was a day to be remembered.

It was not long before I paid my first visit to Rhiwbina to see my new home. This was in a small-scale garden village development on the fringe of open country, run by a trust, in imitation of Ebenezer Howard's work at Letchworth. It was a contrast with other Cardiff suburbs, with its uniform cream rough-cast houses, hedged front gardens and spacious layout. The estate architect was Alwyn Lloyd, a close friend of Cyril's, who lived nearby. Our house was called Four Elms, from the surviving old hedgerow trees, including one magnificent wych elm at the bottom of the garden, a joy in spring with its yellow flower bracts. It was an attractive three-bedroom house, small by The Grange standards, but with a quarter-acre garden backing on to the Whitchurch golf course, just the right size for me. I was rather taken aback to see the initials of C. and O. F. permanently built into a panel over the front door. Inside there were polished oak floors and stairs, grey pine doors with blue paint surrounds, and cream walls. The exception was the dining room, which was a bright yellow; the painter had been heard to exclaim as he splashed it on, 'They won't want no canaries here'. Cyril had given me a free hand with redecoration, so I decided to whiten it in line with the rest. There was a lot of fine antique oak furniture in the house and, apart from new beds from Heals, curtains and loose covers, little change was needed. I resolved to remove Olive's pictures in oils to the girls' bedroom and to replace the prim elderly housekeeper as soon as possible. My wedding presents supplied us lavishly with new china, cutlery, glass and real linen; Uncle Alan McLean provided me with twelve of everything in glass, including finger bowls, ice plates and champagne glasses, rather unnecessary luxuries, of which there are several survivors in my cupboard after fifty-three years and two house moves.

I helped my mother choose a trousseau with lots of lace-trimmed underwear in coral pink crêpe-de-chine, made to order at Harvey Nichols' in Knightsbridge. I recently gave the last pair of camiknickers, carefully preserved in tissue paper, to Exeter Museum. I did not want a conventional white wedding dress, but felt the need of something beautiful for the occasion. I chose a long dress of periwinkle blue lace over a pale pink silk, with a silver Russian style headdress and short blue tulle veil, and I carried a sheaf of pink gladioli.

We were married on a fine July morning in 1933. Cyril's favourite younger sister, Mary Gotch, 'Babs', an accomplished musician, played her violin; my sisters and close relatives were there and my intimate friends, Pam and Sophie. The girls, Felicity and Penelope, had a day off from school. I remember being eager to begin my short walk up the aisle on my father's arm to where Cyril was waiting.

Afterwards we went back to Trafalgar Square, where I changed, and then left with a picnic lunch which we ate in Richmond Park. Rather selfishly I had declined to join a family lunch party at the Rubens Hotel, because I felt we needed to escape and be together as soon as possible; it now seems a bit unkind. We spent a blissful weekend in a Surrey house and garden among the scented pine trees near Farnham, before returning to London and sailing from Tilbury for Vigo and Santiago de Compostela for our honeymoon.

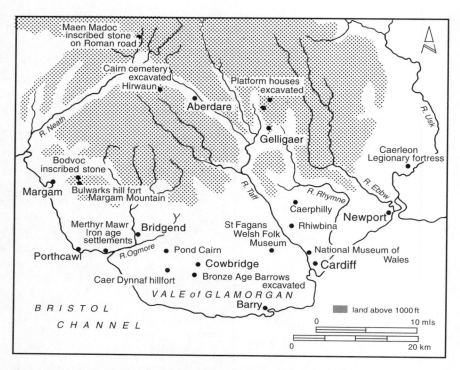

Diagram map of South Wales, marking sites in Chapters 4,5 and 6.

Chapter Five

South Wales
Before the War

1933 – 1939

We came back to Rhiwbina having landed at Plymouth from three weeks' honeymoon in Galicia. I was confronted by the challenge of converting myself from an archaeological career girl of twenty-five into a 'godly matron', as the Prayer Book has it, and the wife of a distinguished man of fifty. The age gap never seemed to matter, but I did often feel regretful that we were not starting from scratch to build our home together, and that there were so many constraints in our daily life. Not only did I have to cope with running a home and garden, two schoolgirl stepdaughters and the needs of a beloved husband, and all too soon my first pregnancy, but there were the demands of Cyril's position as the Director of the National Museum of Wales to be met. My predecessor, Olive, had opted out, but having already been involved with museum work I was determined to take part, both on social occasions and in archaeological work in Wales.

At the museum there were the formal meetings of the Court of Governors, a large representative body who met to receive the Annual Report. I was present in my best dress at the tea party afterwards in the museum library, where I met the President, Lord Plymouth of St Fagan's Castle, and other officers. I made it my job to get to know members of the Museum Council, who met monthly; some were rather sticky, but before long I learnt to appreciate the good company of Leonard Twiston-Davies at Rockfield, his Monmouthshire home, and of the Raglans at Cefntilla, who became real friends. I made every effort to be on friendly terms with Archie Lee, the efficient Museum Secretary, an ex-army captain, a power in the organisation and a loyal supporter of the Director, though we had little else in common. It was easier to relate to the keepers of the departments: Dr F. T. North, the geologist; A. H. Hyde, the botanist; L. G. Cowley, the zoologist, as well as the rather stolid Victor Nash-Williams, the archaeologist, and his lively red-haired assistant, Peter Grimes. Only Iorwerth Peate, the arrogant Welsh-speaking Welshman in charge of Folk Life defeated me. It was not long before I felt I was generally accepted at the museum, though I remember overhearing a rather disparaging remark about 'the Director's girl-wife'.

Other duties were formal lunches and dinners to which 'the Museum Director and Lady' were invited by the City's Lord Mayor on suitable occasions, which were usually very boring: a bad meal concluding with long rhetorical speeches. More interesting were the summons to dine at Cardiff Castle; my telephone would ring and a voice announce, 'This is Lady Bute's secretary,' and then invite us to a meal usually no more than a couple of days ahead. On one occasion, I replied accepting in the third person, posing as 'Lady Fox's secretary'. Still, it was well worth the effort of dressing up, and going to eat in style in the magnificent painted Gothic Hall, redecorated by William Burgess in the nineteenth century. There were footmen wearing white gloves behind the elaborate high-backed chairs, a succession of courses and wines, ending with some of the best Madeira in the world, which came from Lord Bute's cellars and vineyards. It usually transpired that there were visitors in the house party who wanted a personal conducted tour of the museum by the Director, or a visit to the ruins of Caerphilly Castle, where Cyril was an archaeological adviser on the repairs. These days are no more, for both Cardiff and Caerphilly Castles are now in public ownership, and succeeding generations of the Butes have confined their interest to their Scottish estates.

There were also evening receptions at the museum for learned societies. I well remember the first occasion, the Cambrian Archaeological Association's meeting in September 1933, when Rik Wheeler came to stay with us in Rhiwbina and was surprisingly kind to me, perceiving I was distinctly nervous. Cyril was the President, and we received the guests at the foot of the stairs in the museum's great entrance hall; I wore my blue lace wedding dress. Soon after we were at Leicester for the British Association's meeting, staying with Alderman Squire, a great supporter of the museums movement, whilst Cyril was President of their association. The meetings of Section H (Archaeology and Anthropology) were dull, but there was a splendid reception at which everyone wore academic dress; I envied Cyril robed in the black silk gown with scarlet facings of a Cambridge PhD. Not until 1985 would I be entitled to wear the red silk with blue facings of an Exeter Honorary DLitt; in the meantime I had to be content with the modest white silk hood of a Cambridge MA.

My ménage at Four Elms rested on the services of Nan Moran, the splendid Cook-General whom my mother had surprisingly managed to find for me whilst Cyril and I were on our honeymoon. She was a cheerful friendly Irishwoman who never lost her soft brogue and flow of conversation, a hard worker and a really good cook. She made entertaining easy, since she thought nothing of producing an evening meal for six, which was all our dining room could hold. I supplemented her efforts by employing a succession of school-leavers, who came daily for three hours to earn 7s.6d (thirty-seven and a half pence) a week and a cooked lunch, much needed in those hard times in South Wales. Nan lived with us until 1945 when she married, but continued to come daily, a real friend of all the family.

All this was very different from life in Trafalgar Square; I missed Pam and Sophie and my London friends, and had problems finding others of my own generation. Cyril's contemporaries in Wales were too old and, though very kind, were set in their ways. An exception were Max and Kathleen Ede, whom I encountered at one of the stylish dinner parties given by Willie James, a retired lawyer in Llandaff. His guests were carefully selected for their literary or artistic interests; good conversation flowed easily, along with fine claret or burgundy. Max was a solicitor and a collector of early printed books in his spare time; Kathleen had read English at Newnham, preceding me by five years, and so had encountered Cyril there. We found we had much in common to talk about. Like ourselves, they were both good walkers and had a cottage in the Brecon Beacons, where we visited them on holiday. I remember Max climbing the hills in an open-necked shirt, looking like one of the Romantic Lakeland poets he so admired, and so different from the conventional Cardiff lawyer. When I found myself pregnant, it was to Kathleen I turned for advice. She recommended me to Dr Loudon, a Scotsman who believed in leaving things to nature whenever possible. I was most terribly sick in the early stages, but at least I avoided the ill effects of the 1930s equivalent of thalidomide.

My other young friends were the Murray-Thrieplands. I learnt from the local papers of the marriage of Peter of New House in nearby Llanishen with Marged Howard-Stepney from Llanelli, and that he had been excavating with Leonard Woolley at Ur. I boldly wrote and invited them to dinner, stressing our mutual archaeological interests and apologising for omitting the nonsense of a formal 'afternoon call', still then prevalent in middle-class Cardiff society. It was a very successful evening, and the beginning of a lasting friendship that weathered the break-up of their marriage in 1936, and was renewed with Marged's successor, Leslie Scott. Peter was a fair-haired, tall and good-looking young man, immensely strong, having rowed for Oxford, and a bit shy and reserved. He had the deferential manners of an Old Etonian, but beneath the veneer he had unconventional ideas which he adhered to with great determination. It is quite in keeping that Rik Wheeler met him travelling steerage on his way to visit Leonard Woolley in the Near East in 1936. He belonged to a wealthy landowning family with considerable estates in Cardiff, which Peter ran with the help of an agent from New House. There were also properties in Scotland to which he was heir, at Dale in remote Caithness, and at Dryburgh Abbey on the Border where his parents lived. His father was Colonel-in-Chief of the Welsh Guards, which Peter had declined to join; his mother was a tyrannical old lady, who for many years kept locked certain of the best rooms at New House full of her furniture, to the justifiable annoyance of Marged. Consequently, when their first son, Mark, was born, his nurseries were in the attics. New House was within walking distance of Rhiwbina, across the fields and along the track at the foot of the Wenallt hill, and we went there on many occasions. It was a rambling early nineteenth-century stone house, built up against the hillside, with a superb view south over the city to the Bristol Channel, the Holm islands and the Somerset coast. Now the green fields have been obliterated by a mass of small houses and the M4 motorway, and the house is a country hotel.

During my early years in Cardiff, South Wales was suffering acutely from the economic depression, which had started with the collapse of the currency and of the coal trade in 1929–30. Unemployment was widespread, particularly among the miners. I remember many shops boarded up in Merthyr Tydfil, and the groups of hopeless men standing at the street corners in the villages up the grim mining valleys. My kind neighbours in Rhiwbina were the Lewises, Edward, a middle-aged solicitor, and his wife, Amy, with four teenaged daughters. She was a Quaker, and belonged to a group of the Friends who had started a community centre in Senghenydd, near Caerphilly, where the mine had closed; it provided relief and some occupation, mainly useful handcrafts, for the villagers. I too had a social conscience, and so offered to go there with Amy. Together we visited the mean terraced houses with their tiny backyards strung along the hillside; in many we saw a feeble sick man or a pale young woman lying in the front room. Lung tuberculosis was rife, with little hope of cure, and was aggravated by malnutrition from life on the dole, as the unemployment benefit was called even then.

In the centre I gave some afternoon classes for the women, using English literature as a basis. It was mostly readings of simple narrative or lyric poetry, which seemed to me to offer some escape from the stresses of their daily life. My audience sat quietly listening, but it was hard to know what they were thinking and to start any discussion. It was my first effort at teaching. Later I arranged with Peter Murray-Thriepland to go down one of the better working coal-mines at Maesteg, so I could see the conditions at first-hand. I found it puzzling that such a hard way of life underground in the dark and the dirt held any attraction for the men. When excavating on Gelligaer Common in 1936, I employed several ex-miners, who walked up daily from Bedliniog, 500 feet below in the valley, and worked an eight-hour day for 36s (£1.80) a week. I found it was possible to get permanent employment and a family house for one of them on a farming resettlement scheme in the Vale of Glamorgan, but none of them wanted to leave the valley or to give up the hope of a return to mining. This was the oppressive background to my first years in Cardiff; gradually it improved during the late 1930s, with a trading estate for small firms opening at Treforest and an ordnance factory started at Bridgend.

Despite the many new demands on my time and energy, I maintained my predominant interest in archaeology. Cyril had been asked by the editor of the projected *Glamorgan County History* to write the prehistory section, and I agreed to co-operate. It was to keep us busy for a very long time. Although our pioneer field work was never written up as a whole, it gave us a real understanding of the region and much enjoyment of days in the open air. The project was abandoned during the war years, and the volume entitled *Early Glamorgan* was only completed by another set of contributors in 1984, with Hubert Savory from the National Museum as editor. I reviewed it in *Archaeologia Cambrensis*. It was clear that very little field survey had been done in the area, so we decided on a systematic inspection and search, working initially westwards from the Rhymney valley, the county boundary, to the Vale of Neath. This included a tract of the high moorland above the mining valleys and of the coastal lowland, the Vale of Glamorgan. At weekends and any other free day we would set off armed with Ordnance Survey maps, measuring tapes, compass, field notebooks and a Voightländer camera. Our starting point was usually a known site, for example, a hill-fort marked on the six-inch map. After walking all round the earthwork and locating the entrance, we discussed and often argued about the meaning of what we could see. Cyril then made a measured sketch plan and I took descriptive notes to be elaborated and written up at leisure next day. We did not limit our field work to prehistoric sites, but recorded everything we saw and presumed to be of pre-Norman date. In this way I acquired working capital for future articles, not only for 'The dual colonisation of East Glamorgan',[1] but also for 'The siting of inscribed memorial stones'.[2] We were the first to perceive the logic of the ridgeways as lines of communication, the first to record the numbers of cairns and barrows in the upland, and the first to study the soil types in the lowland in relation to the sites. We also made some important new discoveries. We found and planned a forgotten Iron Age hill-fort, Caer Dynnaf at Llanblethian in the Vale of Glamorgan, with an inturned entrance and an outer enclosure.[3] Our friend Bryan O'Neil, then the Inspector of Ancient Monuments for Wales, jokingly suggested we should christen it Vulpidunum, or Fox Fort. The remains of stone structures in the interior have proved to be of Roman date.[4] We studied and planned the interior of an unusual small fortified enclosure close by, known as Mynydd Bychan, with its three or four stone-based round huts and courtyards. Excavation by H. N. Savory was to show it was of late Iron Age origin and had been occupied from 50 BC until AD 100, as well as in medieval times.[5] It was not all plain sailing; we were taken in by an extensive system of small fields visible on an aerial photograph, and obviously unrelated to the existing large hedge banks. The area was known as The Corrwg, Penllyn. We spent a considerable time doing a chain survey, with the help of Peter Murray-Thriepland, but after digging some test holes we realised that the fields were smallholdings of eighteenth-century date, and not of the Iron Age or Roman period as we had expected.

Inland we walked along the grassy high moorland ridges of Pennant sandstone which divide the coal valleys, noting the large round barrows and cairns strung out along the crest, and finding others not marked on the maps. There were also cemeteries of small cairns at the edge of the plateau: some, with a small cist, were undoubtedly sepulchral; others were probably stone heaps, from clearance from ancient cultivation. A war-time excavation of some of these at Hirwaun, at the head of the Aberdare valley, with Leslie Murray-Thriepland produced no finds, but the outline of a possible shallow grave was sometimes visible beneath the stones.[6] The cairns still remain a puzzle, both in Glamorgan and in the upland elsewhere.[7] Another new discovery was a series of nine cross-ridge dykes, earthwork barriers strategically placed at the narrowest places in the hill system.[8] Most were low banks and ditches which would need a palisade or thorn fence to make an effective barrier. All faced north, and we interpreted them as check points to control movement along the ridgeways in the direction of the coast. They would also be useful as boundaries of tribal grazing on the open moorland above the tree line. Cyril had encountered similar works in mid-Wales when surveying Offa's Dyke, and so had no hesitation in assigning the Glamorgan series to the post-Roman period.

Our most significant discoveries were made almost at the outset of our campaign in 1933–4, on Margam Mountain, the upland north-east of Port Talbot, where we re-examined three peculiar hill-forts and four sites of platform houses, new to Welsh archaeology.[9] The principal hill-fort Y Bwlwarcau, The Bulwarks, consisted of four concentric sub-rectangular enclosures and, like the two other less elaborate examples, was placed not on the summit but on the hill slopes, and clearly was not designed for warfare. The earthworks were all small-scale, the entrances simple and on the lower side. We interpreted the unusual fortifications as being of post-Roman date, mainly because of the nearby Bodvoc stone, a sixth-century memorial stone recording three generations of Celtic rulers, the first with the Roman name of Eternalis. However, we were wrong: excavation in Devon in 1937–8 of a very similar earthwork on Milber Down, Newton

Abbot, produced pottery and other finds of middle and late Iron Age date, from 300 BC onwards.

I was to return to the subject some twenty years later, when we had left Cardiff for Exeter, and after I had seen many more such forts in Devon and Cornwall. Gradually my ideas clarified; I realised that there were several varieties of the type, which was confined to south-west England and South Wales, and that the salient feature was the provision of multiple enclosures. The explanation I suggested was that the principal occupation of the inhabitants was cattle-keeping, well known to be important to Celtic peoples.[10] Finally in 1958 I concluded that these forts were an insular regional development with a logic of their own, being designed to provide a defensible central dwelling place for a chieftain and his kin, and a place of security for their stock in adjoining enclosures.[11] Such ideas are now generally accepted, though they still need testing by a large-scale excavation. At the time, Wheeler and other archaeologists only thought of hill-forts in terms of military architecture. Thus Y Bwlwarcau provided a seed which germinated after an interval and, when transplanted, blossomed in my later work.

The discovery of platform houses had a more immediate effect, for it resulted in my first single-handed excavation in 1936 and 1938, of which more later. On Margam Mountain Cyril noticed the first examples, which had been inserted into the middle enclosure of Y Bwlwarcau, blocking an original entrance, and so clearly of later date. They characteristically consisted of a pair of rectangular platforms about 50 x 20 feet levelled into the hillside, with the long axis at right angles to the slope. Usually there were indications of opposite doors, and often a protective low bank round the upper end to divert surface water from the timber long house presumed to have been erected on the platform. We interpreted them as upland farms of pre-Norman date; excavation was to show that some on Gelligaer Common were occupied in the late thirteenth and fourteenth centuries. Further field work with Peter Murray-Thriepland, who shared my love of hill walking, revealed twenty-six sites in East Glamorgan. We located them on the ridges by following the contour just above the change of slope to the valley, where the lower ends of the platforms stuck out like a sore thumb.

Our field work, however, was interrupted in 1934–5, first by the birth of our eldest son, Charles, and then by Cyril's illness. Admittedly I kept going until almost the very last minute, with a very prim maternity nurse from Cambridge, recommended by Peggy Burkitt, trailing behind us on Margam Mountain when we went back to check some measurements. I then entertained Ake Campbell and two other distinguished Scandinavian archaeologists to tea the day before the event, which happily coincided with my own birthday on 29 July. Aided by Dr Loudon and chloroform, I had an almost painless labour at home, and was delighted to have produced a son. It then became obvious that the little house in Rhiwbina was too small to hold another family, so we decided to add on a nursery flat over the garage. As soon as I was allowed to travel – four weeks in those days – I went with the baby to my mother's at The Grange and the builders moved in. A devoted first-time Granny and the old Nanny thoroughly disapproved of the Truby King clothing and feeding methods I had been taught and adopted, leaving Charles to cry in his pram in the garden until the end of the stipulated four-hour interval. The pendulum has now swung the other way and babies are breast-fed on demand. Charles, however, was a happy and lively baby and thrived on the regular routine. I found a nice young nanny for him through advertising in *Nursery World,* and we came back to Rhiwbina in October.

Cyril had been weakened by two stressful years: he had lost a wife in tragic circumstances and acquired another; he had produced a book, an acknowledged small masterpiece, *The Personality of Britain*, and with the indefatigable Lal Chitty was working on another, a prehistory of Britain to be published by Methuen. He was President of the Museums' Association and of the Cambrian Archaeological Association, frequently travelling to London and Shrewsbury for meetings, as well as attending to all the routine work of the museum in Cardiff. He quickly wrote an account of our field work on Margam Mountain, which was published in *Antiquity* in December 1934, but by that time he had succumbed to a violent infection, ultimately diagnosed as a Norwegian form of dysentery. He had to be nursed at home – the hospitals in Cardiff were not very pleasant – and for some days the outcome was uncertain. I have never forgotten or forgiven the high church Anglican priest, Father Clark, who came and then told me in the sitting room that suffering was a good thing. Cyril's recovery was slow, but helped by the news, in strict confidence, that he was to receive a knighthood in the New Year Honours List for his services to archaeology and to the National Museum of Wales.

Soon after Christmas, when I had weaned the baby and the stepdaughters had come home, another misfortune occurred; both Felicity and Penelope developed measles. The nurse, dear Gladys Davies, was recalled and we coped with the high fevers in darkened rooms, fearing that little Charles might become infected. Ultimately all was well, but Cyril was still very languid, unable to concentrate, feeling faint and sleeping badly, and quite unable to enjoy the flood of congratulatory letters which arrived in the new year. It became apparent that he was having what was then called 'a nervous breakdown' and that the local doctors could do nothing for him. My parents were very sympathetic and suggested I should take him to The Grange in Surrey when they went off to the Italian Riviera in February. I got advice from a Harley Street specialist, and he was placed in the care of a Dr Abbot in a Surrey nursing home. After a couple of months he began to mend, and his convalescence was completed at Tenby, Pembrokeshire, where Leonard Twiston-Davies kindly lent us his early nineteenth-century terraced holiday house facing the North Sands. I have very happy recollections of us playing with baby Charles on the beach in the early summer, and of visiting the flower-studded valley of the Ritec, Bishop's Palace at Lamphey and the Castle at Manorbier. Cyril's self-confidence gradually came back and he returned to work at the museum in August, but it was never quite the same for me thereafter. I had had to cope with so much on my own, anxiously to manage our finances and to make all decisions. The days of 'the first fine free and careless rapture' were over, but had I known that there would be many productive years ahead for each of us, both together and individually, I would have been less apprehensive.

Collaboration between two kindred minds is not easy to assess, and the balance varied over the years. Initially Cyril was the leader, and I looked up to him and whole-heartedly accepted his ideas. Unlike wives of several distinguished academics I have known, I was not jealous of his achievements or reputation, though I often regretted I had not been able to share in his field work on Offa's Dyke. I candidly acknowledged his influence in my first major published paper, 'The dual colonisation of East Glamorgan',[12] in which I applied the concepts of *The Personality of Britain* to our field work in Glamorgan. Had it not been for his illness it would have been a joint publication. Later I participated in most of Cyril's excavations of Bronze Age barrows in the Vale of Glamorgan, still playing second fiddle. These were what are now termed 'rescue' excavations, organised and funded by the Ministry of Works, undertaken because the mounds were about to be levelled by the War Office for a new ordnance factory near Bridgend in 1937, and for an aerodrome near St Athans in 1939–40. We employed two or three workmen, who became highly skilled with pick and shovel, whilst Cyril and I did most of the fine trowelling. He planned the features and the general layout, whilst I recorded the finds and supervised their packing and transport to the museum and to its skilled, if unqualified, archaeological conservator, Fred Gay. We found that the best way to move the fragile coarse pottery burial urns was to free them carefully from the surrounding earth and then to bandage them so that they could be lifted in one piece. Our second son, Derek, was born in late September 1937, which limited my activities, but I well remember sitting in the hot sunshine at Pond Cairn that August, laboriously picking out carbonised grains of wheat and barley that I had detected in the dark soil filling a 'ritual pit', the first ever recovered from a British barrow excavation.[13]

The previous year I had embarked on a full-scale excavation of the platform houses to try to determine their structure and date. Cyril was tied up by his work at the museum and Peter Murray-Thriepland and Audrey Williams, later Mrs Grimes, joined me on Gelligaer Common, which was accessible daily by car in about three-quarters of an hour from our home. In 1936 we uncovered at Dinas Noddfa an elaborate stone-and-timber longhouse with central roof supports and a smaller turf-walled building on the platform above it, but no dating evidence.[14] In 1938 we investigated three platforms on the east side of the common and were fortunate in finding medieval potsherds of late thirteenth- to fourteenth-century date, as well as a stone mould for a bronze pendant, and iron slag, evidence for metal working and for permanent occupation.[15] The houses were poor constructions with low walls of turf and timber, and several central post-holes aligned to carry the ridge pole; their excavation was technically difficult and, in attention to detail for a medieval site, in advance of its time. On a fine summer morning, perched on the side of a ridge at 1,200 feet, it was enjoyable and satisfying work.

The settlements are now generally accepted as upland pastoral farms of early medieval origin: 123 sites have been recorded in Glamorgan.[16] The five excavated structures do not conform to the established types: they are not aisled houses nor cruck constructions, neither are they 'longhouses' with a byre at one end, a type which still survives in West Wales and on Dartmoor in Devon. It is now doubtful that they are the houses described in Welsh laws of the tenth century, despite some special pleading to this effect in the report. Iorwerth Peate wanted to dismiss them as *Hafods,* temporary summer dwellings, but their grouping in pairs and distribution is against that. I have a suspicion that Peate, an ardent Welsh Nationalist, disliked the idea of an English woman discovering a Welsh house. The status of their occupants and their economy has yet to be elucidated, and I regret that no one has followed up my pioneer work.

I have never been able to draw freehand and it has always been a struggle to produce an adequate record. I need to take an awful lot of measurements. Cyril re-drew my plans and sections and lettered them in his characteristic style, and we put our heads together to produce a reconstruction of the Dinas Noddfa lower house.[17] I can see no harm in such collaboration, since the credits were clearly displayed (A F *mens*, C F *del*), and we continued to use it throughout Cyril's working life. When he was too busy, I employed a professional draughtsman. In return, I helped him with indexing and proof correcting, and by putting forward suggestions, sometimes accepted and re-minted, sometimes discarded and forgotten. For example, I introduced him to the works of the Newnham Fellow, Jane Harrison, a classical anthropologist, in which he found sources in early Greek ritual for the interpretation of funeral rites in the Bronze Age barrows in Glamorgan that we had excavated.

My other major pre-war excavation was at the Roman legionary fortress at Caerleon in the early summer of 1939, after we had returned from a visit to America. Dr Nash-Williams had been busily engaged there since 1927, uncovering the remains of the barracks and other military buildings, and elucidating the history of the fortress, garrisoned by the Second Augustan legion from AD 75. When it became apparent that Myrtle Cottage and its two-acre orchard in the north-east corner of the fortress was to be built over, Nash was already committed to digging an Iron Age hill-fort at Sudbrook on the Severn, and accordingly suggested I should be given the task. It was made relatively easy by the back-up of the museum and the Office of Works, but even so it was a tough assignment. I had to employ about a dozen local workmen for eight weeks, and had the help of the students in supervising and recording. I felt very strongly that the time had come for selective excavation; the main history of the site had been established, and at Prysg Field Nash had uncovered ten barracks in their entirety; there was no need to duplicate his work. Accordingly I set out three long parallel trenches right across the site and demonstrated the position of nine stone barrack blocks arranged as usual in pairs, back to back, with a metalled roadway between each pair. Much of the masonry had been removed, but I cleared the centurion's quarters in two of the barracks, and four of the men's cubicles, *contubernia*, where the walls were still standing four feet high, one with a latrine recess built in; at both there was evidence of a third-century rebuilding of the second-century originals. In the fourth century the legion was reorganised and part probably transferred to the Saxon Shore Fort at Richborough in Kent, but I discovered that one of the barracks had been patched up, re-roofed and a fire lit on the concrete floor. A moulded altar base had been used as a gaming table, whilst household refuse had been tipped into the adjoining rooms, a sad commentary on the lowering of standards and lack of military control. I have often been asked what was the most exciting find I have ever made on an excavation, to which I usually reply, 'The Roman gold coins at Myrtle Cottage,' because that is what the questioners expect. It was a chance discovery; I was about to draw a section across the rampart and the adjoining barracks, so I asked a student, a cheerful Scotsman from Aberdeen, to go and give the side of the trench a final scrape. Soon he came running back to the hut, announcing he had found gold coins; I guessed it was one of his jokes, and collecting my gear, I slowly walked across the site to inspect. To my amazement, there they were, five of them lying in a hole on the side of the trench, as fresh as the day they were buried, for gold never decays. They had been hidden beneath the earth floor of one of the early timber barracks, presumably by a soldier killed in action. The hoard consisted of issues of the Emperors Nero, Vespasian, and his sons Titus and Domitian, of AD 55–74, and is an important piece of evidence for the foundation of the fortress soon after AD 75.[18] I managed to complete the report during the winter and it duly appeared in *Archaeologia Cambrensis*. In retrospect, it was a competent piece of work, though I missed the significance of some of the divergent cobble foundations which were in evidence for the earlier timber barracks. Our dear friend Ian Richmond wrote me an appreciative note approving of my methods; it was probably why he thought I was the right person to invite to excavate at Exeter after the war. So one thing led to another.

We had some splendid pre-war holidays, usually with an archaeological flavour; we left the little boys and their nanny with my mother at Walton, where they were very happy. The first was to Normandy in the spring of 1934, when the cider apple orchards were in full bloom. I remember looking down from the battlements at Falaise at a waving sea of pink and white. The grandeur of French medieval architecture at Caen and Rouen was a revelation to both of us. We visited Bayeux to see the famous tapestry depicting the Norman Conquest of England. Cyril was much impressed by the narrative technique of the 230-feet-long colourful embroidery with its inscriptions and borders, and afterwards was inspired by it to make a similar record in pen and ink for our scrap-book of our various excursions at home and abroad. My favourite shows our crossing of the Severn in the old ferryboat from Beachley to Aust in our Austin Ten, as we set off to visit Rik and Tess Wheeler digging at Maiden Castle in 1937. There we saw Peter Murray-Thriepland, rather forlorn after the break-up of his marriage, and there he met Leslie Scott, the golden-haired girl supervising the work at the east entrance of the great hill-fort with the utmost efficiency. They were married two years later.

In 1936 we went to Stockholm for the second meeting of the International Prehistoric Conference. On the boat to Göteborg we found Sir Charles Peers, the head of the Ancient Monuments Inspectorate, and Roger, one of his twin sons; Peers was rather stuffy but Roger was good fun. I have no recollection of the conference but I thoroughly enjoyed Stockholm, with its blend of land and water, and the new architecture that Manny Forbes had told me about in my Cambridge days. In the Town Hall we saw the great gallery where the guide told us, 'This is where the councillors walk after dinner'. We went out to Sigtuna with the Peerses and while Cyril and Sir Charles studied the early Romanesque churches, Roger and I managed to buy a picnic lunch without a word of Swedish between us! We finished with a visit to Uppsala with its row of magnificent royal graves under enormous mounds dating from the sixth to the tenth centuries. Cyril had an introduction to Professor S. Lindquist at the university with whom he found an instant affinity; he had been familiar with the Norse sagas and the buried kings since his days with Professor H. M. L. Chadwick at Cambridge. Lindquist not only came with us to the cemetery and museum but gave us his book, *Uppsala Högar och Ottars Höge*

(1936), a magnificent volume now at Newnham College. Cyril commemorated the trip with a tapestry-type narrative drawing with a border of seventh-century Norse interlacement.

In the spring of 1938 we had our first visit to Italy together, staying with Ralegh Radford, then the Director of the British School at Rome. It was good to be back and to revisit my old haunts with Cyril. Ralegh took us to Veii, the Etruscan city with an enormous circuit of ramparts and only green fields within, and to Norcia with its fortifications, carved tombs and temple. We returned via Rimini, then a poor little town with the great monuments of the Malatesta family and no tourist hotels, and finally across the marshland and the pinewoods to Ravenna, to glory in the mosaics.

Later that year we had a trip to Brittany. Rik Wheeler had finished at Maiden Castle and had embarked on an extensive field survey of hill-forts in northern France, coupled with selective excavations. He wanted to find the cultural links between southern England and the opposite coasts during the Iron Age, and the structural differences and resemblances in the hill-forts' construction.[19] Leslie Scott was much involved in the survey, together with Peter Murray-Thriepland, and was in charge of the excavations at Kercaradec, a multivallate inland promontory fort near Quimper. We crossed from Southampton in the *Queen Mary,* which took a few deck passengers to Cherbourg on the way to New York. Peter met us in his big Armstrong-Siddeley and drove us first to Huelgoat to see Rik at work, and then to Quimper. Leslie was rather put out at her second-in-command taking several days off from the dig, then in its frantic closing stages. It was all highly competent work in the familiar Wheeler style, with wide section trenches across the big defences and meticulous cleaning of the stonework. It must have been a revelation to the French archaeologists, who had made so little technical progress since the time of Napoleon.

Before we returned to St Malo, we managed to have a day with Peter and Leslie visiting Mont-St-Michel. It was a marvellous September day, with bright sunshine and great clouds that cast their moving shadows across the wide expanse of sand. The view was unforgettable, gradually developing as we climbed the winding ramp and steps up to the church astride the rocky summit. We lunched together afterwards at a modest establishment away from the tourists, which nevertheless produced an elaborate meal of six courses, the first to our amusement being merely a bunch of radishes. It was obvious that Peter and Leslie were in love, and we were delighted to watch their growing happiness. They were married in London the following November.

Our final overseas trip in March 1939 combined museum business with pleasure. Aubrey Morgan, one of the sons of William Morgan 'the shop', founder of a big department store in Cardiff, took a great interest in the museum. He had married into a distinguished American family, the Dwight Morrows, who lived at Englewood, New Jersey, just outside New York, but he visited his home in Llandaff each summer. He was concerned at the lack of space for the art collections in the museum, particularly the Swansea and Nantgarw china, which was his special interest, and thought he could raise money in the States to pay for a new 'Welsh–American' wing. The Museum Council naturally welcomed the project with enthusiasm and agreed that the President, Lord Harlech, and the Director, with their wives, should visit the eastern cities where Welsh people, mostly steel workers, had settled in the nineteenth century, and attend their St David's Day banquets as a culmination of the appeal. Aubrey was already one of our friends; I found him easy to get on with, stimulating as a talker and such fun. Cyril and I went to London to meet Mrs Dwight Morrow, who would be our hostess, and her youngest daughter, Constance, whom Aubrey was about to marry as his second wife. Charles Lindbergh, the famous aviator was also there; he had married Anne, the elder daughter and a writer, who was still recovering from the kidnapping and loss of their only child and remained at home. Mrs Morrow took an instant liking to Cyril and I felt the same for Con, a very intelligent young woman. Aubrey was optimistic that the financial prospects were good, since the Munich Agreement in September appeared to have removed the growing threat of war, and it was settled that he should go ahead with the appeal. For our own arrangements, my mother cheerfully said she would have Charles and Derek for the six weeks we would be away. Charles, aged four and a half, was at a most engaging stage and loved staying at The Grange. He started at a little nursery school at Walton of which he tells me he has the happiest recollections. My mother also helped me with the several new outfits I needed. I remember choosing in London three long evening dresses, a rich dull red silk with a shirred waist to be worn with my antique garnet necklace, a striped flowered Italian cotton with a flared skirt and a little matching jacket and hairband, and a classical draped *eau-de-Nil* gown with silver trimmings worn with a spray of real gardenias on some occasions. Cyril and I each bought a large solid trunk; mine subsequently functioned as a school trunk for my boys at Bryanston, and took my possessions on the sea voyage to New Zealand in 1973, and back ten years later. Still intact, it reposes in my Topsham storeroom, a tribute to its pre-war workmanship.

We sailed on the *Queen Mary*, first class this time, arriving in New York on 23 February. I was, as usual, dreadfully seasick when the ship ran into some dirty weather in mid-Atlantic, so the food and the luxury were rather wasted on me. On arrival at Englewood, New Jersey, we were each presented with a schedule of our engagements for the next four weeks, which included four successive St David's Day banquets, various formal dinners and businessmen's meetings, and, for me, ladies' luncheons. Lady Harlech had been unable to come, so I had to take the lead. Fortunately time was allowed for us to see something of New York and its museums whilst we were staying with the Morrows at Next Day Hill. The house was an ideal base, a place of elegant luxury without ostentation and a very friendly atmosphere. I was impressed when the dresses I had worn, and my nightgown, were ironed each day. New York was marvellous; I never ceased to wonder at the fantastic skyline of tall towers as we drove across the suspension bridge over the Hudson river from Englewood. The Rockefeller Centre had not long been completed, towering over a miniature ice rink with skaters at its base. Of the museums, I liked best the Cloisters with its display of the colourful 'Lady and the Unicorn' French Gothic tapestries. Nowadays I would be more interested in the Metropolitan's display of American colonial furniture, and of artefacts of the Native American cultures which are rarely seen in Europe.

We were acutely aware of the growing international tension in central Europe, culminating on 15 March when Hitler's armies went into Czechoslovakia ostensibly to protect the Sudeten-Deutsch. The New York Stock Exchange fell dramatically, and several of the wealthy businessmen and corporations which Aubrey had lined up felt unable to contribute to the museum's appeal at that time. Nevertheless, we carried out our engagements of St David's Day banquets in New York, Scranton, Pittsburg and Philadelphia, meetings in Washington, and a dinner at the British Embassy. The banquets proved to be much of a muchness, starting with a formal grace, a succession of courses of dull food, and then toasts and speeches from Lord Harlech and Cyril, punctuated by bursts of song by a soloist performing popular Welsh airs, and invariably finishing with 'Men of Harlech' and 'Hen Wlad fy Nhadau', in which we all joined. It seemed even then a very old-fashioned affair, but was nevertheless a tribute to the strength of Welsh sentiment: it was the 104th annual occasion for the St David's Society in New York, and the 210th for the Welsh Society of Philadelphia. In each city we stayed with the society's chairman, or with an important potential donor to the appeal fund, and we were overwhelmed by the generosity of American hospitality. I remember two extremes: finding in our cabin on the return voyage, a large can of maple syrup to which I had taken a fancy, sent by our hosts in Scranton, and a serious offer to care for our children during the war from the Snowdens in Maryland, by which we were deeply touched.

After our engagements in Washington we had a few days of relaxation in Virginia, visiting Mount Vernon, the home of George Washington; Richmond, the capital, with its Jefferson buildings; Jamestown, and Williamsburg, and so seeing a sample of American colonial architecture. Unfortunately we had no time to see Jefferson's Monticello, or Carter Hill, which I have often regretted and know now that I shall not achieve a visit. Williamsburg, the former colonial capital of Virginia, named after William III, had been splendidly restored by John D. Rockefeller from 1926–37, and then opened to the public. It was a new concept of an open-air museum designed to teach history in its broadest sense, based on thorough detailed archaeological and documentary research. It was an attractive place, architecturally all of a piece. The public buildings, the Capitol, the Governor's Palace and the Court House, were built of warm red brick with slate roofs, the many domestic buildings were timber-framed with a cladding of horizontal timbering painted white, and a brick chimney stack. All were finely proportioned in the classical style, with sash windows, columned porches and balustrades. The interiors had the original panelling and stairs carefully restored and were authentically filled with fine contemporary furniture. The custodians, both men and women, were in eighteenth-century costume. It was a chilly March day when we stayed there, and the trees and the gardens were bare, but I retain the impression of an harmonious small town in a fine setting and justifying its restoration. As we wandered from building to building, it certainly gave us new ideas about future museum developments and how to cater for an intelligent public, ideas that were later to be incorporated by Cyril in the Welsh Folk Museum at St Fagans.

Our final engagements were at Boston, where we stayed with our friends, Hugh and Thalassa Hencken, both archaeologists: he an American with a Cambridge PhD, she, an English blonde with her hair cut short in an Eton crop, an experienced excavator. Whilst Cyril lectured at Harvard, Thalassa took me to Salem and Marblehead to see the ship museum and the houses of the sea captains. We experienced some formal hospitality at the house in Chestnut Avenue of Charles Adams, member of an upper-crust Boston family which in the nineteenth century boasted a President of the United States. I was taken into dinner arm-in-arm with our host to a table resplendent with silver, glass and fine china, and engaged in animated conversation. Cyril was at the far end, next to a daughter of the house; after a pause she said to him, 'Oh dear, father has forgotten to turn the table; I must signal to him'. Instantly my host cut short his remarks and turned to talk to the lady on his left, to be followed by everyone else at the table, a curious if logical American custom.

Reflecting during the voyage home, Cyril and I concluded that, all in all, it had been an enjoyable trip, even if it had not achieved its purpose of raising enough money for the museum. We had done what was asked of us without any mishaps, we had made firm friends at Englewood, and we had seen a good sample of both the past and present in the eastern states. Now we were returning to Cardiff to face the growing tension of an approaching war.

Chapter Six

In Transition
The War and After

1939 – 1948

The summer of 1939 was a busy one; Cyril was hard at work preparing emergency plans for the evacuation of the museum, and I had the Caerleon excavations to carry out. On the home front, we built a concrete air raid shelter under the new nursery wing, designed to withstand blast and possible collapse of the building. We fitted black-out blinds to all the casement windows of our little Rhiwbina house. Hopefully we entered Charles, aged five, for a small mixed private school, Norfolk House, at Llanishen, and bought him the regulation bright green blazer, cap and grey jersey, in which he looked rather ridiculous. Felicity, aged eighteen, had just finished a year's domestic economy course at Harcombe House near Lyme Regis; she had set her heart on going on the stage and was accepted as a trainee assistant stage manager by the Oxford Repertory Theatre, to her great delight.

Penelope, aged fifteen, was now settled in at Howell's School, Denbigh, a very efficient girls' boarding school in North Wales, run by the Grocers' Company. It got her through her School Certificate, which, much later, qualified her to do university work. Previously, at the East Grinstead Convent School, she had wound the nuns around her little finger and had done no work. Despite the tension, we managed to find time for some happy holiday picnics on the beach at Southerndown, at Merthyr Mawr and with the Blundells at Nottage, Porthcawl.

During July and August, it became increasingly obvious that there would be no escape from confrontation with Hitler's Germany. We were issued with gas masks and I went to some evening classes at Rhiwbina school for instruction. I concluded that the known effects of mustard gas were so frightful that no one would dare use it, and I felt the same about nuclear missiles.

I spent some time in the archaeology department at the museum, helping the staff to list and pack up the best of the collections in large labelled boxes ready for transport to a secret destination in mid-Wales. Sadly, Cyril was too busy to accept a pressing invitation from C. W. Phillips to go to Suffolk to help with the excavation of the royal Anglo-Saxon burial at Sutton Hoo. In the event, it was Peter Grimes, then at the Ordnance Survey, together with Stuart and Peggy Piggott, who did the delicate work of uncovering the treasure. The many fine objects of gold, silver and garnet jewellery were removed to the British Museum where, after first-aid treatment at the laboratory, it was all packed away in a safe place for the duration of the war. Short reports were produced by Tom Kendrick, C. W. Phillips and others whilst the matters were fresh in their minds 'Done hastily and trembling in the first week or two of the war when everyone assumed that each day might be their last', as Kendrick wrote in a note to Cyril.[1]

War was declared on September 3; we listened to the radio and so heard of the false alarm of an air raid on London. The next few days were an anticlimax, for in Cardiff as elsewhere nothing happened. Early in October when the first shock had worn off, I drove Felicity to Oxford where she was to stay with Cyril's sister, Babs Gotch, whilst working at the Repertory Theatre in Beaumont Street. I had some time in hand next day so I drove out to Woodstock and walked through the park to Blenheim in the fine autumn weather. I saw Vanbrugh's masterpiece for the first time under strange circumstances. A boys' school evacuated from London was moving in, and everywhere there were the removal men busy covering and shifting the fine eighteenth-century furniture to make room for piles of desks. I wandered at will through the great rooms on the ground floor and no one questioned me. In a mood of pleasant melancholy, I felt sure I was seeing the splendours for the last time.

The impact of the war was gradual. The introduction of food rationing was not much of a problem for a household of six. The local Welsh butcher often had some surplus meat, and was generous with offal, liver, kidneys, tongue and even a sheep's head, which Nan cooked very well. It was possible to get a Bath chap, a delicious bacon joint, by post from the Wiltshire suppliers, and there was plenty of fish in Cardiff, though not much variety; we seemed to get nothing but herrings and hake. Later on, I had to queue in the market to get a rabbit, a pest to farmers in West Wales but very good for a family meal. The buxom young woman named Ivy, who chopped up the bloody carcasses, often would slip me some ducks' eggs to supplement our meagre ration, at one time only one egg a week each. Dried-egg powder made a barely tolerable substitute for scrambled egg. Butter became permanently short, and I hated the taste of margarine. Nowadays the improved polyunsaturated versions are said to be good for you, but I have never overcome my long-time prejudice and can usually taste the difference. With hungry boys to feed, I increased our jam ration by taking extra sugar, and learnt to make delicious jam from Amy Lewis, our kind neighbour. We started with the easy-setting plum, fishing out the stones from the boiling pulp. It was a new skill which I still retain, that gave me great pleasure. I continued to exercise it in New Zealand on the fine strawberries, quinces, and the local grapefruit that made delicious marmalade. Later on, when things were very tight, I once found poor Penelope eating dry bread in her bedroom; everyone had to learn self-restraint and to avoid waste. It is only recently that I have been able to throw away dregs of milk or scraps of butter without a qualm.

Petrol rationing certainly affected us; there were no more of the enjoyable long trips to North or West Wales. Holidays had to be taken within an easy distance of Cardiff, in case of an air raid or other emergency at the museum. Amy Lewis lent us her cottage at Brockweir, perched on the hillside in idyllic surroundings above the Wye valley. There we walked along Offa's Dyke, explored Tintern Abbey and Chepstow Castle, and enjoyed the simple life. I learnt to manage the coal range to heat the water, but failed to cook anything except a rice pudding in the oven after a long time.

All this lay ahead; for the next eight months it was the phoney war and business as usual in Cardiff. In December Cyril started the first of several excavations of the Bronze Age barrows near Cowbridge, finding a complex of stake circles, a novelty at the time, beneath the mounds, and I assisted. It turned bitterly cold, and after Christmas it was impossible to continue because the exposed surfaces were deeply frozen. So Cyril went back to the museum and I went skating with Leslie Murray-Thriepland on a small lake near Pendoylan, taking Derek, a sturdy two-year-old, whom we pushed around well wrapped up tied on to a wooden kitchen chair in the wintry sunshine.

One evening Cyril came home and told me that Nash-Williams was about to be called up, having volunteered for war service, and had asked whether I would consider taking over his lecture courses at University College, Cardiff, for the rest of the session. There was a long-standing arrangement whereby the Keeper of Archaeology at the museum was also the Lecturer in Archaeology at the college. Cyril was rather astonished when, after a brief pause, I jumped at the offer; somehow I knew intuitively that it was what I really wanted to do, though I had no idea that it was going to be my life's work. The Principal, J. F. Rees, later explained that as the college was obliged to make up Nash's service pay, there would only be a small balance left for me, amounting to £75 for two terms' work. He also accompanied me in a highly nervous state, both of us suitably gowned, down the long dismal corridors of the college in Cathays Park and introduced me to the class before I gave my first university lecture. I had previously only given occasional lectures to the local archaeological society, the Cardiff Naturalists, and now found it hard going to prepare two or three lectures a week on British Prehistory and Roman Britain, to select and project the lantern slides and to establish contact with the undergraduates. It was a challenge to remain one jump ahead of the class. I had no room in college, only the austerity of the Women's Common Room, strictly segregated from the male professors on the other side of the corridor. Nevertheless, I still managed to have an occasional day working with Cyril on the Glamorgan barrows, and in the Easter vacation I spent some time on the elaborate Sutton 268 barrow with its spectacular Beaker burial and successive interments.[2]

It was Whitsun when the storm of the real war broke; Michael Zvegintzov, an ex-Russian scientist and the husband of Diana Lucas of the British School of Rome days, was staying with us. He was always politically minded and he explained the logic of the German onrush through eastern France, after the outflanking of the Maginot line, and how the fall of the key fortresses made the encirclement of the British forces, and their retreat to the coast, inevitable. He could not foretell the miracle of the evacuation from Dunkirk which followed.

After the fall of France, it was obvious from Churchill's brave words that there was now real danger of invasion. Cardiff as a key port and an administrative centre was a legitimate target. I determined to remain with Cyril but we decided that it would not be right to keep Charles, a sensitive little boy of six, in the danger zone. After much heart-searching, we declined the two kind offers from America, from the Dwight Morrows and the Snowdens, to take our children. We sent Charles for safety during the late summer months to friends, the Lloyds, at Court Henry in remote Carmarthenshire. I found an advertisement for a school for young evacuees at Nailsworth, near Stroud in Gloucestershire, which was not too far from Cardiff, and which on inspection seemed suitable. Charles happily joined the group of ten small children living in part of a big house, surrounded by a park and gardens. He wrote us his first letter saying he was having a lovely time, but that Simon, a new boy, was his 'worst friend'. He stayed there for a year, whilst London and the cities were blitzed. In Cardiff the sirens frequently sounded and we trailed down to the shelter in the dark, Nanny carrying the sleeping Derek wrapped in blankets. There were many nights when we could see Bristol burning, but Cardiff suffered only one major attack. The next morning Queen Street was littered with broken glass and debris, but the museum and the fine civic buildings in Cathays Park escaped. For the next few days we cooked on a Primus stove and kept the coal fire burning, since there was no gas.

Despite the trauma, Cyril managed to produce his masterly summary of his ten years of field work on Offa's Dyke, which he gave as the Sir

John Rhys memorial lecture to the British Academy in London in October, surprisingly soon after the Battle of Britain. He had been elected a Fellow earlier that year, an honour which pleased him very much. In the same month he also lectured to the Antiquaries on the Glamorgan barrow excavations, subsequently published in the society's *Journal* (1941), *Archaeologia* (1943) and *Antiquity* (1941). Afterwards Jacquetta Hawkes wrote, 'What a marvellous lecturer you are; no one else could make a barrow so enthralling'. The articles contained many new observations concerning the structure of barrows, such as the prior erection of stake circles, the building of turf stacks, trodden areas, and the digging of ritual pits, and their relationship to the primary interment. The fundamental novelty was the interpretation of such features as ceremonial ritual acts carried out by members of a Bronze Age community. It is not too much to say that these ideas have changed the attitude of subsequent barrow excavators, although some have cavilled at his vivid imaginative interpretations despite the supporting evidence in the reports.

Cyril's research was not achieved without much hard work in addition to the demands of the museum's wartime routine. He regularly got up before 6 a.m. to make a cup of tea, and then wrote rapidly or did some drawing in the study until breakfast time. The untidy manuscript was handed to his devoted secretary on arrival at the museum, and he expected to have the typescript before he left at 4.30 p.m. This he often discussed with me before revising it drastically during the evening, though he made time to play with the children before their bedtime. As Director he went through a very bad patch in the summer and autumn of 1941 when, after much discussion, the Museum Council felt obliged to dismiss Iorwerth Peate, the Keeper of Welsh Folk Life, on the grounds that he had failed to register as a conscientious objector and had thus deceived them about his intention of avoiding war service when called up. He had said that when the time came, he would do his duty, which was very ambiguous. Cyril prided himself on his good relations with his staff and took the matter very much to heart. Feelings ran high, and I had to listen to the many twists and turns of the argument and the problems that beset the Director. In the end, the case was reviewed by the museum's governing body, the Court, in October; a packed meeting with a strong Welsh element present decided in Peate's favour, and he was reinstated in January 1942. Relations naturally remained strained for some time.

Another by-product of war conditions in Wales was the amazing recovery of a mass of Iron Age fine metalwork from Llyn Cerrig Bach in Anglesey. It happened when peat had been dug by heavy machinery from the edges of the little lake and spread on the surface of the runways of the RAF airfield at Valley nearby. The resident engineer informed the museum of the strange assortment of objects appearing in the peat, including an iron gang chain with collars. Cyril went to see the site in August 1943 and, realising its immense importance, arranged for the whole collection of objects to be transported to Cardiff. He worked on the material for the next three years and found it utterly absorbing. It consisted mainly of Celtic warriors' weapons and equipment, horse harnesses and parts of chariots, a bronze trumpet and other panoply of war, and an enigmatic crescentic plaque, with an embossed triskele, new to Celtic art. I remember carrying a succession of precious packages in the train to London for drawing and for laboratory treatment by Dr Plenderleith at the British Museum. Then there was much lively correspondence for Cyril with Christopher Hawkes, Stuart Piggott and Ian Richmond, and there were many times when he came home with yet another bright idea to be discussed at the fireside. His interpretation of the find in the Final Report [3] as a succession of native offerings, deposited in a sacred pool, probably under the aegis of the Druids who are known to have had their centre in Anglesey, has found general acceptance. Stuart Piggott wrote after reading the proofs, 'I'm now quite enthralled by the Iron Age in Britain in a way I never was before. Why did nobody before you appreciate the essential excitement and interest in the metalwork and its connections in carpentry and coachbuilders' craft?'

For my part the war years were not productive, being mostly taken up with university teaching and with the arrival of a third son, George, in January 1943. I found that Nash-Williams had handed out full cyclostyled notes for each of his lecture courses; consequently, when the students were asked to write essays, all I got were slightly different versions of the same impeccable originals. It was a job to set subjects that demanded more reading from the students and some evidence that they could think for themselves. There were a few able young men awaiting their call-up in the class, including one, Peter Leech, who sent me a Christmas aerogramme from South Africa wittily decorated with Bushmen-style figures. There were also some duds, like Gwilliam Jones from rural Carmarthenshire, who failed his subsidiary examination three times, but somehow managed to pass by averaging with other subjects when I declined to raise his abysmal marks. I used a room in the museum for tutorials, and there built up a teaching collection of potsherds, coins and other odds and ends for the students to handle, feeling that black and white slides were a poor substitute for the real things. I also instituted 'field days', visiting local sites such as Tinkinswood long cairn, Caerau hill-fort and the Roman fortress at Caerleon, when relevant to the lecture course. These were ideas I developed later at Exeter University. There was a brief interruption to my lectures in January 1943 after the birth of George, when Cyril acted as a stopgap. I had kept going until the end of the previous term in December, going about burdened with a box of slides, my lecture notebooks and the babe up front beneath my gown. I don't know what the students thought but I was determined to carry on. Pregnant women were not then expected to appear in public in Cardiff.

My teaching of Roman Britain brought me into contact with the Latin department and Professor Roland Austin, son of R. G. Austin of Gloucester, who was a co-editor of *Antiquity*, the archaeological magazine. Roland became a firm friend who introduced me to the devious ways of academics and university administrators. Thanks to him, I became a member of the Arts Board, and had successive rises in my salary when it became evident that the war was to be a long one. He was a delightful person, pretending to be prematurely aged and impractical but actually extremely sharp. He never believed how little Latin I really knew, and often floored me with quotations. He was exceedingly fond of my home-made fruit cake, which was denied him by his wife, Violet, since he had a tendency to overweight and high blood pressure.

My teaching sadly came to an end in 1945 when after VE Day, Major Nash-Williams was released from the Army Supply Service. Before I left I wrote a memorandum to the Principal of the college summarising my wartime work, and tactfully suggesting that the time was coming when the archaeology lectureship should be detached from the museum keepership, since each was really now a full-time job. I have no idea whether it had any effect, though I like to think that a seed was implanted in the Principal's mind. Certainly Nash found the work of reorganising the archaeological galleries at the museum was exacting, in addition to his research for his major work, *The Early Christian Monuments of Wales* (1950). After we had left Cardiff in 1948, Leslie Alcock was appointed as his Assistant Lecturer, and after Nash's sudden death in 1955, he became the Acting Head of an independent department at the College. Finally, in 1958, Richard Atkinson became the first Professor of Archaeology. The department has developed from these modest beginnings into one of the most successful in the country, with a staff of five or six specialists, and with spacious conservation laboratories and work-rooms in a new Humanities building. My connection with the college was happily renewed when I served twice as the External Examiner for Archaeology, from 1966 to 1972. I was delighted to be elected an Honorary Fellow in 1981, and have since attended several of the annual Fellows' dinners at the college. Another link with the department has been the creation of the Cyril Fox Memorial Fund, to which I and many of his friends contributed after my husband's death in 1967. It was designed to make grants for travel and archaeological field work to outstanding students in their third year. I have met several of the new generation of professional archaeologists who felt they had benefited from it at a crucial stage in their career.

During the summer of 1943, it became apparent that the tide had turned and that the Allies would win the war. Montgomery's victory over Rommel in North Africa in May was followed by the invasion of Sicily and southern Italy, and the problem of supplies across the Atlantic was being overcome; unbeknown to the public, a landing in northern France was being planned for 1944. It was possible then for archaeologists to look ahead with some confidence, mingled with apprehension, to what would happen after the war. Accordingly a conference was staged by London University's Institute of Archaeology in Regent's Park to discuss *The Future of Archaeology*. Over 280 people attended; Cyril and I both went, I to represent University College, Cardiff, he, a speaker, the National Museum of Wales. It was the first occasion for four years that so many archaeologists had been able to get together and the atmosphere was exhilarating. I left inspired by a sense of missionary zeal and a feeling that there were good times ahead. A wide range of subjects was discussed. The emphasis was on the unity and comprehensive nature of archaeology; 'it does not stop anywhere or at any time but goes on until yesterday'. As Tom Kendrick proclaimed in unforgettable terms, it even may include 'the study of hassocks as well as Victorian church architecture'. Such ideas have continued to influence the practice of archaeology today with the development of medieval, post medieval and industrial archaeology, and by the study of, for example, vernacular architecture. Kendrick's plea for more comprehensive local guide books was soon to be satisfied by Nikolas Pevsner's county series, *The Buildings of England*, published by Penguin Books from 1950 onwards. Similarly, Christopher Hawkes's demand for 'total' excavation of sites has been a characteristic development, made possible by mechanical diggers, whilst Cyril's proposal for a National Record of archaeological material has since developed in a modified form into the Sites and Monuments Record, financed by the county councils. Looking to the future, it was generally agreed that some state control and finance for excavation would be needed for salvage work in the bombed cities, and for its publication. No one proposed what has proved to be the solution, the creation of permanent archaeological field units to undertake rescue excavation and survey, funded by local authorities, with additional grants from the Department of the Environment, now 'English Heritage'.

Throughout the conference the need was expressed in the discussions for more understanding of archaeology by the general public, and hence for its inclusion in some form at all stages of education. This has now been brought about by the increase in the number of practising trained archaeologists, by the production of numerous reliable popular books, well written and illustrated, and by some outstanding series of television programmes. Communication is now recognised to be part of an archaeologist's work, and consequently people are now much better informed and more sympathetic.

After the conference, there was a new mood and sense of purpose; everyone realised there was need for a central body representative of all branches and aspects of British Archaeology which could speak with authority when the time came for planning the rebuilding of the bombed cities, and which could ensure that the need for excavations was not overlooked. The Society of Antiquaries under its President, Sir Alfred Clapham, took the lead in establishing a new Council for British Archaeology, which held its first meeting in March 1944. The new organisation consisted of representatives of the national societies and museums, of the universities teaching archaeology, and of the numerous county archaeological societies, arranged in thirteen regional groups, which also functioned locally. The first secretary was Kathleen Kenyon, from the London Institute of Archaeology; the President was *ex officio* that of the Society of Antiquaries, Clapham being succeeded by Cyril the following year. I was involved in the Council's affairs as a member of the Education Sub-Committee and, after my move to Exeter, as Convenor of Regional Group XIII, a member of the Central Executive and ultimately as Vice-President.

Looking around, I now felt myself committed to work for British archaeology as a whole in the post-war period, whether by teaching and public education, by site preservation, museum work, or by rescue excavation, as and when the need and opportunities arose. I felt secure and accepted by the professionals, and no longer considered as Cyril's shadow. I first concerned myself with education; stimulated by the conference, I clarified my ideas in an article for *Antiquity* entitled *The Place of Archaeology in British Education,* which I still find full of good sense.[4] I defined archaeology as 'a method of recovering, studying and recreating the past, with its subject matter the very diverse material that has survived to the present time, man himself, his belongings and his handiwork'. Its educative value lies in the demands it makes for a mixture of intellectual and practical qualities, requiring a trained eye, a good visual memory, close reasoning and inductive powers, and imagination allied with common sense. I followed up this didactic essay with its application to the school teaching of Roman Britain to a gathering of classical teachers in Oxford.[5] I urged them to try out the effects of visits to local sites and museums, coupled with class displays of slides and reconstructions. These would show the children that the Latin language with which they were struggling belonged to a widespread Roman civilization present in this country, of which many traces survive today. I finished off my missionary efforts with editing *A Book List for Teachers,* published by the Council for British Archaeology in 1949. It was a pioneer work, well organised but now totally superseded; it was produced after many amicable discussions by an Education Sub-Committee consisting of myself, Jacquetta Hawkes, Dinah Dobson and Margot Eates.

At the same time (1945–6) I started to work with Alan Sorrell on a children's book about Roman Britain, which I knew was very much needed. I wanted to express in simple language and in illustrations the ideas I had developed in my wartime lecture courses. I had taken several groups of ten- to twelve- year-olds around the museum galleries and the local Roman and Iron Age sites and felt I knew what would interest them. I also had a critic in a lively intelligent son, Charles, of the same age. I had kept in touch with Alan since our time at the British School at Rome, and indeed had suggested to Cyril that he would be a suitable artist to produce the reconstructions of the legionary fortress at Caerleon and the Roman town at Caerwent that Nash wanted for the archaeology gallery in the museum. Before the war Sorrell stayed with us in Rhiwbina several times. I remember taking him to see the Dark Age memorial stone of Dervacus, son of Justus, set up on the edge of the Roman road, Sarn Helen, on the bleak high moorland above Ystradfellte. The remote scene fired his imagination and the result was a fine reconstruction which he gave us, and which Cyril used to illustrate his account of its recent re-erection.[6] It is a typical Sorrell painting with its sombre tones and stormy sky, and the group of figures around the stone in the foreground.

Together we planned the Roman Britain book and the illustrations; we used several of the previous reconstructions Sorrell had done for the *Illustrated London News* and for the museum, but most were new, tailored to my text. Sorrell demanded precise answers to many questions of detail. I remember hunting out the figure of a blacksmith in his leather apron, and the use of flails and winnowing baskets from provincial sculpture in the Rhineland; I never wholly approved of his version of the excavation of a late Roman buried treasure, but in most of his pictures accuracy of detail was successfully combined with imaginative scenes and with a wonderful feeling for landscape. It was a great disappointment to us both when Allen Lane, the publisher, decided that his new series of Puffin Books for children, for which our *Roman Britain* had been commissioned, was to be limited to fiction, and although he gave us our advance royalties it was no compensation. The book had to wait until 1961 before it was published by the Lutterworth Press, in a revised and extended version and an attractive format. It was well reviewed and has stood the test of time, being reprinted eight times; unfortunately it was produced before the availability of inexpensive colour printing made it possible to do justice to Sorrell's work.

My next task was a surprise, an invitation out of the blue from our friend, Professor Ian Richmond, the leading Romanist, to undertake trial excavations in the war-damaged areas of Exeter. The city had been subjected to one of the 'Baedeker raids' in May 1942, when the German air force had been directed to bomb defenceless cathedral cities in southern England. Much of the historic centre had been laid waste, and offered a wonderful opportunity for archaeological investigation. A high-powered Excavation Committee had been formed in January 1945 with Professor R. Darlington, the medieval historian from the University College at Exeter, as secretary, and with Richmond representing the Society of Antiquaries: he had put forward my name from his personal knowledge of my pre-war Caerleon excavations. I felt some hesitation about leaving the family for any length of time, but agreed to go down to Exeter to meet him and some of the committee for a discussion. So in April I found myself on a train travelling down the Exe valley in the evening sunshine and gliding into St David's Station between the green hills of Exwick and the wooded slopes of Duryard, coming upon the city unawares; the contrast with the close-packed terrace houses on a similar approach to Cardiff was striking. I fell in love with Exeter and its environs from that moment. The next day I met Ian, and together we looked over the flattened expanse, extending from the ruins of the eighteenth-century Bedford Circus (now Bedford Street) right up to Rougemont Castle. Not a shop in the upper High Street had survived the city's clearance after the bombing, and the same was true of South Street down the hill as far as the remnants of the Lower Market in Smythen Street. The excavation was a daunting task but, encouraged by Ian, I accepted the challenge.

There was a lot to do before the starting date in July, so much so that I find I have no recollection of what we did to celebrate VE Day in Cardiff on May 8. My father became seriously ill that summer and died in August, which added to my cares. I could safely leave Cyril and the children for a month: Charles, a bright boy of ten, was now a weekly boarder at a good small preparatory school, Westbourne House in Penarth; Derek, aged five, later accompanied by George, went to Rhiwbina Infants' School, running happily down the sheltered footpath from our house. I still had Nan coming daily to cook, and a devoted young nanny, Betty Henney, who had been with us all through the war; she was a charming Welsh girl from a mining village. Both Cyril's daughters had joined the forces and had married, so I was freed from any responsibility for their welfare. Felicity, a Wren, had married a Canadian naval officer, Patrick Redgrave, and had returned with him to Toronto; Penelope, in the WRAF, married an army officer, John Gray, but soon had to get a divorce. She took a secretarial course in Oxford and became assistant to Professor Alan Gardiner, the Egyptologist at the Griffiths Institute. Later she married John Eames, a classical archaeologist, and they moved to Liverpool on his appointment to the university.

Returning to Exeter in July, I faced a housing problem; after some trials and errors, I found accommodation as a paying guest in the lovely late eighteenth-century red brick terrace of Southernhay West, facing on to the communal gardens with its splendid trees. The house belonged to two elderly ladies, Miss Sybil and Miss Ethel Bankart; I can't imagine why they put up with my irregular hours, and dirty boots and dungarees. The atmosphere and the furniture were Victorian, but there was good conversation in the first-floor drawing room after the evening meal, when I had time to spare. My first season was difficult, as I was starting from scratch, and there was some local hostility to the project. Passers-by told me that it was a waste of money, and asked why the city council was not building houses instead. The only labour obtainable was six Italian prisoners of war from Poltimore, who needed close supervision; I found two of them asleep under a buddleia bush one warm afternoon. My only regular assistant was a young medical student, Dr Walter Chisholm-Batten, who had excavated with St George Gray and who was very keen otherwise it was the occasional elderly volunteer from the Devon Archaeological Society, for whom it was not always easy to find a suitable job. I was also at the mercy of the local cranks, such as the witch-like Miss Lega-Weekes, a learned old lady, who kept popping up unexpectedly at the side of the trench to ask me difficult questions. However, the city officials were helpful with the loan of equipment, including an old air raid shelter in which the Italians cooked their midday spaghetti; they also provided an assistant to help with the planning and surveying. The two following seasons were much easier. I began to know what I was doing, and I had adequate British labour as well as the help of university students from the history department, organised by Norton Medlicott who had succeeded Darlington as Professor and as the Secretary of the Excavation Committee. It was not long before we became good friends. I also discovered Alison Leadley-Brown, a Cambridge biologist, married to an Exeter solicitor, who proved to be a highly competent volunteer and who undertook much of the daily organisation of the dig. We were joined by Richard Goodchild, returned from war service in North Africa, with his detailed local knowledge of Roman Exeter, who gave me much moral support, as well as Leslie Murray-Thriepland, who undertook the planning.

To my mind, there were three outstanding problems which I had to try to solve; first, the origins of the Roman city, whether it started as an Iron Age settlement, or as a Roman military post or as a civil establishment; secondly, the character, date and sequence of the defences, which included the magnificent circuit of the standing town walls; and thirdly, the whereabouts of its principal buildings and its road system. I felt there was no need to investigate the medieval or later town plan, though, of course, I would record any relevant discoveries. At the end of the work, I came up with answers to the problems, some right, but others proved to be very wrong some twenty years later. The practical difficulty was to find any

sizeable area where the Roman deposits were intact; all too often the
ground had been disturbed by the foundations of recent buildings, or cut
up by ancient cellars, or by rubbish pits. Furthermore, unlike most walled
cities where soils have accumulated over the centuries so that the Roman
levels are only to be found at great depth, in Exeter, the ground has frequently been levelled off for medieval or subsequent buildings, so that the
early Roman layers may lie close beneath the present-day surface, and the
later ones may be completely missing. It was difficult to make sense of
short lengths of wall foundations, or to identify a road from small patches
of gravel; I realised that only the discovery of more pieces would eventually reveal the picture of the Exeter jigsaw puzzle. I have had the satisfaction of producing a framework, and of seeing most of my bits and pieces
subsequently fitted in by the Exeter Archaeological Field Unit, ably led by
Chris Henderson.

I was lucky in finding significant Roman stratification near the ruins
of the Saxon church of St George in South Street. Beneath the recent
debris, a spread of solid gravel had been laid down *circa* AD 75–80, and
had obliterated the remains of earlier rectangular timber buildings and a
narrow road. The first two periods in the development of the city were
thus apparent, and have proved to be of fundamental importance. I tentatively identified the gravelled open space with the Forum, an essential part
of the civic centre of every cantonal town. Since nothing was found to
suggest the presence of the military, I concluded that the earlier occupation in the wooden buildings was civil, and rashly stated in the Final
Report, 'the idea that *Isca* may have been a fortress of the Second
Augustan Legion must now be given up'.[7]

I had to wait to prove myself wrong until 1964, when I found a ditch
of definite military character and early date outside the south gate of the
city.[8] In 1971 the discovery, by the newly-founded Exeter Archaeological
Field Unit, beneath the recently-demolished Church of St Mary Major in
the Close, of a great military bath house subsequently converted into the
Basilica and civic centre, clinched the matter. The Second Augustan
Legion is now firmly established as having been stationed in a forty-acre
fortress at Exeter from about AD 50–55 to AD 75–80, before it was moved
to Caerleon in South Wales.[9] The wooden buildings in South Street can
now be identified as possibly part of the *praetorium*, the commander's
house, succeeded by a gravelled market place, an extension rather than the
centre of the Forum.

My work on the city defences was successful in firmly establishing a
sequence of a second-century earth rampart, cut back later for the building
of the city wall in the local volcanic stone. Subsequent work by myself
and by the field unit has refined the dating to the end of the second or
early third century, in line with several other Roman town walls in

England. One special small find sticks in my memory: a dirty black potsherd with markings on it, handed to me by a student volunteer in South Street. When washed, it revealed an incised Christian symbol, the Chi-Rho, a monogram formed from the first two Greek letters of the word 'Christ'.[10] This was striking evidence of a Christian community in the city in the fourth century AD. I suggested that this humble vessel held an offering of food or drink, set aside to take to a church on feast days.[11] The Christian tradition may well have been unbroken in the city, since cemetery burials of the fifth to sixth and of the seventh to tenth centuries have now been found in the Cathedral Close, beside the foundations of the Saxon Minster.[12]

All in all, my three short seasons of excavation were judged successful by the committee, though now I feel they were rather inadequate, and I was instructed to prepare a full report. There were to be far-reaching consequences for me and Cyril in the near future, which will be described later.

Cyril, of course, was very busy, travelling frequently to London to preside over meetings of the Society of Antiquaries and the Council for British Archaeology. In Cardiff he had succeeded in the delicate negotiations with Lord Plymouth concerning the transfer of St Fagan's Castle and its surrounding parkland for a Welsh Folk Museum. It was a project he had long wanted, ever since he had visited the Folk Museums in Scandinavia, because he was well aware of the wealth of vernacular buildings and crafts still surviving in Wales.[13] I remember him telling me of his visit to a weaver's house in Anglesey, which was later to be transferred to St Fagans. When he asked to buy a specimen of his work to exhibit, the old man replied that he hadn't any, but 'If you give me a fleece I will make you a blanket'; obviously he had managed with the local farmers by a barter economy. At the opening in 1946 only the sixteenth-century castle house was ready, furnished from the museum's collection and by Lord Plymouth's generous gifts. Now there are small farmhouses and cottages characteristic of different Welsh regions, a row of miners' houses, a chapel, a tannery, as well as the weaver's shed and woollen mill. These have all been carefully recorded, taken down and rebuilt in a woodland setting. Iorwerth Peate was the first curator. Though semi-independent, St Fagans remains part of the National Museum of Wales and is greatly appreciated by the Welsh people.

As soon as possible we had a proper summer holiday, in August 1946, crossing the Irish Sea from Fishguard to Cork, where we made friends with Brian and Claire O'Kelly at the university's archaeology department. I shall never forget the two eggs and bacon provided for each of us at our first breakfast in a rather shabby hotel, more than enough for a week's ration at home. The O'Kellys took us to Garranes, a multivallate hill-fort where Dubliner Sean O'Riordain had been digging, and had established from his finds of imported amphorae and the manufacture of *millefiori* glass, that the fort had been occupied in the fifth and sixth centuries AD. This was the first time I had seen relics of Dark Age fortification, and these later enabled me to identify similar sherds from settlements in the sand-hills on the coast of South Devon at Bantham and Mothecombe.[14] We went on westwards by slow train and country buses to stay in Dingle. The remote countryside was idyllic, with its red fuchsia hedges, the sound of corncrakes in the small fields, the rocky coasts and hills. There were the long black currachs, the skin boats, parked upside down on stone blocks in the coves. The fishermen walked to the water carrying them on their shoulders, and rowed them with stick-like oars over the heavy Atlantic swell. They looked like black water-beetles skating over the waves. There were many antiquities for us to visit and for Cyril to draw: memorial stones with ogham inscriptions, groups of stone huts on the rocky hill-sides, and primitive churches built of drystone masonry, including the famous oratory of Gallarus, with its remarkable corbelled stone roof. Though there were some days of soft driving rain, I recollect the landscape in bright sunshine, with white clouds and blue sky.

Somehow during the post-war years, I fitted in another task, the rearrangement of the Corinium Museum at Cirencester. I owed the invitation to become its part-time Honorary Curator to Mrs Elsie Clifford, a notable and enthusiastic Gloucestershire archaeologist and a dear friend of Cyril's, and to Dr F. S. Wallis of the Museums' Association and Director of Bristol Museums. The museum, first opened in 1938, was a spacious one-room building, with good cases and fittings provided by the Carnegie Trust Fund. It housed an exceptionally rich and varied collection of Roman finds from the town, which had been the cantonal capital of the local tribe of the Dobunni, and known as *Corinium Dobunnorum*. During the war, everything had been packed away and the building requisitioned by the Air Ministry and then used as a Food Office. I made successive short visits over the next five years, first to get the main exhibits in place, and then to organise the reserve collections. It was exciting to uncover and clean the elaborate floor mosaics, with pictures of the heads of the Seasons, and of Orpheus surrounded by a circle of pacing beasts. I was immensely pleased when I discovered a coin of the Emperor Allectus (AD 293–6), which had been found in 1909 beneath the Orpheus pavement and so established its early fourth-century date.[15] This dating can also be applied to other similar pavements in the neighbourhood, now recognised by David Smith as the products of a Corinium school of late Roman mosaicists. The fine quality Romano-British sculpture and architectural fragments were arranged in triple concrete tiers across the angles at the far end of the room, flanking the unique carved capital of the free-standing

Jupiter Column. Jocelyn Toynbee, my old friend of Newnham days, came over from Oxford to identify some unusual figures of Celtic deities, including a serpent-footed god, Cernunnos. My aim was to produce a coherent display that would be attractive both to the general public and to the student coming purposefully to study the collections. I learnt a lot from organising and labelling the material. However, museum displays, like those in gardens, are transient and changes are inevitable. The fashion is now for exhibits in darkness lit by artificial light, for reconstructions with figures, a return to the peep-show and everything made easy.

The post-war years were overshadowed by the thought of Cyril's approaching retirement. He thought of our moving to a country house in Monmouthshire, where he was developing a project of recording rural vernacular architecture in co-operation with Lord Raglan, but I doubted whether I wanted to commit myself to the isolation of country life or to county society. I thought of settling in Cirencester and making the museum into a full-time job. However, our change of location was decided when in August 1947 I was offered a Special Lectureship at the University College of the South West at Exeter. I owed the appointment, of course, to Norton Medlicott; he had come to Exeter from Swansea and knew of my work in South Wales and my teaching at Cardiff. He was sympathetic to archaeology and he had seen me in action at Exeter. He was anxious to expand and to vitalise the history department. The Principal, John Murray, was also ambitious, trying hard to make Exeter into an independent university, instead of a college attached to London University. He was an autocrat, who got his own way with his Senate and Council, and consequently my post was not advertised, but went through with several others. Although I had given Medlicott a list of my publications, and other credentials, I was not interviewed. This was counted against me for some time. I could not understand the opposition to archaeology I encountered from the irascible Professor of Botany, and the cunning politically-minded Professor of Philosophy.

I had made it clear that we were unable to move to Exeter until 1948, when Cyril retired, and that with my family commitments it had to be a part-time post initially. When Christopher Hawkes congratulated me, he asked me whether it was a life sentence, and after a little hesitation I answered correctly, 'Yes'. Bryan O'Neil, now Chief Inspector of Ancient Monuments, said he was glad to learn I was to become another tassel on the same Celtic fringe, recognising the affinities between South Wales and south west England. He had wanted me to dig at Sutton Walls, a formidable Herefordshire hill-fort, which I had to decline; he got the equally formidable Kathleen Kenyon instead. During the 1947–48 session I went to Exeter each term to give a short course of lectures, and I continued to work on the excavation report. I also had an important article on settlement in Wales during the Early Christian period, which Nash-Williams had asked me to write for the centenary volume of *Archaeologia Cambrensis – A Hundred Years of Welsh Archaeology* (1949). It was my first attempt at an historical synthesis, and I had been allotted the most difficult period, which even now eludes the archaeologist because of the lack of datable material. It was a pioneer work, hunting out pieces of evidence from old excavation reports and from museum stores, and assessing the possibilities of survival of a variety of sites from late Roman times onwards into the Dark Ages. I sent Ian Richmond an offprint; he highly approved, finding it '... so full, so well stated, so rich in suggestive lines of thought, and all documented in so detailed a fashion', which was welcome praise.

We planned to move during Cyril's leave, in July 1948, giving me time to settle in before the university term began in October, though he would have to return to Cardiff for a couple of months to complete his museum service. We put Four Elms up for sale and I went house-hunting in Exeter. I knew that we would like one of the late Georgian houses still surviving in the city. I was very attracted by a small one in Pennsylvania Crescent, but it was quickly snapped up by another buyer. The house-agent then directed me to St Leonard's Road, an early nineteenth-century development of stuccoed houses on the former Baring Estate. As I went up the path to the front door of No. 28, I realised that this shabby house with a fine ironwork verandah and porch might be the answer. It was divided into two flats, it had a dark basement kitchen, there was brown varnish and embossed lincrusta paper on the stairs, and it was really a bit too big for our requirements. But the rooms were well-proportioned, with original marble fireplaces, and I was attracted by the walled back garden, which had a grapevine in a conservatory and lots of fruit trees. The more I thought about it, the better I liked it. Fortunately the price, £6,000, was within our means; Cyril saw it and approved, and we lived there happily for nearly twenty years.

Before we left Rhiwbina, we asked Alan Sorrell to paint us a 'Conversation Piece', an informal family group at home in Four Elms. It shows Cyril in his study with a spread of maps and drawings, Charles beside him looking at his stamp album, Derek with his favourite toy engine and me, holding young George, aged three, who would not stay still, with a bunch of lilac from the garden. Sorrell insisted on painting in oils, which makes it rather sombre, but he did a delightful series of preliminary studies in chalk which I cherish. The portrait of Cyril was curiously prophetic, a good likeness of what he became, rather than as I then saw him.

There were many tributes paid to Cyril that year for his successful administration of the museum and for fostering its development as a national institution, and for his outstanding research achievements during his twenty-four years in Wales. He was greatly pleased to receive an Honorary Doctorate from the University of Wales, sponsored by Professor William Rees, the Welsh historian, at a colourful ceremony in the Brangwyn Hall at Swansea. After the final meeting of the Court at the museum, he was presented with a fine Welsh landscape by Cedric Morris; it was a view from the Gower peninsula with the rural houses in the foreground and the smoking industrial chimneys of Llanelli across the water behind, symbolic of the two aspects of South Wales that Cyril wanted to remember, for he never cared for the mountains as I did.

We left Cardiff with few regrets, though retaining happy memories of friends, field work and the young family. Cyril was now convinced that it was best to make a break and that to hang around in South Wales, watching a new director at work, would be a mistake. He had plenty of archaeological business to attend to in London, and he planned to come back regularly to continue his Monmouthshire field work with Lord Raglan. For my part, I was delighted at the prospect of more university work, and of exploring new country in south-west England.

Chapter Seven

The University College of the South West
The Pursuit of Archaeology

1948 – 1956

In 1948 Exeter was still only a university college, which prepared students for the external degrees of London University. Although the purchase of the Streatham Estate to the north of the city in 1922, coupled with the gift of Reed Hall, a magnificent Early Victorian mansion, had assured the long-term future for a university campus, only the Roborough Library and the Washington Singer laboratories for chemistry and physics had been built on the hundred-acre estate. The architect was Vincent Harris, who decided that seventeenth-century-style brick buildings complete with oriel windows, were appropriate, regardless of their function. The administration and all the arts departments were crammed into a tall mock-Georgian building in Gandy Street in the city centre, supplemented by a row of wartime Nissen huts, and the York Wing of the adjoining Royal Albert Museum. There were some 900 students, including many ex-servicemen, and a number from overseas, mostly living in well-regulated single-sex halls of residence. The Principal, John Murray, had set his heart on the college becoming an independent chartered university, but it was generally recognised that it had some way to go, academically and financially.

When I turned up at Gandy Street, I found my accommodation consisted of a school desk, a chair and a filing cabinet in the middle of a large ground-floor room, in which there were eight other new members of staff. I had already acquired a quantity of heavy two-and-a-half inch glass slides, and a bulky set of six-inch maps of Devon presented to me by the Ordnance Survey as their new county correspondent, as well as material for a teaching collection. For most of that year, I sat with my feet on the heap of maps and slide boxes, until the college carpenter had time to make me a chest of map drawers. The next year, I shared a decent room temporarily with Mary Coates, a retired historian from Somerville College, Oxford, and then with the newly-appointed Joyce Youings, a lecturer with special interest in local history, with whom I had much in common and who became a great friend.

I managed to get surplus material for my teaching collection from friends amongst museum curators: decorated Samian and Anglo-Saxon pottery and metalwork from Geoffrey Bushnell at Cambridge, early Iron Age pottery from Ken Annable at Devizes, Gallo-Belgic wares from M. R. Hull at Colchester, as well as unstratified Roman coarse pottery from my Exeter excavations. I bought a set of inexpensive Roman coins from Seabys, a London firm, and so had enough for demonstrations. I then obtained a good secondhand case with storage drawers beneath a sloping glass top, and this was placed on the upstairs landing adjoining the lecture room which housed the departmental projector. I felt it was very necessary for students to see original material, since the Exeter Museum was useless, with more space given to ethnographic material from the Pacific, Africa and the polar regions than to British or local antiquities.

I had agreed to give courses in Roman Britain and in Anglo-Saxon archaeology to a mixture of History and English students as well as a few lectures on British prehistory in the geography department. Numbers were small, but I found the standards required by London were higher than in Wales, and I had to raise my sights. Professor Medlicott was rather surprised when I decided to attend regularly the history departmental meetings, but I felt it was essential to integrate archaeology into the curriculum, instead of it being regarded by my colleagues as a strange sort of optional extra. I was the only woman at the large table in the professor's room on the top floor; there were five others: easy-going Bill Handcock and George Greenaway, who had been there for a very long time, Professor Frank Barlow, the medievalist, F. Schenk and Donald Southgate, all recent appointments like myself. I listened attentively to the cut and thrust of academic argument, presided over kindly but firmly by Medlicott. Other social contacts were made informally over lunch in the refectory, in a shabby Nissen hut, patronised by both arts and sciences, so in a short time I came to know most members of the small staff in a way that is no longer possible in the large provincial universities today. The Principal was frequently to be seen at lunch; he always bought a packet of chocolate biscuits and bestowed one on any female sitting within reach, which I found rather embarrassing. He also organised formal afternoon tea for junior members of staff parties at the grandiose Rougemont Hotel; these which were rather a trial. There was an unexpected streak of whimsy in the man, outwardly an ambitious administrator, which led him to produce fanciful literary effusions; I was given a copy of one to present to my husband, who did not know what to make of it any more than I did.

My teaching commitments were light, and I soon began to take stock of archaeology in south-west England and to set myself objectives. I sensed that there was something wrong because, in comparison with the adjoining counties, the prehistoric and early civilizations in Devon had been so little studied, with the exception of Dartmoor by Hansford Worth. No inventory had been produced by the Royal Commission for Historic Monuments, and the first volume of the Victoria County History published in 1906 was inadequate and out of date. There was no archaeologist on the staff of the museums in Exeter, Torquay or Plymouth, and whilst the learned independent scholar Dr Ralegh Radford was always generous with good advice, he had published very little. There were two county societies, the Devonshire Association established in 1862, large and wealthy but old-fashioned and inert, and the small Devon Archaeological Exploration Society, founded in 1929 for the practice and publication of excavations in the county, the 'new archaeology' of its time. Both societies had contributed to my Exeter excavations, and I felt I needed to be involved with both in the future. Accordingly, I took on the production of an annual report, for the Devonshire Association *Transactions* on the Early History of Devon, extending its subject matter to cover the prehistoric period from the Neolithic onwards. As I wrote in my first number, 'It is now generally accepted that a study of the material remains of a period, i.e. its archaeology, is one way in which its history may be built up, and that 'early history' no longer need be limited to the time of written records'.[1] This sounds now only too obvious, but it must have been news to most members of the Devonshire Association at the time. Over the years, the record proved useful in attracting contributors from various parts of Devon, and gradually it became known that the new archaeologist at the university was interested in all sorts of chance finds.

By recording the sprats, I attracted some larger fish, namely finds that were of more than local interest and that deserved publication in a national journal. For instance, two Greek silver coins from Holne, found separately; a worn one of Alexander the Great, and the other of Aesillas, a Roman quaestor in Macedonia in 90 BC. I visited the farmer who had dug them up, and concluded these were genuine discoveries from the southern fringe of Dartmoor, and indicative of trading contacts with the

Mediterranean in the first century BC.[2] Later, in 1959, I was informed of the discovery of a fine bronze bowl on Crooked Moor, Rose Ash, north Devon. The farmer had turned it up when cutting drainage channels at a boggy stream-head, where 'it shone as though it were gold'. It had a stylised animal head mount for a ring handle in a characteristic late Iron Age style. It gave me an opportunity for a comparative study, and for my first attempt to describe a Celtic art object and to relate it to the surroundings. I concluded that it was probably a votive offering at a spring-head, a sacred site, or *nemet,* suggested by the nearby parish place names such as Kings Nympton and Bishops Nympton.[3] When the Exeter Museum committee declined to pay £50 for it, the bowl was bought by the British Museum.

Another time a member of the Devon Archaeological Society brought me a cardboard shoe-box full of alleged Romano-British pottery from the sand dunes at Bantham, at the mouth of the river Avon, which she wanted identified for a local history exhibition, celebrating the Coronation of 1953 by the villagers. To my astonishment the sherds were mostly pieces of imported Mediterranean wine-jars of fifth- to sixth-century date. I recognised them from those I had seen on our visit to Garranes in Ireland. I boldly suggested that they indicated a Dark Age trading settlement on the south Devon coast.[4] At that time the only other similar material had been recorded from Tintagel by Radford, but subsequently more was found on the south Devon coast at Mothecombe on the Erme, and at High Peak, Sidmouth. The trade is now regarded as well established in the south west and in other Celtic realms around the Irish Sea, with sources in the eastern Mediterranean and North Africa.

My other concern was with the recording and protection of earthworks. In 1949 I was horrified to learn from a newspaper cutting that a farmer in the South Hams had levelled a small hill-fort enclosure known as Burleigh Dolts despite the fact that it was a Scheduled Ancient Monument and, as such, required notification and the consent of the Ministry of Works. I wrote to *The Times*, I reported it to the Archaeological Societies and to the county council, but no one seemed unduly worried. The ministry took no action, and declined to prosecute on the grounds that more than six months had elapsed since the offence had been committed. However, I had maintained my contacts with Bryan O'Neil, Chief Inspector of Ancient Monuments at the ministry, and he appointed me their county correspondent, charged with the care of the Scheduled Monuments in Devon.

I then made a point of visiting, usually with Cyril, all the hill-forts and the outstanding groups of Bronze Age barrows marked on the six-inch Ordnance Survey maps. I revised the plans and the inadequate descriptions on the record forms I had inherited from my predecessor, a curious elderly lady, Miss Cicely Radford, who was no archaeologist. I added many new sites to the schedule, which nowadays is included in the Sites and Monuments Record maintained by full-time officers of Devon County Council. My recommendations were accepted without question in Whitehall; at present only a visit by an inspector from London can ensure the modest degree of protection for a site that 'scheduling' provides.

It became obvious that more positive action was needed to enlist support for archaeology in the west country. When I was asked by the Council for British Archaeology to reorganise the local regional group, I readily accepted with the strong support of Professor Medlicott, who was willing to be its chairman. Group XIII was the association of archaeological and kindred societies from the counties of Cornwall, Devon, Gloucestershire and Somerset. It had been started by Mr St George Gray of Glastonbury Lake Village fame, a veteran of the Somerset Archaeological Society and curator of their museum at Taunton, but it had failed to take off. My first concern was to increase its membership by drawing in representatives of the smaller local societies, for example, the Torquay Natural History Society or the Cotteswold Field Club, as well as from museums with archaeological interests. We decided to hold regular meetings twice a year to discuss regional problems. As convenor, I represented the group on the council's executive meetings in London, and so could make our views known and ask for national support.

Protection of earthworks came high on our agenda, and in 1949 the group published a pamphlet summarising, in simple language, the legal position, the dangers from agriculture and local development, and what action archaeological societies might take. We followed it up with others dealing with *Chance Finds* (1951), and *The Care of Churches* (1953), both packed with useful information. Members were asked to distribute the pamphlets with their proceedings. These leaflets were a pioneer attempt to make known the resources generally available nationally and locally, and aimed to create an informed public opinion. There was no means of knowing whether our efforts were successful, but there is no doubt that over the years an understanding of the value of archaeology and the need for conservation have grown.

Turning to domestic affairs, the family settled happily into the new home at 28 St Leonard's Road. Cyril and I each had a study, on either side of a dividing wall in the big front room, opening on to the verandah; both were lined with bookshelves, and Cyril had his big new drawing-desk with storage drawers below, where he worked on his *Monmouthshire Houses*, whilst I had the Jacobean oak refectory table on which to spread my papers. The sitting room with its shallow Regency bow window faced the garden, which was entered from the basement door below. The boys had a small playroom on the ground floor and the eldest, Charles, had the doubtful privilege of sleeping in an attic bedroom. All three were now at school: Charles a boarder at a public school, Bryanston in Dorset, Derek and George at day school in Exeter. We had given a lot of thought to Charles's education; neither of us liked the conventional public schools with their emphasis on the classics and games and still practising corporal punishment and 'fagging'. I am not sure how we heard about Bryanston as a progressive school possibly from Jacquetta Hawkes who sent her son, Nicholas, there, but a visit to Blandford Forum and an interview with Mr Coade, the headmaster, confirmed our good opinion. It was situated in the lovely Dorset chalk country beside the river Stour; it offered freedom for the boys, fostered the creative arts and provided good teaching. Charles was very happy there, experimenting with acting and painting, and he eventually passed into Dartmouth and the navy without much trouble in 1951. Derek was not suited to the Episcopal Boys' School, and was soon transferred to a small private boarding school in nearby Newton St Cyres. We found a vacancy for George, aged five, at St Margaret's Girls' School in nearby Magdalen Road, which accepted small boys in the lowest form. As a young man he amused his girlfriends by claiming to have shared their education. I had some domestic troubles before I got settled with a staid cook-housekeeper, including an episode with an unmarried mother, and with another girl who had concealed the fact that she had recently been discharged from Exminster Mental Hospital, and whom I had allowed to take George to Paignton Zoo; she finally ran away and was picked up behaving very eccentrically by the police in Sidmouth and was returned to hospital. There was no social service or after-care in Devon in those days.

George was always a bit delicate and had a succession of illnesses, jaundice, measles, and appendicitis. People on the beach used to stare at my skinny child, although he was very active and cheerful. His sudden attack of jaundice coincided with our evening party at St Leonard's Road for some of the distinguished archaeologists attending the Exeter meeting of the Prehistoric Society in September 1949. I had been asked by Sir Lindsay Scott, the president, to help organise the meeting to be held at the university, and it really was quite a big occasion. I experienced the familiar tug-of-war between my maternal feelings and the demands of my archaeological profession; in the event, I compromised by omitting the Sunday Dartmoor excursion in order to remain at George's bedside.

I gave the first paper on the Farway (Broad Down) barrows and the Wessex culture in Devon, having been inspired by the rich grave goods characteristic of the early Bronze Age which lay neglected in the Exeter Museum, including two fine shale cups from Broad Down.[5] I had visited the Farway cemetery, where over sixty mounds were strung out along three miles of the 700 foot ridge of the Greensand plateau of East Devon, inland from Sidmouth. This was quite an effort, as we then had no car and I had to take a bus to Sidford and walk up the Roncombe valley to the site. Other exotic finds from Devon now fell into place, and I was able to establish a cultural province analogous to and contemporary with the second phase of the Wessex culture of the southern chalk, as defined by Stuart Piggott in 1938. At that time archaeologists thought in terms of invasions from the continent to explain cultural change; now local developments are favoured instead, stimulated by trading contacts and gift exchanges between chiefs. The diversity of grave goods, the variations in barrow construction and in ritual acts evident in the Farway cemetery certainly suggest prolonged use by different local groups.

The conference was not without incident. I remember the growing impatience of the audience listening to Mr G. L. Carter, a local solicitor, of 'the lunatic fringe', airing his theories about the significance of the blue stones in the geologically-mixed Bunter Pebble Beds on Woodbury Common, until several people, including me, walked out. I felt the conference was important, because it had brought leading archaeologists like Stuart Piggott, Christopher Hawkes, Gordon Childe and Grahame Clark, to Exeter, and had bolstered my position at the university.

The next step was to plan a campaign of excavation, in addition to supplementary small digs that would be needed in Exeter. It was Stuart Piggott who stimulated me to tackle the prehistoric settlements on Dartmoor. 'I do wish,' he said, 'that you would try to knock some sense into all those stone huts'. I was attracted in any case to the hill country and had already realised the inadequacies of previous investigations by the Devonshire Association. I decided in 1951 to start at Kestor, on the eastern side of the moor, which was accessible by a steep, narrow, granite walled road from Chagford. On the slopes below the tor there was an extensive field system with drove-ways and some twenty large huts scattered singly and in small groups in the fields. The site had been surveyed by Dr Cecil Curwen, a leading Sussex archaeologist, on his honeymoon, with Mrs Curwen holding the tape,[6] and he kindly let me use his original plans. July in 1951 and 1952 was fine and warm, and it was most enjoyable to be working in that attractive upland at 1,200 feet, with a party of friends and students. Visitors were rare, but occasionally a herd of ponies came by headed by, a wild aggressive stallion. I had engaged two local workmen who knew how to move the large fallen granite slabs by 'trigging' them up with small stones, and how to 'walk' them zig-zag fashion with an iron bar. The results were very satisfactory; by careful scraping we found a ring of postholes, as well as a central one which showed how these large round huts were roofed, and enabled Cyril to draw a convincing reconstruction.[7] The association of the huts and fields was demonstrated, and stratified pollen grains were obtained from a lynchet, showing that shallow ploughing had taken place after some peat had formed: a quern-stone from the hut confirmed that grain had been ground.

The second season we dug at Round Pound, a large hut in a concentric walled enclosure with an entry from the drove-way through the fields. It proved to be a metalworker's hut, complete with a bowl furnace and lumps of slag, a forging pit and a quenching place with a covered drain, a most exciting discovery. As the slag was being collected and the structures recorded, a holiday visitor stood by and expressed much intelligent interest. He introduced himself as Sir Allan Grant, a director of the Firth Brown Steelworks, and offered to get samples analysed at their research laboratory in Sheffield. Naturally I thought that I had found the long-sought evidence for prehistoric tin smelting, but the slag analyses proved that iron was being extracted from a local haematite. This confirmed my belief that the settlement was of late date, and in existence in the first half of the first millennium BC.

My next task was to find out the distribution of similar field systems, with the help of aerial photographs, the six-inch Ordnance Survey maps, and many fine winter days walking on the moor when the undergrowth was down. As a result, I wrote an article, 'Celtic farms and fields on Dartmoor', embodying my new ideas about early agriculture and settlement patterns on the moor.[8] Times have changed, and fresh discoveries by Andrew Fleming have demonstrated that the small field systems which I defined are part of larger layouts, bounded by long walls known as 'terminal reaves', and that the larger parallel fields, then generally thought to be medieval, are contemporary with the Bronze Age huts.[9] In archaeology changes are inevitable, and I remain content to have started the concept of Bronze Age farming communities on the moor.

To continue the research, I felt it was necessary to investigate another variety of settlement, the enclosed hut groups locally known as 'pounds'.

My field studies had shown that they were the predominant type on the southern and western part of the moor. I was lucky in that the siting of a new reservoir in the Avon valley coincided with a well-preserved enclosed settlement of nine huts on Dean Moor, and that the Ministry of Works was willing to finance a full excavation. This was to be spread over three summers from 1954 to 1956.[10] The upper Avon valley was a remote place, over-shadowed by the heights of White Barrows at 1,540 feet. There was no road beyond Shipley Bridge until one was made to the reservoir by the contractors, and then there was no way of getting equipment to our site, except by wading, until the Ministry had built a footbridge over the river. The first year was very wet, and it was only with the greatest difficulty that plans and sections of the huts were completed following day after day of driving rain. The small student party put up at the little Pack Horse Inn at South Brent; it included Desmond Bonney, a promising student geographer, who became my assistant supervisor, and later had a career with the Royal Commission on Historical Monuments of England. Our only entertainment was a once-a-week ancient movie in the dilapidated village hall, where I remember hearing Doris Day singing 'Che sarà, sarà', in Hitchcock's film, *The Man Who Knew Too Much*, and laughing helplessly throughout the misadventures of *Genevieve*, the vintage car on the way to Brighton. The second season was briefly interrupted by an accident to my youngest, George, who was now at the local Exeter Preparatory School; he had climbed an old apple tree in a neighbour's garden on his way home, and had fallen and broken his arm. I dashed back to Exeter to see him in plaster in hospital, and to find that Cyril, with the housekeeper, was able to cope with him for the few days until the dig was finished. After that it was my turn to sit and wait for an hour or more with a fidgety ten-year-old in the basement corridor of the old Royal Devon and Exeter Hospital in Southernhay, where the fracture clinic was held.

Returning to Dean Moor, there were some interesting sidelights on human life from the nine huts that we excavated. The lower half of each hut floor was dirty, and could be identified from the hearth as the kitchen and working place. There were also small pits in which food had been cooked in hot ash or heated river pebbles: others which probably held a sunken pot in which milk could have been set to curdle for cheese. The upper half of the floor was clean, and was the sleeping quarters; one had a bed recess, another a small store cupboard in the wall. Someone must have searched in vain for two small cornelian beads fallen on the floor. When I swept the interior for a photograph, I often thought of other women who had swept it in the Bronze Age. There were many whetstones, showing there were metal tools to sharpen, and, most surprisingly, about 50 lb of small pieces of iron ore were embedded inside one of the hut walls. Their nearest source was near Buckfastleigh some six miles away; this suggested that the inhabitants had recognised the mineral and transported it, but unlike the people at Kestor, did not know how to smelt it and extract the metal. It was then discarded as so much waste and built into the wall. Although there were no signs of fields in the valley, pieces of saddle querns showed that some grain was obtainable. The acid soils on the granite had destroyed all ancient bones, so no details of domestic animals were known; nevertheless it was apparent from the surroundings that the economy of the Dean Moor settlement, and of the Avon valley generally, was based primarily on stock keeping.

On the whole I was satisfied with my five years of field work on Dartmoor, which had concluded with an excavation of a unique medieval monastic homestead on Dean Moor, identifiable from documentary evidence as that of a lay brother of Buckfast Abbey in the fourteenth century.[11] I had defined the different types of hutted settlements, and stressed their economies; I had demonstrated their different distributions and had dated them to the Late Bronze Age and Early Iron Age. Later I revised this to the Middle Bronze Age, in consequence of the back-dating of the pottery series in southern Britain generally.[12] Subsequently radiocarbon dating of charcoals from excavations by Geoffrey Wainwright and Andrew Fleming have shown that 1600–600 BC is the most likely time range for the settlements. Now I had gained a really good working knowledge of the moor, I felt I should turn to other things, and leave it to others in the future to reassess the problems. I busied myself with a study of the hill-slope forts in Devon and Cornwall, already described in Chapter Five.

Cyril, too, was busy and productive during the ten years after his retirement, so I had no cause to worry about a lack of occupation; I think of him standing at his slope-top desk in his study, hard at work drawing, writing, proof correcting or sitting in the elegant iron-work verandah reading in the morning sunshine. In 1952 the Society of Antiquaries presented him with their highest honour, the Gold Medal, and Magdalene, his old Cambridge college, elected him as Honorary Fellow, which greatly pleased him and brought new friends in the Master, Sir Henry Willink, and his wife. He also served on the Gowers' Committee on houses of outstanding historical architectural interest. In Exeter he busied himself with work for the Cathedral and the Diocesan Advisory Committee: he urged Dean Wallace to wash the west front and get rid of the accumulated soot of ages. Afterwards Mrs Wallace was heard to say that she liked it better black, but

Aileen's mother – Alice Livingstone Henderson née McLean.

Aileen's father – Walter Scott Henderson.

Aileen (centre) with her sisters Mari (left) and Sheila, 1921.

Aileen, aged 2.

The Grange, the Henderson family home at Walton on the Hill in Surrey.

Aileen on the occasion of her presentation at Court, 1926.

In the Alps above Bonneval, Savoy in 1927.

Aileen and Cyril, 1933.

The wedding of Cyril and Aileen, Chelsea Old Church, July 1933.

Four Elms, Cyril and Aileen Fox's home in the Cardiff suburb of Rhiwbina, 1933–1948.

Kenneth Clark (Director of the National Gallery, later Lord Clark), standing on the steps of the National Museum of Wales with Members of the Museum's Council, circa 1935.

From left to right: Sir Cyril Fox (Director), the sculptor Goscombe John, Kenneth Clark, the Earl of Plymouth (President of the Museum), W. G. A. Ormsby-Gore (later Lord Harlech, Vice-President) and Archibald Lee (Secretary of the Museum).

Cyril and Aileen examining a bronze age urn during excavations at Simonstown Farm, 1937.

Sir Cyril Fox speaking to the Cambrian Archaeological Society at Tretower, 1949.

The Avon Valley, looking towards Dean Moor.

Hut 7 with storage pit at Dean Moor.

Kestor hut with postholes, 1951.

'Trigging up': the Dartmoor method of raising massive granite slabs with a bar and then pushing small stones underneath. Kestor, 1952.

Excavation in the bomb-damaged areas of Exeter, 1945–7:
the General Post Office site behind the City Wall.

Excavations in progress in Bartholomew Street, Exeter, in 1959.

Exeter University, Department of History, June 1956.

Mrs Gilbert   Mrs   Kenneth   Peter   Mrs Rowe   Col.   Commdr.   Cyril and Aileen
     Creasy   Rowe   Grimes   Creasy   Gilbert   Fox
     (Mayoress)   (Sheriff)   (President)   (Mayor)

A function at the Royal Archaeological Institute, Exeter, July 1957.

The Retreat, Aileen's home on the River Exe, 1967–1998.

Aileen at Te Awanga, New Zealand, 1974.

The staff of Auckland Museum, 1983.

A cold, windy day at Hawkes Bay, 1983.

Aileen with members of the New Zealand Archaeological Association, at Hawkes Bay, 1983.

Mount Eden, a terraced *paa* in Auckland, New Zealand.

Aileen and Michael Hordern having received honorary degrees of Doctorate of Letters at Exeter University, 1985.

most thought it a great improvement. He was also concerned about the destruction of late medieval merchant houses in the city, and together with W. G. Hoskins, then living in St Leonard's Road, protested at several public inquiries. It was a triumph when an exceptional timber-framed house in Frog Street, on the line of the inner by-pass, was moved bodily to a new site and so preserved intact. It is still popularly known as 'The House That Moved'.

He completed his survey with Lord Raglan of *Monmouthshire Houses*, which was published by the National Museum of Wales in three slender volumes in 1951, 1953 and 1954, with a second edition in 1994. He was at once inveigled by Rik Wheeler, then the Secretary of the British Academy, to revise and reprint his work on *Offa's Dyke*, previously published annually in *Archaeologia Cambrensis* from 1926 to 1934, together with the summary he had given to the Academy in 1940 as the Sir John Rhys Memorial Lecture. Rik, when Director of the National Museum, had instigated the project for Cyril when he was appointed Keeper of Archaeology at Cardiff in 1925, knowing of his previous work on the dykes in Cambridgeshire. With a foreword by Sir Frank Stenton, the historian, and an enlarged format, the fine volume published in 1955 by the Academy is a worthy tribute to his six strenuous years of pioneering field work, his acumen and his original ideas. It remains a monumental work of reference. How often have I regretted that I was not with him to share the field work!

Fortunately there was an opportunity for a new joint venture, a survey of the Wansdyke: it is a magnificent linear earthwork, a single massive rampart with its ditch on the north, presumably defining a post-Roman frontier. It extends from Savernake Forest across the chalk hills of north Wiltshire and continues, it was then held, though diminished in size, over the broken Jurassic country to the south of Bath ending at the Iron Age hill-fort of Maes Knoll in Somerset. Our interest was aroused in 1955 when Cyril led a group from a summer school at Urchfont, Devizes, to see the dyke at its best on Morgan's Hill nearby, and we realised that it offered a challenge and the need for a fresh approach. Accordingly we started on a programme of systematic field work and research; it was truly a work of collaboration in the field and in the study. Cyril was now in his seventies and visibly ageing, but his enthusiasm carried him up and over the chalk hills of Wiltshire. I remember him on the summit of Tan Hill, over 900 feet, exulting in the panorama of downland and declaring that it must have been from here that the course of the dyke was planned. I also remember anxiously hastening down the hillside when dark thunderclouds were gathering, to get to the car before the storm broke.

At the outset we had doubts about the continuation of the dyke across the low-lying land west of the chalk and in the Avon valley; I was convinced that the reduced earthwork was no more than the remains of the Roman road to Bath. Oddly enough, a young archaeologist, Tony Clark, had the same idea unknown to us. It was all rather awkward, and bad luck for him, but we paid him a friendly visit when he was digging a section across the earthwork in Spye Park, Sandy Lane in 1957. He demonstrated to everyone's satisfaction that it was the *agger* of the Roman road to Bath and not the Wansdyke.[13] We had already perceived, after a lot of concentrated field work, that the builders of East Wansdyke had dug away the same Roman road at the head of a combe on Morgan's Hill, and that the dyke actually ended with the chalk plateau 200 yards to the west. We planned the vital complicated junction of the road and dyke with the help of Desmond Bonney, then with the Royal Commission for Ancient Monuments in Salisbury, so our interpretation became plain for all to see.[14] It is now accepted that East and West Wansdyke are separate earthworks in Wiltshire and Somerset respectively.

It was Cyril, of course, who assessed the evidence of the local Saxon charter boundaries of the ninth and tenth centuries, and of the related entries in the Anglo-Saxon Chronicle, for the conquest and early history of Wessex in the sixth century. Remembering his Cambridge days with Professor Chadwick, he realised the significance of the unusual Woden place-names, Woden's Valley (*dene*), Woden's Mount (*beorge*), Woden's Gate (*geat*), grouped around the ridgeway crossing of East Wansdyke (Woden's Dyke) at Red Shore.[15] He considered that these implied there had been a sacred precinct dedicated to Woden, the dominant Saxon god, intimately connected with the building and naming of the dyke. An old friend, Dr Kenneth Sisam, drew attention to the poetical heightened language of the Chronicle when referring to Ceawlin, the dynamic ruler of the West Saxons in the late sixth century. Though well aware of the difficulties and uncertainties of correlating early history and archaeology, we bravely stuck our necks out, and tentatively identified Ceawlin as the builder of East Wansdyke in the sixth century. We spent a long evening with our friends, Nowell Myres and Christopher Hawkes in Oxford, describing our findings and discussing our interpretation. Both were impressed, but Nowell rightly thought other solutions were possible, though none could be proven, and there the matter rests.[16] Our report was closely modelled on that for Offa's Dyke, with a systematic description of the earthwork related to strips of the six-inch Ordnance Survey maps.[17] It fell to me to draft much of the text, whilst Cyril concentrated on the illustrations, which have the hallmark of his distinctive lettering. By this time he was preoccupied with preparations for *Pattern and Purpose, A Study of Celtic Art,*[18] and *Life and Death in the Bronze Age*[19] each a reworking of his earlier writings. Soon after the stress of so much work he began to show a loss of memory, and the signs of Alzheimer's disease.

The first ten years in Exeter were not all work; we had some very good family holidays as well as others on our own, such as a return visit to Eire to meet with Sean O'Riordain in 1953. He took us on to the Hill of Tara, to see the Rath of the Kings and the outline on the grass of that strange long building known as The Hall. It was May, and the whole countryside was white with blossoming hawthorn. In Dublin we absorbed the riches of the museum: Bronze Age gold and Iron Age Celtic art. We also managed a visit to the Abbey Theatre to see O'Casey's play, *Juno and the Paycock*, and I went to Trinity College to hear Alfred Deller singing madrigals and Elizabethan airs. It was the first time I had heard a counter tenor, and the combination of music and poetry in the setting of the College Hall was unforgettable.

Memorable, too, were visits to Peter and Leslie Murray-Thriepland's holiday home in remote Caithness, where they owned Dale, an old farm on the Thurso river, near Halkirk. It was wild country, a flat peaty expanse, part moorland, part reclaimed stonewalled pasture, with views of the distant hills, Morven and the aptly named Maiden Pap. It was on the way to Duncansby Head that I saw at close quarters a peregrine falcon make a kill, and a hen-harrier hunting low over the moor, as well as the crowd of puffins, fulmar and skuas on the cliffs. There were many stone towers, brochs, and wheel-houses as relics of the past for us to visit. Cyril was much interested in the local vernacular architecture with its inhabited two-room crofts. In 1953 there were three of the four Murray-Thriepland boys holidaying at Dale together with our two; their consumption of baps, treacle scones and oatcakes was prodigious. A succession of wet days induced them to entertain us with a play of *Odysseus* in five scenes. Each boy had to take several parts except David, the twelve-year-old eldest who, as Odysseus, appeared in every scene. George was allotted all the female roles – Circe, Nausica and Penelope. Leslie had written an outline text for the plot, but most of the words were made up as they rehearsed. It was not a very polished performance, but full of zest. Alas, that was the last happy year at Dale for us, for Peter died very suddenly in 1957. An old Etonian and an Oxford Blue, he was rowing with David on the Thames at Eton when he suffered a massive heart attack and collapsed into the river, and was dead when David pulled him to the bank. I was very grieved, for he was a true friend on whom I could always rely, even if he had some of the prejudices of a wealthy landowner.

On another northern holiday we took our car on the sleeper train from Exeter to Newcastle, and George and Derek, now teenagers, brought their bikes. After a night in Hexham, we set off for Kelso, giving the boys a good start. Climbing up over the Cheviots we reached the border at Carter Bar with its hairpin bends, where we found a disconsolate George and a damaged bike on the roadside. Travelling too fast downhill, he had mis-judged the bend and shot over the edge. Derek, who followed more slowly, failed to see the accident and had pedalled on, thinking George was ahead. It took us quite a while to catch him up, and we couldn't help laughing at the mishap. Kelso was an excellent base for visiting the Scottish border country; we managed also to get to Lindisfarne, which we found so fascinating that we stayed extra hours whilst the causeway was submerged at high tide. It was a very hot day, and the boys swam along-side an inquisitive seal which was bobbing up and down in the chilly water. We stayed in the Ednam House hotel, which was excellent but rather expensive, so I firmly said we would omit afternoon tea, with its delicious scones and cakes served in the hotel lounge. On the last day I relented and we all indulged. When it came to pay the bill, there was no charge, tea being included in our 'pension' terms; I never dared tell the boys what they had missed!

To my great delight, George shared my liking for wild flowers, which he collected and pressed, winning a prize for his efforts at the Exeter Preparatory School. I was able to introduce him to the glories of the Mediterranean spring flowers in Sicily in 1956, and to the Alpine flora in his summer holidays from Bryanston in 1958. We went to Syracuse with Peggy Piggott, now separated from Stuart, and her adopted niece, Sue, who was fifteen, the same age as George. Sicily was then unspoilt and lit-tle visited, apart from Taormina. There was a profusion of flowers around the Greek theatre and temples, and the sinister quarries where the Greeks were imprisoned outside Syracuse, and on the walled slopes of Epipoli. I remember specially the little blue irises (*Gynandriris sisyrinchium*) among the ruins, and golden Coronaria daisies (*Chrysanthemum coronarium*). Everywhere the orange and lemon trees were laden with fruit. We jour-neyed in a little train over the hills to see the temples at Agrigento and Selinunte and then back to Piazza Armerina to visit the imperial Roman villa, with its well-preserved mosaics, recently excavated. Neither Peggy nor I were classical archaeologists, but the Greek and Roman architectural achievements are a part of the English cultural heritage in which we both delighted.

For the Alps, George, Derek and I went to Binn in the Valais together with my sister, Sheila; there we alternated leisurely flower hunts in the valley with some strenuous walking up to the higher Alpine pastures and the screes at 3,000 metres. Sheila, always overweight, found it hard going at times. In late July the meadows were coloured by misty blue campanula (*Campanula barbata*) and brilliant orange daisies (*Arnica montana*). The trip revived my memories of the early expeditions with my father.

Meanwhile Charles had left Bryanston and, after three months at Grenoble to improve his French, he joined the navy at Dartmouth in May 1952. Thereafter we saw little of him, as he was stationed at Malta, where I visited him in 1957, taking the opportunity to look at the splendid walled defences of Valetta constructed by the Knights of St John, and the mega-lithic chamber tombs and temples. Eventually he opted to join the now-extinct Fleet Air Arm as a navigator, and consequently was stationed at Culdrose in Cornwall. One weekend he unexpectedly blew in with a rather silent good-looking girlfriend, Jane, on their way to the Farnborough Air Show; on their return, greatly to our surprise, he announced their engage-ment. The poor girl obviously had been apprehensive of Charles' inten-tions and of her future in-laws, both archaeologists. However, all was well, and they were happily married at Gulval Church, near Penzance, in proper naval fashion in March 1959.

At 28 St Leonard's Road, there was a steady stream of visitors, old friends like Sophie Fry and the Burkitts, the step-daughters now with their small children, archaeologists who came to lecture to my students, such as Glyn Daniel, or just to talk to Cyril, such as Maurice Barley and Stuart Piggott. Stuart, now Professor of Archaeology in Edinburgh, invoked the attractions of his proposed spring visit in light-hearted rhyme with allu-sions to Celtic art and vernacular architecture:

> Warm west winds in an Exeter garden
> Far from Scotland's Calvinist gloom,
> Ere my Celtic arteries harden
> while the snowdrops are still in bloom
> How I gasp for it, eagerly grasp for it
> A spring resurrection from winter's tomb.
>
> Talks Dobunnic, and walks Dumnonian,
> Crucks and mirror style, chamfrain and bowl
> Façade and pediment (quite Summersonian)
> Each one blowing his own trumpet scroll.
> Hint of the sun in it, glint of fun in it

A light-hearted banquet for reason and soul.

With the help of photographs and the family album, I have set out here a small selection of trivia and travels to show that though the pursuit of archaeology was predominant in both our lives, we had other interests as well, and that now our sons' company and doings added to our enjoyment. For me, it was a very varied life, teaching and examining at the university, lecturing in the county, serving on committees, doing my field research, excavating and writing, as well as organising the home and garden and our finances, and meeting the needs of Cyril and the family. Like many other women in the post-war epoch, there were many strands for me to weave into a satisfactory pattern, and I had to work hard to get my priorities right.

After we had been ten years in Exeter, there came an invitation from Glyn Daniel to write a book about south-west England in the new series of Ancient Peoples and Places which he was editing for Thames & Hudson. It was to be a short book with many illustrations, aimed at students and general readers rather than the specialist academics, what Glyn called '*haute vulgarisation*', in effect. I felt this would be a good opportunity to pull together my ideas and the results of my field work and to produce the first synthesis, long overdue, of early human settlement in the south-west as a whole, ignoring county boundaries. The absurdity of the Devon–Somerset boundary bisecting Exmoor is obvious. It took me two or three years to write it, to collect the numerous illustrations and to fill some of the gaps in my knowledge. My working method during university term was to keep one day a week clear of teaching and distractions, and to settle down to write at home. Creative work for me is best done in the morning, revision in the afternoon or early evening; I cannot work at night. The intervals between the end of the university term and the school holidays were also good for concentrated work. For one such fortnight in July we were lent a cottage on Dartmoor at Jordan, near Widecombe, where Cyril and I led a quiet simple life. There was no telephone, we drew water from a spring and cooked with Calor gas; it was wonderful to be free of distractions. I sat at the window looking out down the peaceful valley and completed the Bronze and Iron Age chapters with little trouble. It was very satisfactory as the typescript mounted up and the book took shape. I took care to make the text clear and readable, even if it meant some simplification. It was essentially a personal book, reflecting the views of an archaeologist working in the 1950s and 1960s.

For the 150 illustrations, I enlisted the help of two talented archaeology students who did most of the original line drawings, since the history department then had no professional draughtsman. I used the university photographer to take new photographs; I think he enjoyed his trips to the various museums as a change from his darkroom. Both the editor and the publisher, Eric Peters, were very helpful, patient and encouraging. Glyn insisted that I added a final chapter to include the Dark Ages to AD 600. Thames & Hudson had made it into an attractive volume when the book eventually appeared in 1964; it sold well, so much so that a second, revised edition was needed: this was published by David & Charles in 1973, and incorporated new discoveries in Exeter and elsewhere. It is now out of print, and has been replaced by Malcolm Todd's more substantial work *The South West to AD1000* (Longman, 1987). I was glad to see that he considered my volume 'deserves a place on any shelf of essential books on the peninsula', alongside Hencken's *Archaeology of Cornwall and Scilly* of 1932.

The writing of *South West England* appropriately forms the end of a chapter. It marks the close of our happiest days in Exeter. Thereafter came the dark days of Cyril's decline, my mother's death, and the frustration of my efforts to establish archaeology as an independent department at the newly-established Exeter University.

Chapter Eight

Exeter University
The Development of Archaeology
and The Making of a Don

1956 – 1973

In 1955 the University of the South West got its Charter at last and became the University of Exeter. The document was presented by H. M. Queen Elizabeth to the first Chancellor, the Duchess of Devonshire, on 8 May 1956, and on the same day Her Majesty laid the foundation stone of Queen's Building in which the arts and social studies departments were to be housed. It was an occasion for decorous academic rejoicing; honorary degrees were awarded in the somewhat inappropriate setting of the Savoy Cinema, and there was a dinner for staff, Senate and Council in the old Civic Hall in the Higher Market; the deficiencies of its decor were skillfuly veiled in a gauze tent. I attended, wearing an elegant long silver-grey embroidered satin dress, which I finally deposited as a dated period piece in Exeter Museum.

Freed from the restrictions of external London degrees, the history department revised its syllabus and the provisions for teaching archaeology. Unfortunately for me, Norton Medlicott had left Exeter for the London School of Economics in 1953, and Frank Barlow had succeeded him as professor and head of the department. A scholarly medieval historian, he had none of the kindliness or tolerance of Medlicott; he mistrusted archaeology which, in some curious way, he felt threatened the integrity as well as the popularity of historical studies. He disliked me too, probably on account of my title, and a feeling that I had got my lectureship, now established as a full-time post, on false pretences. Whilst he always supported my requests for research funds, he hardly ever expressed appreciation of their promptly published-results. He had a sardonic manner, and at times a cruel tongue. A shrewd and effective politician, dominant in the

Senate, he built up the history department and ruled it tyrannically in the style of the day. Now, heads of departments are elected and concern themselves with administrative chores, from which most professors are glad to be free.

Under the new university regulations, I was able to teach 'British Prehistory' as an option, and to continue with 'Roman Britain' as a special subject for students in their second and third years of a history Honours course; the latter was also available for classics students. I was anxious to foster my links with the geography department, and Professor Arthur Davies, always sympathetic, and supported by Bill Ravenhill, agreed to include British archaeology as one of the choices for an additional subject; similarly I got the Arts Board to include archaeology as one of three subjects for a new General Degree at a rather lower level than Honours. My intention was to build up the subject and to make it available to more students outside the history department; it seemed that the number of those taught was the only thing that mattered to the powers-that-be when considering the progress of archaeology. I was rewarded by attracting some bright students, including one girl who got a first class degree in all of her three General subjects, and by some able geographers who are now professional archaeologists, including my good friends, Desmond Bonney and Graeme Guilbert, as well as Desmond Walling, who became a professor at Exeter. A further development within the history department was the introduction of medieval archaeology as a Special Subject in 1963, consequent on the appointment of Martin Biddle as a lecturer, of which more hereafter. In 1968 the Arts Board, after much discussion, agreed to start Combined Honours courses, in which two relevant subjects were studied in tandem at the same high standard as for Single Honours. The combinations of history and archaeology, and geography and archaeology, were approved, necessitating the appointment of an external examiner and a third archaeologist, John Collis, a prehistorian from Cambridge in 1970. My contribution was a course on 'The Celts', which I taught in alternate years. This bald recital of a successful expansion conceals a prolonged and uphill academic struggle.

There was also the problem of getting adequate premises for archaeology. When we moved in 1958, into the new Queen's Building for the Arts, designed by Sir William Holford, I had one of the many small rooms on the second floor, along with other lecturers in the history department, with the professor in the large corner room at the end. I could gaze out of the window westwards towards the Exe valley and the little green hills above Exwick; in the foreground at the top of the grassy slope, there was a group of three shapely old Scots pine trees with their warm reddish trunks, beside which a bronze figure sculpture by Barbara Hepworth later stood. The whole staff had the advantage of a large ground-floor common room with a big picture window framing the same fine view, a great improvement on the old cramped quarters in Gandy Street. I managed to get the use of a small seminar room where the archaeological teaching collection could be installed and the projector permanently set up, and I normally lectured to my small groups there. Though I did not have the exclusive use of the room, it was the first step in getting a special place assigned to archaeology.

When the expansion of staff and arts students occurred in the sixties, as a result of the Robbins Report, Queen's Building was overflowing, and the administration asked for volunteers to occupy temporary accommodation elsewhere. Together with Martin Biddle, the newly-appointed lecturer in medieval archaeology, I decided to move to a converted stable block in a quiet courtyard at the back of Reed Hall, now changed from a Hall of Residence into the Staff Club. Here we had a small but adequate lecture room, a lobby for the teaching collection, and rooms for ourselves and a typist, whom Martin kept fully employed on his Winchester excavation work. There were both advantages and disadvantages on being distant from our colleagues across the gardens in Queen's Building. The students loved it; one of them remembered how I always lectured in a gown, as most people did in those days, and how in the confined space of the room in Reed Mews they were worried lest it caught in the trailing flex of the projector, or slipped right off my shoulders; somehow I always managed to hitch it up in time.

The ploy of going out into the wilderness paid off. When the archaeologists returned to Queen's Building in 1967, we moved into a spacious language laboratory on the first floor, which was converted into three staff rooms and a big workroom, with tables for seminars and demonstrations and with space for the collections and other equipment; we also had the use of an adjoining lecture room with a projector. By now, 1968, Ann Hamlin had replaced Martin Biddle as the medieval archaeologist, and we had acquired a young departmental technician, a talented draughtsman, so one of the staff rooms became his drawing office and a slide store. Historians occasionally asked him to draw them a map, but most of his time was taken up by the archaeologists. Thus little by little, along with the growth in student numbers, the development of the degree courses and field work as well as the new premises, archaeology acquired a visible identity in the university.

The final move came only after I had retired, but Ann and I had thought it out previously. The geography department, accommodated in the east wing of Queen's Building, was due to move into the large new Amory Building in 1975. Their rooms were well equipped with ample storage space, a dark room, a small laboratory, sinks and display cases. We perceived it was the right size, and well suited to the future needs of archaeology, and with the support of Bill Ravenhill, later the Reardon-Smith Professor, it was so agreed with the administration. Malcolm Todd occupied the professor's room, with a secretary in a room adjoining; there was a drawing office for two technicians, with rooms also for three or four lecturers and space for research students. It has become a satisfactory base for an archaeological concern that aspires not to become equipped as a science department, but to be a partner in an arts Department of History and Archaeology, as it was renamed in 1979.

The special feature of all archaeological courses at Exeter was field work. It was laid down in the syllabus that 'field work was an essential and integral part of the course'. This formula ensured that students were eligible for a grant for their expenses from their local authority, and that money could be allocated from departmental funds. During the term, field work consisted of one or two days of site visits by coach, for example to Dorset to see Maiden Castle, Martin Down long barrow, and the field systems in the Valley of Stones, or to Dartmoor, walking up the Avon to the complex Ryder's Rings settlement, or to Kestor with its huts and fields as well as the nearby stone rows. At Easter there was a three-day field course based at Devizes to visit the classic Wessex sites, or at Bodmin for Cornwall, or at Caerleon for South Wales. I found small cheap hotels that in March welcomed a student party, and though it was rather an effort, it was very worthwhile. It was the field work that students remembered about archaeology at Exeter: rain on Dartmoor, snow one bitter March day at Avebury, solitude at Stonehenge and an experience which one student described later as 'A marathon mind-expanding and physically exhausting exercise'. I did not intend it to be very strenuous, and was always rather surprised when I was the first up a hill-fort, and when some students found it difficult to keep going across a pathless heather-covered moor. There are photos of me in a check skirt, blue anorak and a white woolly hat, pointing out the details of an earthwork and no doubt asking the group what they signified.

In the summer term there was practical instruction in elementary surveying for first-year students including the use of a level, and the planning of one of the more accessible Dartmoor huts, plotting the wall-face stone by stone. I remember one girl who came wearing toeless sandals, until I reminded her that adders were not uncommon on Dartmoor; we had killed two of them during the Dean Moor excavations. During the long vacation, students spent at least a fortnight on an approved excavation. Some went with Martin Biddle to Winchester, some came with me to Exeter or Dartmoor or to the Roman signal stations in North Devon. Others went to a variety of sites, including Cadbury, the great hill-fort near Ilchester, to work for Leslie Alcock from Cardiff. In return I had students from University College, Cardiff, from Leicester and other provincial universities: a useful exchange on both sides. At the beginning of the Michaelmas term, we held informal seminars at which people could compare notes, show slides and photographs and discuss critically the methods and results of the excavations. Everyone kept a field notebook, which was handed in for inspection at the end of the academic year. Most included sketches of objects studied in the museums, as well as site plans and descriptions. I always emphasised the importance of recording a real object at first hand, even by a poor drawing, because the effort imprints it in the memory in a way no slide or book illustration can do. Some students developed a gift for archaeological drawing, and two girls were talented enough to produce illustrations for my book, *South West England* in 1962–3.

Over the years there were a few who got a first class degree, after some heart-searching by the examiners, because the history department was always scrupulous in maintaining high standards. There was usually a lively and responsive group of upper seconds, who made teaching enjoyable and worth while. I always had to emphasise the difficulties of getting a permanent job in archaeology; for example, one man with a first, who tried very hard to get accepted, finally had to settle for the well-paid post of an income tax inspector. In contrast, his contemporary, Bob Higham, became a lecturer in the archaeology section at Exeter. I did not encourage the best students to undertake postgraduate research; after three years at Exeter, I felt they needed to widen their experience, and go to a well-staffed specialist centre, such as the Institute of Archaeology in London. If there was local research to be done, I wanted to do it myself. Quite a number were attracted to museum work and were successful in obtaining posts in small local museums, where they could apply their general knowledge of prehistory, Roman Britain and early history to a specific new district. Others have found congenial work with local authorities as archaeology officers in the planning departments, looking after the Sites and Monuments Register for the county council, and making a case for conservation of threatened sites when needed. All in all, my twenty-five years at Exeter produced quite a few dedicated people, well qualified to assist with the expansion of British archaeology in the 1970s and 1980s, and to foster its growth in the public esteem.

I have always thought that membership of an institution, whether a university or an archaeological or other society, carried with it an obligation to take part in its administration if required. Accordingly I went to the annual meetings of the Arts Faculty, and in due course was elected to the board; I joined the Readers' and Lecturers' Association, and became one of its six representatives on the Senate and Council in 1962–5 and finally was elected its chairman for 1964–6. I remember waiting with another candidate in the hall of the staff club for the result of the vote and saying to myself, 'Che sará, sará'. Senate meetings I found incredibly tedious with long drawn-out discussions and lasting for hours. I sat nervously anticipating the right moment to intervene on an issue on the agenda that concerned the association. I am not a good impromptu speaker, but I do try to be brief and to stick to the point. Would that others had done the same! Still, it was interesting to be at the centre of power during a period of rapid development and university expansion. I also enjoyed the formal occasions of Degree Day and the like with their academic processions and the doctors in their colourful fancy dress. I only had the modest white hood and black gown of a Cambridge MA until given an Honorary DLitt in July 1985 on my return from New Zealand, which greatly pleased me.

One of the consequences of the move from Gandy Street was that there was a place for a Staff Club which the new Vice-Chancellor, Dr James Cook, was anxious to establish. A large private house, Knightley, in Streatham Drive had been acquired and altered, and a lump sum allocated for its furnishings – it now houses the music department. I can't remember exactly how I found myself on a small executive committee together with my friend, Ewart John, from the geography department, a talented artist. Knightley was a handsome Edwardian house, but we were determined to get away from mock Tudor or Georgian and to have furniture and fabrics of modern design. Ewart and I worked out the colour schemes, and the committee literally chose each piece of furniture, carpets, chairs, glass and cutlery from samples obtained through the university administration from wholesalers, including specialist firms like Gordon Russell. I well remember tackling the Vice-Chancellor for his approval of a fine Wilton patterned carpet as a centrepiece for the spacious oak-panelled hall, which was not included in the original budget. Cook was a parsimonious Scotsman but I managed to convince him of its necessity, for the carpet gave just the right touch of sophistication and colour at the cost of £80.

Perhaps it was that encounter, as well as the scarcity of women academics, that prompted him, in 1961, to ask me to join a working party of four to consider the university's policy for the halls of residence. I had long been interested in the subject since serving on the Aberdare Hall for Women's committee at Cardiff. Thanks to Principal Murray, Exeter had been well provided with Halls, Reed, Mardon, Hope and Lopes to name a few, some purpose-built, some converted from large old houses providing accommodation for about 60 per cent of the students. All were staffed by wardens, mostly from the academic staff; all were subject to stringent rules and regulations which the students resented. The old ideal of making residence in a hall an agreeable educational experience with contact between dons and staff at formal evening meals was rapidly being eroded, and students wanted more freedom to come and go as they pleased. With the rapid growth in numbers in the 1960s, new halls, Duryard and Birks, were being built on the campus, each with three or four separate houses for men and women, but with shared communal dining rooms, cafeteria and common rooms. Such mixed halls were then a novelty.

In retrospect, the working party's report seems rather equivocal; on the one hand we favoured more staff/student contact, and on the other we urged the need for more experiments in student freedom. Many of our practical suggestions for staffing and accommodation have become standard practice. Residence in hall is now popular and the atmosphere, I am told, is relaxed. Everyone has a front-door key; formal meals are few and appreciated. Halls are increasingly truly mixed, following the Oxbridge pattern. A significant new and popular development which we did not envisage is a block of self-catering flats at Lafrowda on the campus. So far as I was concerned the report ensured me a place on the newly-formed Residence Committee and thence to its Furnishing Sub-Committee, providing me with work which I both understood and liked. We had control of the three Birks Halls, opened in 1966 and named at my suggestion after the Devon hills, Haldon, Raddon and Brendon. We chose modern furniture and fittings for students' study bedrooms, staff accommodation and common rooms, and approved the colour schemes. I remember vetoing one that included scarlet, which I felt would be difficult to live with, and I induced the architect to add a flight of steps and handrail from the garden to one warden's flat, which differentiated it from others in the severe grey concrete block.

Research excavation was not neglected, though from 1962 onwards it was increasingly difficult to leave Cyril, aged 80, alone, and I had to ask for help from his relatives whilst I was away. Very little was known about the Roman occupation of the south-west and so, in partnership with Bill Ravenhill of the geography department, I embarked on a series of excavations of the few suspected military sites. Bill and I made a good team, along with his wife, Mary, a good troweller and our caterer. Bill was a skilled surveyor, and was responsible for all the plans; I looked after the finds, and together with a varied student party and volunteers from the archaeological societies, we discussed endlessly of an evening the problems of the site. We began in a small way on Stoke Hill above Exeter in 1956–7 where aerial photographs had revealed the outlines of a double rectangular enclosure, resembling the Roman fourth-century signal stations on the Yorkshire coast. Its situation commanded a fine view of the Exe estuary and the Creedy valley, not obtainable from within the Exeter city walls. Unfortunately we found no sign of a timber watch tower, and no satisfactory dating evidence; we were handicapped by the stubborn nature of the Culm clay: it held water after heavy rain which had to be pumped out by the fire brigade, and it bleached and baked hard in the heat.[1] Nevertheless we determined to go on and in 1961–2 turned our attention to the two analogous earthworks on the North Devon coast,

Martinhoe and Old Burrow, both with stupendous views over the Bristol Channel. Here we were successful, though the results were a surprise. Instead of being fourth-century structures, keeping watch for Irish or Saxon pirates, both were first-century fortlets, designed to keep an eye on the unconquered Silures, the aggressive Celtic tribes in South Wales, and presumably working in conjunction with ships of the Roman fleet. At Martinhoe we found the foundation trenches for two wooden barracks housing some eighty soldiers, a forge for the armourer, and cooking ovens. At Old Burrow, the earlier of the two, the only structure was an outsize field oven, so the garrison must have been living in leather tents, quite an ordeal at 1,100 feet, as we found to our cost in a wet July, though we had the comfort of a guest house in the Oare valley to return to. Martinhoe was more enjoyable, though in the Land Rover we had to navigate a narrow lane where once we encountered a large bull head-on; we stayed very quiet and apprehensive until he had passed by in search of his cows. The view from both sites was fascinating, ever changing, with the cloud shadows over the sea; on a clear day I could see the villages and fields in the familiar territory on the South Wales coast, fifteen miles away.[2]

It was now becoming obvious that the Roman conquest of Devon had not been a pushover of the allegedly friendly Dumnonian tribes. I myself had found an early military ditch beneath the Roman South Gate in Exeter in 1964; aerial photographs had located the outlines of a likely fort at North Tawton, and Graham Webster had sectioned the defences of a turf and timber fort at Wiveliscombe in West Somerset. We now took a long hard look at the Nanstallon earthwork near Bodmin, where first-century Roman coins and pottery had been found in the nineteenth century, and liked what we saw. The site was right for a fort, on an interfluvial spur with wide views; it was accessible from the river Camel and strategically well placed to control the narrow Cornish isthmus in an area full of Iron Age settlements. Bill and I went into action with our usual team in 1965, and in our first season re-established the position of the levelled rampart, uncovered two of the timber gates and the foundations of a wooden barracks. It took another three seasons to work out the details of the headquarters building (*principia*), the commander's house (*praetorium*), and sufficient of the barrack blocks to show that we had here an auxiliary fort for a mixed unit of cavalry and infantry (*cohors equitata*), occupied from about AD 55–65 until AD 80.[3] The western half of the fort was left for future archaeologists to explore. We thought that we had done enough to show that there had been a regular military occupation of the south-western peninsula at least as far as the Camel–Fowey narrows. A few years later the elaborate bath house and the defences of a legionary fortress was discovered in the centre of Exeter, and Nanstallon and other discoveries fell into place, greatly to our satisfaction. I am not really military-minded, but there was plenty of human detail to record at Nanstallon, such as the fine leather belt with conical iron studs that someone had let slip into the latrine pit, or the phantom-like impression of the tip of a post that had broken off whilst being pulled out from an angle tower when the fort was evacuated.

From the academic point of view, the mid-sixties saw the peak of my achievements. I was a senior lecturer, Chairman of the Readers and Lecturers, and external Examiner in Archaeology successively at Leicester and Nottingham Universities, which was unusual for someone in my position. My successful book, *South West England,* had appeared, my excavations in North Devon, Exeter and Cornwall, had yielded good results, and my publications were up to date. Increasingly Martin Biddle and I were producing good students, and numbers were growing, though limited by the quota system. For some time I had thought that archaeology would be better served by becoming independent of the history department. Expansion was in the air; a new department was planned at Southampton, and new appointments affecting the South West were to be made at Reading and Bristol. At Exeter new departments were being created for Spanish and Russian, replacing previous lectureships in the French and German departments respectively, and economic history was about to be detached from history and become a separate department in a social studies faculty. Martin and I put our heads together and decided to make a case for an archaeology department, providing teaching for Combined and Single Honours, after the appointment of a professor and another lecturer.

Needless to say, this did not meet with the approval of Professor Barlow, who was already losing two of his economic historians to social studies, and he worked very hard on Martin, whose work at Winchester as a medieval historian he respected. He liked also the kudos his major excavations had brought to Exeter. Martin finally succumbed to the pressure, and on the morning of the day of the departmental meeting which was to discuss our proposition, he told me with some embarrassment that he could not support it. Dreadfully taken aback, English words failed me and all I find to say was '*Tiens*'. At the meeting I did the best I could to convince my colleagues whilst Martin remained silent.

However, that was not the end of the matter, because, greatly daring, I insisted on putting the proposals to the Development Committee of the Arts Faculty and went in person to present my case. I also exercised a lecturer's right of talking to the Vice-Chancellor; Cook was always very fair and listened carefully, but we both knew that he could not intervene to overrule the wishes of the head of a department. I destroyed my papers relating to this unhappy period when I retired, so have no detailed records of what I said. The tense atmosphere reminded me of the intrigues in a Cambridge college vividly described in C. P. Snow's novel *The Masters*.

Barlow brought his influence to bear on the Dean of Arts, the ineffectual Professor of Classics, whilst I sought support from the liberal-minded Professors of Geography and French. Finally a compromise was reached, when the English professor, an ebullient Welshman, the Revd Moelwyn Merchant, became the new Dean of Arts. I agreed to withdraw the demand for a separate archaeology department and for Single Honours, in return for the introduction of Combined Honours in History and in Geography with Archaeology, and the appointment of an assistant lecturer early in the next quinquennium.

No one can foresee the future; at the time I felt very bitter and conscious of failure, but my struggle bore fruit once both I and Professor Barlow had retired. In 1979 Malcolm Todd was appointed as Professor of Archaeology, and the department was renamed as 'History and Archaeology'. In the financial crisis of the eighties, archaeology had been saved from cuts or the threat of closure by being part of a large department at Exeter, and is now in good shape.

Whilst the struggle at the university was going on, I had other troubles to contend with at home. In May 1964, my mother suffered a severe stroke which left her paralysed and speechless. At the time I was visiting her at Walton and slept in an adjoining room. I woke in the night hearing a curious noise which I thought was the twittering of birds, but she must have been calling for help. Tired after my long drive from Exeter I slept again, only to find her semi-conscious next morning. The doctor did not expect her to survive, but she lingered in that distressing state for another two years, cared for in her own home at Walton by my sister Sheila, and a succession of nurses. Fortunately there was no problem with the finances, for which I had to resume responsibility.

Cyril's work had finished by 1960, after the publication of his books: *Pattern and Purpose: A Study of Celtic Art,* and *Life and Death in the Bronze Age*, and the first sign of Alzheimer's disease were apparent before his eightieth birthday in December 1962. We celebrated with a small family party at the Clarence Hotel in Exeter, joined by the Raglans, and by Cyril's daughter Felicity who came over from Toronto. He was delighted by a sheaf of congratulatory telegrams, and in the following year by a *Festschrift*, entitled *Culture and Environment* a volume of essays by twenty of his friends, headed by a sensitive appreciation by Rik Wheeler. He suffered a steady decline thereafter, but retained his charisma to the end. I remember a young man, Bruce Eagles, just starting work with the Royal Commission for Historic Monuments, who came to call briefly at St Leonard's Road, and who stayed for a long time completely fascinated by a talk about vernacular buildings. Cyril died peacefully in an Exmouth nursing home in January 1967, after a series of strokes, the first on our return from my mother's funeral at Walton the previous July. On a dark

January day in Exeter cathedral the Dean performed the funeral service which was well attended: a few days later Charles and I walked across the fields to the isolated small church at Nether Exe, where we scattered Cyril's ashes in a corner of the churchyard amongst the wild snowdrops; it had been a favourite part of the Exe valley for our afternoon walks.

Long ago I had accepted the fact that I would outlive my husband, but it was still a shock that affected me deeply. I went to stay with Leslie Murray-Thriepland at New House, Llanishen, where in familiar surroundings I found some solace in answering many of the letters of sympathy and appreciation from friends and institutions. After a fortnight, I went back to my university work. The three sons were a real support at this time. Charles was now accessible, at Gwithian living in Cornwall with his wife and three small daughters, whilst pursuing his naval career at nearby Culdrose. He had given his father much pleasure in 1961 by bringing his little ship, HMS *Tilford*, his first command, up the Exeter canal for a three-day visit to Exeter, with a reception by the mayor in the Guildhall, which we both attended. Derek, after some farm training at Wallingford, Oxfordshire and several false starts, had found a satisfactory job at Matford Farm near Exeter, travelling there on his moped from home. The volatile George had acquired fluent French after a course at the École du Commerce at Neuchâtel in Switzerland. He first started in advertising with Masius & Ferguson in London, then worked with Sichel in the wine trade at Bordeaux and Mainz, and in 1967 was working with Rank Xerox in South Wales.

It was obvious that the large house in St Leonard's Road was no longer needed, and I started on the task of sorting, clearing out and disposing of the accumulation of Cyril's books and papers over twenty years. There was a bonfire burning at the bottom of the garden most weeks until Easter. I also asked estate agents for particulars of flats or small houses in Topsham. Quite soon I had a letter from Jack Simmons, the history professor at Leicester, enclosing particulars of a new Chair in Archaeology, and suggesting I might like to apply; I realised then how anxious I was to get away from Exeter. Though Leicester was not my favourite city or provincial university, nor the East Midlands my chosen countryside, I felt that there was a challenge for me in the job during my last five years in university service. I knew from my experience as their external examiner that the three lecturers in archaeology at Leicester were at loggerheads with each other, and consequently non-productive, and that local archaeology had been neglected. So I applied, was short-listed, and went in April for an interview, straight from my field school at Bodmin.

I had never been formally interviewed for a job before: they had always been offered me on a plate, and I was ill-prepared for some of the questions from the panel. I had expected to be asked about the development of research and excavation rather than of local radio; my support for the new Museum Studies Diploma sponsored by the university drew a blank. When pressed about what I intended to do for the department, I could only reply that in the light of my Exeter experience financial stringency would limit any new appointments. I could hardly say that I hoped to instill a better spirit in the department for soon afterwards one lecturer committed suicide. It was really too soon for me to have overcome my trauma, and by the time I had met up there for a meal with W. G. Hoskins, I knew I had failed; I did not blame the adjudicators for preferring the lively young Charles Thomas.

Nevertheless, there was a consolation prize. Fulford's agency had come up with a first-floor flat at Topsham in The Retreat, a fine eighteenth-century house on the Exe. I had seen it before I went to Leicester, and as soon as I went in and looked out of the window, I knew it was where I wanted to live. There was the river curving around a little island and cutting into the extensive reed beds: beyond were the Exminster marshes and the Haldon hills under the wide sky. Cyril and I had often walked along the riverside footpath and wondered who lived there behind the fine iron garden railings and the elegant Victorian balcony. As soon as possible I bought it for the modest sum of £5,250, having sold 28 St Leonard's Road for £11,500, and with the help of my 'daily', Mrs Dart, I moved in August 1967 and was there until 1998. I loved the spacious well-proportioned rooms, with the Adam-style fireplaces, and the wide panelled doors with their original brass drop handles; they provided a fine setting for my books and antique furniture. I kept my binoculars by the window, from where I watched the birds on the river. In the winter, there were regular visitors of parties of goldeneye ducks and of red-breasted mergansers, as well as the locally resident shelducks, herons and cormorants.

In 1967 I had five more years before retirement from the university. My first concern was to organise a special subject, 'The Celts', to be introduced for the new Combined Honours in 1969–70. I had already done some work in 1964, when I had revisited hill-forts on the Upper Danube and seen Professor Kimig at work on the magnificent defences of the Heuneburg, where he uncovered a rampart of mud bricks on a stone foundation with a row of rectangular bastions in the Mediterranean style, dating from about 600 BC. It was over thirty years since I had been there. I had also been to an international Celtic congress at Épernay and visited the classic early La Tène sites on the Marne, and studied the material, poorly displayed, in the museums. It was in the town hall at Épernay that the delegates were offered the best champagne I have ever drunk, from the mayor's special reserve. Then in 1969, with Leslie Murray-Thriepland and her youngest son, Patrick, aged sixteen, I went to see the Iron Age walled settlements in the south of France, St Blaise, Constantine, Enserune and Entremont, as well as the obvious Roman towns like Arles, Nîmes, Orange and St Rémy. With difficulty we managed to find the peculiar Celtic sanctuary of Roquepertuse, near Aix, tucked away in scrub and seldom visited. It was a terraced hemicycle at the foot of a low limestone cliff, which acted as its back wall. In front of it there had stood a portico crowned by a sculptured bird, with the supporting pillars with niches containing human skulls, now in Museum Borely at Marseilles. There were also seated cross-legged figures of gods or heroes, and a frieze of horse-heads in profile. It must have been an awesome place. It is still inadequately published except for the statuary.[4]

Leslie and Patrick left me at Dijon, where I hired a car and drove on to see the spectacular finds from the Vix royal burial in the museum at Châtillon-sur-Seine. These had been excavated from a large barrow at the foot of the nearby contemporary hill-fort of Mont Lassois, and belonged to a lady buried in the late sixth century BC, wearing a gold neckband, together with her jewellery, her silver and bronze table service, and a dismantled wagon. Nothing I had read had prepared me for the sight of the great bronze crater, over five feet high, which dominated the display. Made in Greece about 525 BC, with a splendid procession of warriors and chariots in relief below the rim, it must have been imported with other luxuries across the Alps via northern Italy, or by way of the Rhône. It is surely the most dramatic symbol of the wealth and power of the early Celtic aristocracy.[5] The reason for visiting these and other continental sites and museums was to gain first-hand knowledge of the archaeological raw material on which the course would be based. I acquired a store of vivid memories to draw on, and without which the lectures using only other people's published work, would have been repetitive, and would fail to interest, let alone inspire, an undergraduate audience. It was time and money well spent. Of course business and pleasure were often combined, as when visiting the opera in Munich, or discovering the beauties of the elaborate baroque churches in southern Germany, or the wildflowers on the Mediterranean coasts.

Alas! The tour of Provence was the last on which Leslie was my travelling companion. Patrick fell sick at Eton that summer, and ultimately his complaint was diagnosed as a form of bone marrow disease, which was virtually incurable. Leslie took it very hard; she was deeply attached to her youngest son who had been some consolation for her at the time of Peter's sudden death in 1957. When Patrick became seriously ill and was moved from Cardiff to the Royal Marsden Hospital, she became very withdrawn and refused to see any of her friends, though I tried hard to contact her. I was not surprised when the telephone rang one day in late January and her eldest son, David, told me that Patrick had died, but I was amazed and utterly horrified when he added very incoherently that Leslie had fled and committed suicide 'in the Roman manner' in a Brighton hotel. It was a tragic end for a talented archaeologist, and a highly competent woman, who with three other sons seemed, despite her losses, to have something to live for. There was no one quite like her amongst my friends, and I still miss the stimulus of her vigorous mind and the sharing of our archaeological activities.

I maintained contact with the Murray-Thriepland sons because I was one of their trustees. Peter had made a strange will, dividing his considerable estate amongst his five sons in varying proportions to be allocated by the trustees according to their merits, when the youngest came of age. The trustees were involved in a lot of trouble, and so were the lawyers, before the will was set aside in 1972 and an equitable division was agreed. I well remember being pressurised by my co-trustee, Leslie's brother, R. McNair Scott, who wanted to exclude the only son of Peter's first marriage, Mark, from a share in the distribution. I was invited to dinner together with the Cardiff solicitor, at an expensive London club, and plied with drink which I did not like, but I stood firm for the principle of equal shares. New House and the Cardiff estate have since been sold; the M4 motorway now runs through their erstwhile fields.

At Exeter the newly-founded Civic Society took up more of my time once I had become chairman in 1967, succeeding W. G. Hoskins who had quarrelled with the city council. The major battle was over the preservation of the Higher Market in Queen Street, a late classical building designed by Charles Fowler in 1838. The intention was to demolish it to make way for a new shopping mall, to which the society was strongly opposed. It took almost ten years to achieve an acceptable new plan, which retained the Doric columns and pediment of the market as a monumental portico and entrance to the new shopping centre behind the Guildhall, and which provided real distinction to Queen Street. The city officials thought the society was an ineffectual nuisance body, so I had to gain their respect. We did this by producing a series of illustrated reports by our architect members for proposed conservation areas in the city, such as St Leonard's or Bury Meadow, which were well received by the planning committee. We invited leading figures in the architectural and town planning world, like Sir John Summerson or Lord Holford, to our annual dinner, together with the mayor and other officials, and we listened to their views on the city developments. It brought a breath of fresh air into a rather heated atmosphere, and before long good relationships between the society and the city officers and the city council were established, and have happily continued to the present day. It is now difficult to recapture the spirit of the 1960s and the sense of urgency and mission which motivated the society and its chairman.

There was also work to do for the Devon County Council, which had appointed me their Archaeological Consultant, together with W. G. Hoskins for medieval and later buildings and Malcolm Spooner for industrial archaeology. For a time our main function seemed to be partaking of a sumptuous lunch with the clerk and the planning officer, but I was called up to vet schemes for afforestation and to report on threats to barrows and other earthworks from time to time. I was also consulted by the Dartmoor National Park Authority where I attended some stormy meetings. It was a useful preliminary to the paid appointments of archaeology officers in the National Park and the planning department in the late 1970s.

In 1969 I was approached by the Plymouth City Council and the South West Water Board to assist them with a report on the Dartmoor antiquities that might be affected by the construction of a proposed new reservoir at Swincombe, and to give evidence to a House of Commons committee in support of their Bill. The site was about three miles south-east of Princetown, at the head of the Swincombe river, and included the infamous Fox Tor mire. It was a remote piece of grass moorland and bog, over 1,200 feet high and inaccessible except on foot. It was a challenging piece of field work which I did mostly single-handed, visiting all the sites marked on the Ordnance Survey six-inch maps, and finding some others. Eventually I enlisted half a dozen keen students and we walked in a line over the central area to ensure that nothing had been missed. This was very necessary because an opponent of the scheme was Lady Sylvia Sayer, acting for the Dartmoor Preservation Association. She was a fanatic who wanted to preserve everything on Dartmoor regardless of other considerations, and everyone was frightened of her. Indeed, when the Plymouth town clerk had invited me to be their consultant, he told me I had been chosen because I was capable of standing up to her and the publicity she could command. 'This is darling Dartmoor, and Sylvia Sayer is saving it', as a caricaturist expressed it. As expected, I found there were a few prehistoric sites, mainly burial places, including the so-called Childe's Tomb; two medieval crosses belonging to a series marking a track across the moor from Buckfast to Tavistock, and extensive remains of nineteenth-century tin workings; none were of outstanding importance. I recommended that all should be recorded, and that some should be excavated and carefully removed and then set up on the margin of the reservoir. These would remain visible to the public in their original setting. Both authorities and the Ministry of Works agreed to this idea.

I went to London in November 1970 to support my evidence, and was heard in a splendidly-decorated committee room in the House of Commons. I was cross-examined by lawyers in full dress wearing wigs. It was quite an ordeal, but I gained in confidence, and more than held my own with the lawyer representing the Dartmoor Preservation Association, who got some of his facts wrong. The committee was amused by my account of Childe's Tomb, a composite monument of Bronze Age origin with medieval and late nineteenth-century additions. It was alleged to be where a traveller called Childe killed his horse, disembowelled it and sheltered inside it against the cold, but nevertheless died of exposure. His body was taken to Tavistock Abbey for burial, but there is no good reason to connect these events with the so-named Swincombe site. However, Plymouth's efforts were all to no avail, for it was decided that another reservoir in the National Park would be inappropriate and after long delay a new site was found at Roadford, West Devon, where excavations of an early farmstead and a mill took place before the place was flooded in 1990.

I like to think that, as an impartial archaeologist from the university, I was of use to various local authorities in Devon, as well as to national organisations such as the Council for British Archaeology, the Ancient Monuments Inspectorate of the Department of the Environment, or the Ordnance Survey, who regularly referred Devon matters to me. I built up a good working relationship with a succession of inspectors, as well as with the Chief Inspector, Arnold Taylor, an old friend from Cardiff days. This is how I was able, in the company of an inspector, to approach the Dean of Exeter in 1966, as soon as it had been decided to demolish the redundant Victorian church of St Mary Major, at the west end of the cathedral; together we got him to agree to a major excavation once the site had been cleared. Archaeological work was not started until 1971, and was carried out by the newly-formed Exeter Archaeological Field Unit, simultaneously with excavations by John Collis, the new assistant lecturer from the university, on the Guildhall Shopping Centre site. I had had to work hard in the committees to get the St Mary's project agreed and financed. It was W. G. Hoskins who had drawn my attention to the potentialities of this central site, for both Saxon and Roman times. The result exceeded all expectations, with the discovery of a large legionary bath-house, followed by its conversion to the basilica in the forum of the cantonal town of Isca Dumnoniorum, and finally the remains of a Christian cemetery and of the late Saxon and early Norman minster.[6] I shall never forget seeing, in one of the first cuttings, the monumental flight of stone steps belonging to the town's basilica, overlying the red tile pillars of the hypocaust of the military baths.

It was a great source of satisfaction that Paul Bidwell, the principal excavator, dedicated his final report to me when it was published by the Exeter City Council and the university jointly in 1979; the partnership symbolised much of what I had tried to achieve in my twenty-five years at Exeter. I have continued to have very friendly relations with successive directors of the Exeter Archaeological Field Unit. Whilst sometimes regretting that archaeologists at the university are no longer involved with excavation in the city, I realise that the change was inevitable, for it is now a full-time task, requiring a team of trained workers available throughout the year both for digging and writing the reports.

Finally, during my last three years at the university I was engaged on the publication of the Holcombe decorated Celtic mirror. This was an amazing discovery made in August 1970, whilst Sheila Pollard, an old friend and skilled excavator for the Devon Archaeological Society, was directing a dig of a Roman villa at Holcombe near Lyme Regis, which had been damaged by ploughing. She telephoned me one afternoon in a state of excitement to say that one of her workers had uncovered a complete bronze mirror buried in a little pit beneath a floor, and would I please come and see it and advise her what best to do. Fortunately it was a solid piece of metalwork, weighing 800 grams, and after photography there was no difficulty in lifting it and taking it for safety to her Sidmouth bank, and later to the British Museum for conservation. It is now there on show in the Iron Age gallery in company with its peers from Desborough and elsewhere.

It is a magnificent piece with an elaborate symmetrical design engraved on the back; it gave me much pleasure to analyse it, to define its motifs, and to make comparisons with other pieces of a south-western school of Celtic art.[7] The heavy handle was uncomfortable to grasp, but it ended in a loop which suggested to me that it was intended to be suspended; when thus reversed, the mount revealed an animal face with eyes of red enamel where it joined the mirror plate, a typical Celtic hidden image. The mirror face was of polished bronze, and I wondered what the lady saw in it, as it hung in her hut. An old friend since Cardiff days, Professor Roland Austin, supplied the clue with a quotation and a colloquial translation from Propertius, a Latin poet, writing in the late first century BC. He warned his mistress, Cynthia, not to imitate the Britons by painting her forehead blue or by dyeing her gleaming hair – which would have been a surprising image to encounter.

As the excavations continued, it became clear that the mirror was related to a late Iron Age settlement of round huts in a small ditched enclosure, which had preceded the villa. Presumably it was buried when the westward advance of the Roman army threatened the region in AD 44–5, after their attacks on Maiden Castle and other hill-forts. Decorated mirrors appear to have been a status symbol in Celtic society in Britain, and most have been found with burials. The Holcombe mirror was the first to be recovered in excavations from a settlement, and demonstrates how modest were the dwellings of wealthy women in the Celtic world. Sheila Pollard and I were able to exhibit the mirror and to give an account of the discoveries and their significance to the Society of Antiquaries in November

1971. It is always rather an ordeal to address the critical audience at Burlington House; certainly I had found it so when talking about the Wansdyke in 1960 – but this time I was buoyed up by knowing I was dealing with a masterpiece of Celtic art.

I was now worrying about what I should do after my retirement in September 1972. I had been twenty-five years at Exeter and knew I was in need of a change, not of a rest. I considered the possibilities of an exchange with William and Mary University in Virginia, USA, with which Exeter had links, and of studying the Native American tribes known to me from the attractive sixteenth-century drawings of John White, made during his expeditions with Walter Ralegh and Grenville to the area. I then realised that field work in Virginia by a lone female might well be difficult or even dangerous, given the prevailing racial tension in the United States. Suddenly I remembered an article by the anthropologist, Raymond Firth, in the first number of *Antiquity*, way back in 1927, about Maori hillforts, and I realised that there might be scope in New Zealand for studying a warlike people similar to the Celts in Britain. I was terribly ignorant about New Zealand; I hardly realised that it consisted of two islands, let alone that it had four major universities. A rapid visit to the Commonwealth Institute in Kensington showed me that archaeology could be studied only at Auckland, situated in the subtropical North Island University or at Otago University in chilly Dunedin in the South Island, so I quickly decided on Auckland. By good luck the new Vice-Chancellor at Exeter, Dr Jack Lewellyn, had come to us from New Zealand, where he had been chairman of their University Grants Commission; he was very encouraging and reassured me that I would be welcomed. He also pulled strings, and in a short time I had the offer of a visiting lectureship for one year in the anthropology department at Auckland, and of a return fare provided by the Grants Committee. I gladly accepted both; I now had an astonishing answer to the many enquiries about what I was going to do when I retired.

The summer term ended in the usual flurry of examiners' meetings, departmental dinner, polite speeches and presentations. The students, remembering my weaknesses on field courses, gave me a crystal beer mug and a packet of ginger biscuits. Ann Hamlin collected some entertaining tributes from generations of former students and bound them up as a personal *festschrift* which I still cherish. I had a few regrets in leaving; I was glad to be rid of the chores of marking essays and attending departmental meetings and committees. Cheerfully I said to myself, 'Tomorrow to fresh woods and pastures new'.

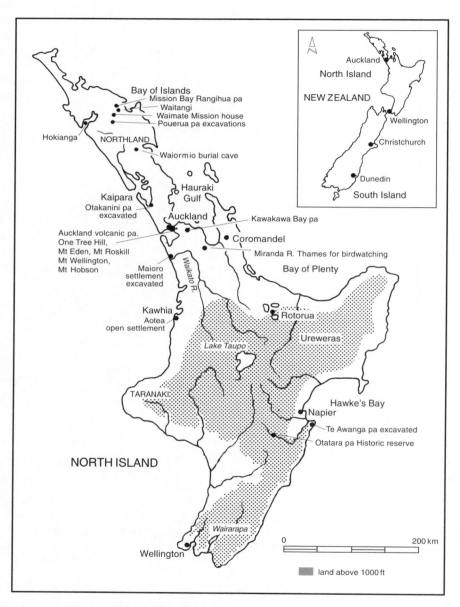

Auckland
North Island

NEW ZEALAND

Wellington

Christchurch

Dunedin
South Island

Bay of Islands
Mission Bay Rangihua pa
Waitangi
Waimate Mission house
Pouerua pa excavations

Hokianga

NORTHLAND

Waiormio burial cave

Hauraki
Gulf

Kaipara

Otakanini pa
excavated

Auckland

Kawakawa Bay pa

Auckland volcanic pa.
One Tree Hill,
Mt Eden, Mt Roskill
Mt Wellington,
Mt Hobson

Coromandel

Miranda R. Thames for birdwatching

Maioro
settlement
excavated

Bay of Plenty

Kawhia

Aotea
open settlement

Rotorua

Ureweras

Lake Taupo

TARANAKI

Hawke's Bay
Napier

Te Awanga pa excavated

Otatara pa Historic reserve

NORTH ISLAND

Wairarapa

0   200 km

Wellington

land above 1000 ft

Diagram map of the North Island showing sites mentioned in Chapters 9 and 10.

Chapter Nine

Indian Summer in New Zealand

1973 – 1977

In the Antipodes the seasons are reversed; the academic year begins in late February, towards the end of a long hot summer, and finishes in November, in late spring. Since I did not have to be in Auckland until February 1973, there were six months to fill in after I retired, in which to plan my new university work and to get ready to go. My concern was to produce a revised text and illustrations for a second edition of *South West England,* to be published by David & Charles of Newton Abbot. A decade had elapsed since the book was written, and much new material was available from excavations, especially in Exeter. As I wrote in the preface, there had been a change in emphasis, with more stress on continuity of prehistoric population in the region, and there was no longer the need to explain every change in pottery as due to another invasion from the continent. The publisher changed the book to a smaller format and a thinner paper, with the illustrations spread throughout the text, instead of being all together at the end. It made an attractive volume, but I disliked the heavy gilt Gothic lettering on the spine. Though in places out of date, I am glad it remained in print until it was remaindered in 1980. I have heard from several people that it was the book that gave them an abiding interest in local archaeology, including one lady from the Devon Archaeological Society, who took it into hospital to read as a distraction during her labour; an author can hardly ask for a better tribute. It now has been replaced by Malcolm Todd's comprehensive regional history volume, *The South West to AD 1000* (Longman 1987).

I decided to go to New Zealand by sea, which enabled me to take books and heavy luggage at no extra cost, and to spend a leisurely month on board Shaw Savill's ship *Northern Star*, broken by calls at ports in the Canaries, South Africa and Australia. I sailed from Southampton on 6 January 1973, seen off by my sons George and Derek. It was a grey day, and passing the chalk cliffs of the Isle of Wight in the mist I wondered if or when I should see them again. *Northern Star* was not a smart cruise ship; the décor was old-fashioned, the food undistinguished, but I had a single cabin in which I could work at the new lecture courses and arrange the slides for Auckland. The people on board were friendly; most were going to visit relations in Australia and New Zealand, including many Scots bound for Dunedin in the South Island. I quickly established a routine of work in the morning, a laze in the sun and a swim in the small pool in the afternoon, and a film or other simple entertainment after dinner in the evening. I was determined not to over-eat and put on weight, so I walked briskly round the deck about half a dozen times each day: here I encountered for the first time a group of joggers in shorts and vests pounding along, a novel activity of New Zealand origin which has since become universal.

The first port of call was Tenerife, where I was taken by car by a would-be admirer, a widowed businessman from Leicester, to see the grass-covered crater of an extinct volcano, a foretaste of those I would find in Auckland. The ship crossed the Equator in a thick warm mist, which was not what I had expected, but we landed at Cape Town in glorious sunshine. There I was met by James Walton, an old friend of Cyril's, a distinguished artist-draughtsman, and a pioneer writer on vernacular architecture in England and in South Africa. He took me to see the elegant Dutch-style homesteads, with their stepped and scalloped gables and decorative baroque plaster-work of seventeenth- and eighteenth-century date, as well as the winery at Great Constantia, featured in his book *Homesteads and Villages of South Africa* (1952).

In the botanic gardens I had my first glimpse of the rich and varied flora of Cape Town in its subtropical abundance, but regretted there was no time to see it in the wild on Table Mountain. There was much that was unfamiliar, such as the blue jacaranda trees, the orange bignonia creepers, and the proteas, which I would meet again in Auckland. From our next stop at Durban, there was an opportunity to visit the Natal animal park, and a Zulu reserve in the Valley of a Thousand Hills. I found the circular kraals with the wattle-and-mud round huts fascinating and very relevant to my Dartmoor studies, though the inhabitants seemed to be leading a rather artificial life for the benefit of tourists such as ourselves. In Durban I was horrified by the segregated counters for blacks and whites in the central post office, as well as by notices on the beach. The ship sailed at dusk, with a recorded band playing, and the air was heavy with the scent of spices from the nearby warehouses, whilst the brilliant stars of the southern hemisphere shone overhead.

It was a long week across the Indian Ocean to Australia, with only a succession of albatrosses, petrels and shearwaters to watch until we reached Fremantle. It must have seemed an eternity to the English settlers, their wives and servants, crammed into the small sailing ships of the 1850s and 1860s. The rest of our voyage went quickly, after a brief stop in Sydney, to be revisited later: and I had my first sight of New Zealand: of Cape Farewell, named, as so many other places, by Captain Cook as he left it on his first voyage in 1770; of the indented coastline of the Marlborough Sound and the many small islands; finally *Northern Star* entered Cook Strait and was slowly manœvered into Wellington harbour. I was met by Peter Bellwood and his attractive Maori wife, Teri; he was a young Cambridge archaeologist who had been doing first-class work on Maori culture at Auckland University, but was about to transfer to Sydney. On a characteristic cool windy Wellington day, they took me up to Mount Victoria for a panoramic view of the city. I was surprised at the number of sophisticated tall buildings, and by the extent of the waterfront, so close to the city centre; the rugged wooded hills beyond the curves of the great harbour were a foretaste of the untamed countryside known as 'the bush' which still survives in New Zealand.

Naturally I questioned Peter about the archaeologists at Auckland, and he encouraged me to think I would fit in, under the direction of the newly-appointed professor, Roger Green, from the United States.

Next day we sailed on up the east coast of the North Island, passing close to Hawke's Bay, which I was to know so well later, and the five weeks' voyage to Auckland was completed overnight. I looked out of my cabin to see the conical humped profile of Rangitoto, the volcanic island, bathed in glorious sunshine. Wearing my new lavender-blue linen suit, I found on the quay Pat Lacey, Professor of Classics, who took charge of me and my belongings. He whisked me off to my motel and then to the university, to be introduced to the staff club in the splendid wooden Old Government House, and there to meet some of his colleagues. He also invited me to an evening meal with his wife and four sons at the seaside suburb of Kohimarama. Within a week I had settled in; I had bought a small green Toyota car; I had leased the ground-floor flat in a house next door to the Laceys, owned by Mrs Jean Preisler who lived upstairs, and who proved to be a kind and sympathetic landlady: little did she or I think that I would be there for the next ten years and that we would become good friends. Above all, I had satisfied myself that I had come to the right place, when I climbed the 600-ft-high green hill, aptly named Mount Eden, which I could see from my motel window. There I found no formal defences, only a puzzling succession of massive scarps and terraces, broken up and dovetailed one into the other, with many pits and indications of rectangular house sites, as well as a large volcanic crater. This was a fine example of a Maori hill-fort, a terraced *paa,* which I had come so far to see; it offered a real challenge, which I took up later.

Let me recall my first impressions of the place in summer, the clear atmosphere, the perpetual sunshine, the warm sea water lapping on Kohi beach, the persistent chirring of the cicadas, but above all the strange mixture of the novel and familiar in the trees, flowers and birds. For instance, there were fine English oak trees and, in contrast, the native *pohutukawa* trees with their crimson tasselled flowers along the Auckland waterfront. In the gardens there were pink oleanders and scarlet hibiscus bushes flowering profusely, trees covered with lemons and grapefruit as around the Mediterranean, and the hairy brown Chinese Gooseberry hanging from its vine, better known now as kiwi fruit. There were splendid English roses in the gardens as well as cinerarias and azaleas. Arum lilies grew wild in damp fields in the country, as did the pink amaryllis lilies with their cloying scent. I was astonished to see sparrows, blackbirds, thrushes and starlings mixing with the parti-coloured Indian mynah birds on the lawn. There were little native silver-eyes and fantails in the shrubberies, besides chaffinches and the occasional greenfinch. The English colonists had brought with them their cage birds, which escaped and rapidly increased in the favourable climate. The swallows, much in evidence, came from Australia, blown nearly a thousand miles across the Tasman Sea; they nested here for the first time as recently as the 1950s.

When I began to explore the nearby countryside I was impressed by the empty roads, which made motoring a pleasure, apart from the unsealed by-roads where the loose surface of small stones was horrific with the car sliding round the corners. I was puzzled by the lack, on the large scale maps of any marking of antiquities; one had to rely on a friend's information and one's eyesight. I shall never forget driving my first Sunday to Kawakawa Bay, Clevedon, and looking up to see a splendid *paa* with three lines of ditches visible in profile on the promontory, and then looking down to the beach to see a blue heron, and a party of elegant black and white stilts, all new to me.

I duly presented myself to the newly-appointed Professor of Archaeology, Roger Green, and was allocated a room in one of the three old timber-boarded houses in Symonds Street, occupied by the anthropology department, of which archaeology was a part, the other two used by social anthropology and Maori studies. It was a cosmopolitan staff; Roger a soft-spoken American with a Harvard background, devoted to his Pacific studies, principally Lapita pottery; Richard Cassels, a young English archaeologist, a product of Cambridge, concerned with the archaeology of Maori economies Agnes Sullivan, a New Zealander working on Auckland's early history, and Harry Allen, a prehistorian, newly appointed from Australia. There was excellent back-up from two technicians: Karel Peters, the draughtsman and Cyril Schollom, the photographer. All were friendly and prepared to take me on trust as an English expert! I had three lecture courses to give: 'British Prehistory', 'The Celts in Europe', and 'Roman Britain', supplemented by discussions. I liked the students and found them more forthcoming than their Exeter counterparts. I was rather put off by a long-haired male wearing striped pyjamas under an ancient navy duffle-coat, but mollified by his intelligent questions. Here, as elsewhere, I felt my title was a handicap; however, it was not long before it was dropped in favour of 'Aileen' by staff and students alike. Fortunately the name cannot easily be abbreviated to a monosyllable, the general New Zealand practice; for example, there are no Davids or Katherines, only Dave and Kath.

In my spare time I read everything I could on Maori fortifications, though there was pitifully little published from recent excavations, with the notable exception of Peter Bellwood's work at Otakanini *paa* and the Mangakaware *crannog* (lake dwelling).[1] There had been major excavations at Kauri Point *paa* and at Sarah's Gully settlement in the Coromandel by Jack Golson in the early 1960s. He had come from Cambridge to Auckland University in 1954 and was the acknowledged founder of modern archaeology in New Zealand, but he left for Sydney, without ever publishing his excavation reports. Others had followed his example, and it seemed to me as though New Zealand archaeology, like Maori genealogies, relied on oral tradition. However, I discovered, through the lectures of a social anthropologist, Dr Anne Salmond, a rich source of information in the journals of the early nineteenth-century missionaries and travellers, principally Samuel Marsden and his companion, J. L. Nicholas, who described in detail the inhabited *paa* that they visited in the Bay of Islands in 1814–15. There were also travelling artists such as Augustus Earle (1826–7) and G. Angas (1843–5) who drew the fortified settlements in their landscape setting, as well as portraits of the Maori chiefs. All these people had seen and recorded prehistory in action, as it had survived as it were, until the middle of the nineteenth century: it was a revelation for an English archaeologist. The New Zealand archaeologists had paid little attention to the wealth of literary and pictorial evidence, and were strangely preoccupied by analysing shells from the many waste heaps (middens) surviving on the sites.

I was determined to see as much as I could of the Maori fortifications during my year's stay, and so under the guidance of Janet Davidson, the Vaile archaeologist at the Auckland Museum, I regularly drove off on my travels at weekends. On our first encounter, Janet and I had found ourselves in accord; like my colleagues at the university, she had expected to see, in her own words, 'a small frail elderly lady', and was agreeably surprised to find 'a vigorous active person' at the main door of the museum, asking where to find the best *paa*. She had very good knowledge of the Auckland region and the far north from personal field work and we visited many sites together. She also sent me off to visit her friends who were the regional file keepers in Northland, Waikato, the Bay of Plenty and Taranaki, and who looked after the archaeological archive for their area on behalf of the New Zealand Archaeological Association. Thanks to their kindness and hospitality, I was taken to see a series of outstanding sites, and had the benefit of discussions with Stan Bartlett, Ken Gorbey, Ken Moore and Alastair Buist.

Because of the sad neglect of archaeological sites by the Government map-makers in the Department of Lands and Survey, the New Zealand Archaeological Association had taken on the essential task of site recording. An admirable system had been established, starting in 1954 with Jack Buchanan in Hawke's Bay and developed together with the national organization, the Historic Places Trust, from 1958 onwards.[2] In each region of the North and South Islands, field workers, both amateur and professional, recorded a variety of archaeological sites, each with a map grid reference, a description and sketch plan on a special form with a duplicate. These were sent to the appointed regional file keeper, where they were numbered and filed; the duplicate was forwarded to the central file in Wellington, which was, and still is, maintained by the Historic Places Trust. In this way a valuable archaeological archive has been built up, accessible both locally and nationally, which anticipated the County Councils' Sites and Monuments Register in England by some twenty years. In due course I found myself a file keeper for Auckland in 1974–6, as a temporary replacement for Janet, and can testify to the efficiency of the system.

In the meanwhile my social life in Auckland was taking shape. I made lasting friends with Richard and Paula Allison, he a tall Scotsman, a newcomer from Edinburgh and Oxford who joined the classics department at Auckland, at the same time as I arrived there, she a school teacher of English. Together we sampled many of the inexpensive restaurants in Auckland and went to orchestral and chamber concerts in the town hall and to plays at the Mercury and Theatre Corporate. Both were repertory theatres with intelligent directors; despite its small stage and cramped auditorium the Corporate produced a memorable performance of Brecht's *Mother Courage*, Ibsen's *Hedda Gabler* and Shakespeare's *Measure for Measure*. I never felt I lacked cultural experience in Auckland, as I now do in Exeter.

Through Janet Davidson I met Paul and Lisl Heller, both of Austrian origin but now naturalised New Zealanders. He, a quiet incisive little man, was an expert on international law at the university, and before that was with the New Zealand consulate in Western Samoa. She, who had started as a dancer, was an exuberant character of striking appearance, with extravagant notions and a wonderful flow of conversation. They lived in the country south of Auckland, in a ramshackle house converted from former outbuildings. Lisl kept sheep, ducks and chickens, to which she was very attached, but that did not prevent her from slaughtering and butchering them herself for the table. Sunday lunch there was an experience, usually with three or four well-chosen guests. In summer it was preceded by a compulsory swim with Lisl in the Manukau harbour, reached by a quarter-mile walk through the fields and a steep climb back through their strip of woodland 'bush'. Lunch finished with an Austrian *torte* and coffee, but conversation flowed on during long lazy afternoons.

A complete contrast was the household of an Auckland solicitor to whom I had an introduction. I was invited at 8 p.m. and assumed it would be an evening meal. I presented myself promptly at a stylish house in the well-to-do district of Remuera, and had a glass of sherry with the assembled company; nothing more happened except laboured conventional conversation in the drawing-room. After nearly two hours I was about to leave, being both tired, bored and hungry, when, as the clock struck ten, the daughters of the house rose and quickly reappeared with trays of sandwiches, cakes and coffee. I had forgotten that most New Zealanders have their full evening meal, which they call 'tea', at 6 p.m. and I learnt that introductions were very 'hit or miss' affairs.

My most successful introduction was undoubtedly to Mr and Mrs Glenny at Te Awanga near Hastings in Hawke's Bay. It meant a long drive of nearly 300 miles, across the North Island via Lake Taupo and the volcanic plateau, and then over the ranges rising to 3,000 feet, through the deep gorge of the Waipunga river on a road that never seemed to stop twisting, even on the descent to Napier and the coast. Though the route became familiar, I always found the journey an ordeal. The Glennys, of English extraction (she, nicknamed Duntie, had lived near Exeter before her second marriage to Jim) made me very welcome to their pleasant home and lovely garden filled with summer flowers and fruit. Knowing my interest, they asked their neighbour, Bill Shaw, to show me the *paa* on his Tiromoana estate. He was a stalwart young New Zealand sheep farmer who drove in his Toyota truck up the steep slopes which scared me, and there, 200 feet above the river, was this amazing place; it was a *paa* with three separate lines of defence across the narrow ridge, a row of possible postholes of a lateral palisade, many pits and terraces in the interior, and the outline of a long house clearly visible in the grass. I had rarely seen a site so well preserved. Bill was clearly interested and shared my enthusiasm; we agreed that it would be a good place to excavate some day. Some months later Roger Green was looking around a training dig for students in the summer vacation (December–February); I volunteered to try my hand at Tiromoana if suitable arrangements could be made, and my university appointment extended to July 1974, to allow time for producing a report.

I told of my newly-discovered Hawke's Bay *paa* with its visible long house at the annual conference of the New Zealand Archaeological Association at Christchurch in the South Island, only to be met with scepticism from some of the contingent from Otago University, Dunedin. 'Did I realise that prehistoric Maori houses were fragile timber structures and had left little trace when excavated hitherto?' Thinking of the many wooden buildings I had excavated in England, I held my tongue and looked forward to the time when I could demonstrate their reality in Hawke's Bay.

In the meanwhile I was busy working on an article on storage pits – a common feature of all types of early Maori settlement, using pictorial evidence as well as common sense to interpret archaeological findings.[3] Clearly these, as the postholes showed, were roofed structures; not houses but cellars, providing the necessary frost-free and controlled humidity for storing crops of sweet potatoes (*kumara*), the Maoris' favourite food. Janet Paul at the Turnbull Library in Wellington had showed me the sketch book of the missionary, Richard Taylor (1846), and an album presented to Mrs Hobson, wife of the first British governor in 1848 (facsimile published 1989), in which there were domestic scenes showing low roofed structures differing from the larger rectangular walled Maori houses. Both were also visible in the drawing of a deserted *paa* at Kahuwera, in the Bay of Islands, by Louis du Sainson in 1827, and provided conclusive evidence for my reinterpretation.

Once the finances were arranged by a grant from the enlightened National Kiwi Lottery Fund, I could start to plan the Te Awanga excavations. First, a detailed survey was needed, because the *paa* was not marked on the maps; for this I had the invaluable services of Karel Peters, the departmental draughtsman. Bill Shaw offered his shearers' quarters for the fifteen to twenty students and other volunteers; these were a range of wooden buildings by the river, divided into cubicles with a kitchen/diner and a shower-room, such as every landowner was obliged to provide for the Maori gang who, rather like the Kentish hop pickers, arrived each year for the sheep shearing. Nowadays they come each day in their own cars and on motor bikes. A student rota was established for cooking the evening meal; I was amazed by the number of possible variants on minced beef, and there was an abundance of peaches and vegetables from the local market gardens, so we fared well. It proved to be an agreeable, cheerful and hard-working group.

The dig went well, despite the great heat, though I felt the usual tension as I started a new site. Karel's accurate work in planning and setting out was a great help. We tackled the defences, found the large deep postholes of a fighting stage, uncovered most of the embanked longhouse, which was superimposed on an early palisade, and found other timber structures, a shed, a storage rack, a cooking place and a sequence of pit cellars. I practised area excavation, albeit on a small scale, to get these results. New Zealand archaeologists had learnt through Jack Golson to dig in three metre squares with baulks between, as Mortimer Wheeler had done at Maiden Castle. This method made the detection of wooden structures extra difficult, because the vital postholes would somehow manage to lie concealed in the baulks. I was always careful not to criticise the earlier archaeologists, but rather to demonstrate that there were other methods. Finds were scarce, mostly scraps of chert and obsidian, and I felt the lack of pottery acutely; the Maoris had ceased to make it before they sailed from east Polynesia in the eighth or ninth century AD. For dating I had to rely on radio-carbon 14 analysis, from eight samples of wood and charcoal, identified by Dr J. Rafter of the Institute of Nuclear Sciences. I well remember carrying a heavy package containing a portion of one of the big posts which supported a fighting stage to the Wellington laboratory. The analyses as well as the stratification indicated a long occupation of three phases, from the tenth to the early nineteenth century AD, with the principal fortifications about AD 1600, on which, after a second season in 1975, I could base the final report.[4]

On my return to Auckland, I was taken by surprise one morning by Professor Roger Green who invited me to give the Macmillan–Brown lectures on the subject of Maori fortifications. These were an endowed series given in each of the four New Zealand universities in rotation, and in 1974 it was Auckland's turn for the anthropology department to nominate a lecturer. I was very hesitant, because I had only been a year in the country, and doubted if I had enough material for three lectures. However, Roger was very persuasive, saying I could use my knowledge of British hill-forts to supplement that of the Maori *paa*. I said I would think it over during lunch, only to find when I came back that he had fixed it with the university authorities. I had to set to work quickly to collect my thoughts and organise the material for new slides to be ready by mid-June. Once started the text came easily; it was designed for an intelligent but not a specialist audience. It was an attempt to explain, in simple language, the methods of modern archaeology, to illustrate the wealth and variety of sites existing in New Zealand, and to analyse the *paa* and its defences and the structures within it. I tried to demonstrate that a Maori *paa* was not the crude haphazard work of a group of bloodthirsty savages, but a sophisticated structure changing over the years in response to the needs of a community for defence, for a living place, and for safe storage of their food supplies. I concluded by comparing the *paa* and the British hill-forts, finding that the striking similarities were due to two people, the Celts and the Maoris, far apart in time and space, having similar social needs and values; each were the product of a tribal warrior-led society. The lectures were quite a social occasion; I wore a long blue patterned dress in fine wool, and the hall was full. An expanded version was eventually published by Longman Paul; it sold well, and I was pleased to find it included in the anthropology students' book list of essential reading.[5]

Thinking that the end of a very agreeable stay was in sight, I fixed the date of my return, though I knew that I had a lot of unfinished business. Suddenly there was an opportunity to extend my stay: Janet Davidson learnt she had obtained a Rhodes fellowship for two years in Oxford. I had strongly supported her as one of her referees and, half in jest, half seriously, I had hinted I would like to take her place at the Auckland Museum if she was successful. The director, Dr Graham Turbott, agreed with her that some temporary help was needed, and offered me a part-time post. So I went back home in late July with the certainty of a return in October after Janet had gone into residence in Lady Margaret Hall. It had been a wonderful year; the escape from routine teaching, examining and committees, as well as departmental meetings run by a tyrant, had given me a new lease of life. A new environment and a new material culture to study had provided a challenge and stimulated my creative faculties surprisingly late in life. I had gained new friends and had been accepted by New Zealand archaeological society.

I flew back to England, breaking the long journey with a week in Tonga where a young friend from Cardiff days, Margaret Blundell, was running a branch of the new University of the South Pacific's adult education programme. The small plane from Auckland was crammed with large black men, gaudily dressed, going back to their island after a spell of well-paid work in New Zealand: I was the only woman passenger. I had some good days with Margaret, swimming in the warm coral lagoons, and visiting some of the small-scale native fortifications as well as the remarkable dynastic tombs at Mua: these were on rectangular stepped platforms faced with large limestone slabs. On Sunday we went to the Methodist church in Nuku'lofa, which was attended by some of the royal family and crammed with men and women wearing their colourful dresses and with the children dolled up to the nines. The sides of the church were open to the tropical air and the singing of the hymns was tremendous. The visit finished with a feast given in our honour. We sat on the ground in a little arbour; the food, which included a sucking pig and a large fish, was laid in front of us and we were helped to choice morsels by our male hosts. We ate with our fingers, with a leaf for a plate. We were told that the women and children would eat later and finally poor relations would finish up the scraps.

I continued my journey via Fiji in a British Airways Viscount, only half-full, so I could stretch out on three seats to sleep. At the refuelling stop at Hawaii Airport I spent an hour in a Japanese-style garden with its little pools and flowers adjoining the departure lounge, long since replaced by tarmac. From Los Angeles, the pilot obligingly flew low to give us pas-

sengers a view of the Grand Canyon: those were the days when it was possible to enjoy air travel. Even so, if I have a window seat, I am happy to
gaze at the clouds, the sea or the landscape below, and to become conscious of the round world from the curve of the far horizons. I have vivid
recollections of seeing northern India spread out like a map, after taking
off from Delhi eastwards in the early morning on my return flight to
Auckland via Hong Kong. There were the straight lines of the railways
and roads across the plain to the foothills and then the great snowy ranges
of the Himalayas, increasingly glowing and becoming pink in the dawn
light.

The three months in England were a happy interlude with my family
and friends, a second summer stolen from the calendar years 1974–5. We
celebrated my return with a family feast at The Retreat, masterminded by
George who at that time had a catering business in Shrewsbury. Janet
came over in September, and I enjoyed showing her a variety of hill-forts
in the South West, and the Bronze Age huts in settlements on Dartmoor, as
well as some of the classic sites on the chalk hills, including Maiden
Castle. I drove her to Oxford in a highly nervous state at the prospect of
her two years in a conventional women's college; however, once settled
down she enjoyed herself, widening her archaeological experience and
making new friends. Finally she acquired a fiancé, Foss Leach, another
visiting New Zealander, a distinguished archaeologist from Otago
University.

Back in Auckland, I was trying to take her place as the Vaile archaeologist at the museum, no easy task as she was greatly esteemed. The
museum is a fine building in the classical style, having an imposing
entrance façade with Doric columns and pilasters; behind it there is a
hemicycle of three storeys housing the offices for the curators and a large
library. It is built on the crest of a low volcanic eminence in the grassy
parkland known as the Auckland Domain, with fine views of the bay and
the islands; I often used to walk there in the lunch interval. The museum
incorporates the Auckland memorial of the two World Wars, in which New
Zealand was involved. On Anzac Day, 25 April, the director is obliged to
attend the 5 a.m. dawn service at the Cenotaph, outside the museum's
front door, which commemorates the landing at Gallipoli in the
Dardanelles. The collections are outstanding, with not only a complete
Maori meeting house, a war canoe and other fine carvings in the main
hall, but also fine English furniture and ceramics, and objects from the
Pacific of real artistic merit; to wander in the galleries was a constant
pleasure. The administrative set-up, like the building, resembled that of
the National Museum of Wales, with a director, Dr Graham Turbott, a lay
council and curators of six departments. I soon felt at home in its staff
room, at 'morning tea', alias a coffee break, though to work regularly

from 9 a.m. until 5 p.m. was a change from the casual university regime to which I had become accustomed.

The museum archaeologist was on her own, though sharing a typist with the ethnologist, Dave Simmons, in the office next door. He was very friendly; he gave me helpful advice in all matters of Maori traditions and behaviour, and encouraged me by his example to take a sympathetic attitude to the growing Maori aspirations. I found I was expected to deal with public relations and correspondence, with accessions of new material and storage, but had little to do with the galleries, where the display was static and rather old-fashioned. Like Janet, I was free to get on with my own work; this included a second season of excavation at Te Awanga *paa,* for which the museum provided some funds, and writing the final report, published by the New Zealand Archaeological Association in 1978.

Thanks to Roger Green, I was invited to join the Archaeology Committee of the Historic Places Trust, meeting four or five times a year in Wellington. The trust, a similar body to the English National Trust, and mainly concerned with historic sites and nineteenth-century houses, was about to become deeply involved with the protection of archaeological sites, Maori as well as colonial. At long last, after years of pressure from the New Zealand Archaeological Association and other conservation bodies, the government had recognised its responsibilities for protecting the cultural heritage, and in 1975 had passed an Historic Places Amendment Act due to come into force in April 1976, as well as an Antiquities Act, concerned with portable antiquities. The first Act instructed the Historic Places Trust to compile a national register of archaeological sites more than 100 years old: the Act made it an offence to damage a site in any way, or to alter it, without a written authority from the Trust, thus checking on developers and government departments alike. If an excavation was deemed necessary for research purposes, an official permit from the Trust was required, which prevented casual digging; and if a site had to be seriously damaged or destroyed, a prior excavation might be required for which the landowner or the developer would have to pay. This proviso was an advance on English Ancient Monument Acts and has now become an accepted practice here.

It was the job of the Archaeology Committee to make this enlightened legislation work. We at once put the case for additional staff, for there was only one archaeology officer, Jim McKinlay, but he was soon joined by Dr Aidan Challis, a young Englishman, to take charge of the site register. We wrangled at length over the paperwork for the authorities and permits; needless to say, some of our detailed recommendations came to nothing, including a plan to peg the protected sites, which was quite unrealistic. What sticks in my memory are the long hours; we worked all the morning until a break for lunch, and stopped only in the late afternoon in time for the participants to catch their planes for Auckland, Christchurch or Dunedin. I have always found committee work tiring, but the New Zealanders seemed undeterred by the marathon discussions and a long agenda. However, it was a good way for me to get to know the leaders of New Zealand archaeology outside Auckland, and I felt privileged to be at the centre of power at the beginning of a new era.

The committee agreed that the site register was the top priority, utilising the records already compiled by the Archaeological Association, together with its organisation of voluntary regional file keepers, and funds were made available for new site surveys. As acting file keeper for the Auckland region, I was soon happily involved. Roger Green supplied keen and competent students; I selected the areas where field surveys were most needed, mostly on the coast; I supplied the couples with maps, guidelines and record forms, and sent them out into the country for two or three weeks. I managed to visit most of them towards the end of their time to discuss any problem sites, and afterward I tactfully kept up the pressure until they produced a report. We also ran a one-day training school at the museum. As a result, the 1,585 sites recorded in the file had grown to nearly 3,000 by the end of 1976, and I had made several good friends in the younger generation.[6]

I also did some field surveys myself in Hawke's Bay, in order to provide the background for the Te Awanga *paa* excavations report. I was assisted by Mary Jeal, a keen amateur, who had proved her worth on the dig and who had the local knowledge of the landowners and the Maori people. She was a good draughtswoman and produced all the necessary sketch plans, always my weak point. This became an annual event for the next six years (1976–82), and, as soon as Mary became file keeper, was to the great benefit of the files. We had good fun together, though there were some stressful incidents, such as being taken up a steep *paa* site as a pillion rider behind the landowner on his powerful motorbike, or encountering an enormous lorry loaded with sheep in a steep and narrow lane. January in Hawke's Bay can be very hot, but we only once gave up, one afternoon when the thermometer stood at 38 degrees centigrade, and there was a scorching north-west wind coming from the tropics. Each year the dots on our local distribution map steadily spread and began to make sense, so that when Nigel Prickett asked me to contribute a regional study of Hawke's Bay to a volume he was editing I cheerfully assented, feeling that basic field work had been done, albeit in a limited area.[7]

As the museum archaeologist, I undertook a study of a Northland estate, asked for by an interested landowner, Mr Douglas Myers. The 850 acres, centred on Parua Bay on the north coast opposite the Cavalli Islands, proved to be a small but rewarding area, which had been densely settled by the Maoris. I was assisted by John Coster and his wife, and we lived amicably and agreeably in a caravan near the beach in this remote uninhabited area reached only by dirt tracks. We got plenty of exercise in the dramatic hilly landscape, planning the six *paa* and seven open settlements, with ever-changing views of the sea, and cliff-ringed coast. In my report, the settlements were reviewed in relation to the topography, and to natural resources, here fishing rather than cultivation; the fortifications were classified and indications for their chronology noted, and a not entirely successful attempt made to relate the district to Maori tradition and history and to estimate the population.[8]

It was in the course of field work for the Auckland Regional Authority that I came to grief, slipping and breaking my ankle. A Chinese orthopaedic surgeon, London-trained, consigned me to the local Middlemoor hospital where the Pott's fracture was set, followed by six weeks in plaster and on crutches. The pessimistic ward sister told me that I would never be able to walk on rough ground again; I proved her wrong, thanks to a lot of therapy and massage. New Zealand has an excellent system of health care; all my treatment was free, and I received financial compensation as well as every kindness and consideration. To cheer me up at Christmas my two sons, George and Derek, came out, followed the next summer by Charles and his wife, Jane, my sister Mari and her husband, Peter Bicknell, and my friend, Professor Joyce Youings, from Exeter University. All these visitors were a good excuse for picnics and swims in warm clear water on nearby beaches, and for visits to places like Rotorua with its hot springs, bubbling mud, geysers and all-pervading stink of sulphur. Travelling in New Zealand is made easy by the ubiquitous motels, which supply not only good basic accommodation but also full kitchen equipment, apparently without much loss. My favourite was one near Keri-Keri, Bay of Islands, set in an idyllic citrus orchard, with the trees laden with oranges and grapefruit which dropped on the grass.

Everyone enjoyed a trip to the north: there is nothing so exciting as the first view of the Hokianga estuary when, after emerging from the tortuous unmetalled road through the Waipoua Forest with its giant native kauri trees, the high dunes flanking the river mouth suddenly appear, with golden sand on one side, dark on the other, and the blue river in between. It is little changed from Augustus Earle's painting in 1827, except that the Maori *paa* he showed are deserted.[9] There was pleasure, too, in repeatedly pottering around the Bay of Islands in the little white steamers, watching the swarms of fish in the clear water, or cattle being made to swim to land on the small islands. The past was evoked for me when the outline of the first church missionary settlement showed up on the grassy slopes behind the beach at Rangihoua, with the cross commemorating the founder, William Marsden, in 1814. There were the house sites and the garden plots, whilst beside them towered the terraced slopes of Rangihoua *paa* where their patron, Chief Duatara, lived.[10]

There are other memorable tourist attractions in the area: for example, the governor's elegant house where the Treaty of Waitangi between the Maori chiefs and Queen Victoria was signed in 1840; the later mission house at Waimate North, and their stone store at Keri-Keri, with Chief Hongi's *paa* of Kororipo across the river, where tall white Chinese lilies have run wild beneath the gum trees. It is unfortunate that the simplicities and fine proportions of classical buildings such as these were soon to be replaced by the ponderous elaboration of the villas of 1860–90 built for the well-to-do colonial settlers. Domestic architecture is not New Zealand's strong point; the main streets of so many small towns are unfortunate examples of ribbon development without a centre or any public building of distinction, just a string of mean shops, cafés, garages and bungalows. The pleasures of exploring an English small town like Totnes or Cirencester was something I constantly missed in New Zealand, though compensated by the enjoyment of unspoilt countryside and the coasts.

My site protection work based at the museum meant that I had to be in touch with the local authorities in Auckland, who were responsible for the management of the volcanic cones as 'public open spaces' known as 'domains' or 'reserves'. These conical green hills around a crater now rise from a mass of small houses, as striking features in a unique urban landscape. In the past, the Maoris had fashioned them into terraced and fortified *paa*, but many had been quarried away for road metal, others seriously damaged by reservoirs, and fewer than a dozen survive more or less intact, so their conservation was of great importance. Some officials were interested and co-operative, with regard to Mount Wellington and One Tree Hill in particular, but vigilance was needed. Cattle instead of sheep suddenly appeared to graze the slopes, motorcyclists tried to race up and down the terraces, or a trench for a new water main needed to be dug, so action had to be taken.

To my surprise, archaeologists had neglected to study the sites in detail; there had been no major excavation, only small-scale digs when damage was threatened, and the results remained unpublished. From my first arrival and encounter with Mount Eden I felt these impressive sites were a challenge; their very size, – One Tree Hill is 1 kilometre long and 50 metres high – made detailed planning a problem, and their complexity demanded explanation.

With the aid of aerial photographs, local authority surveyors and a succession of university students organised by Roger Green, we produced detailed plans which were fitted together by a fine university draughtswoman, Caroline Phillips, and the complete contour plans of five major *paa* were achieved: Mount Eden, Mount Hobson, Mount St John, Mount Wellington and One Tree Hill. For my part, I walked the sites time and again, checking the plans and thinking, until slowly they began to make sense. I distinguished a series of 'strong points', utilising knobs of scoria (solidified lava) on the crater rims, which were defended by short lengths of transverse ditches and by scarps. In several cases these defences appeared to be a late feature, cutting into or superimposed on the living terraces. Only on One Tree Hill was there a comprehensive linear defence, facing the relatively easy approach from the Manukau harbour, in addition to four 'strong points' on the crater rim and a citadel on the summit. Here the 'One Tree' stood, a pine planted by Sir John Logan Campbell but since replaced, as successors to the sacred totara tree of the Maoris, together with Campbell's grave and an obelisk dedicated to the Maori people.

'Only connect', wrote E. M. Forster, so I tried to match the sites with Maori tradition and with the tribal history of the Auckland isthmus, in the light of the evidence given to Justice Fenton in 1868 in the Native Land Courts. It was apparent that the area had been peopled by the Waiohua tribes, certainly before the fifteenth century, as attested archaeologically by a radio-carbon date of AD 1430 from excavations on Mount Wellington. The attractions were the accessible north-south waterways linked by a short portage across the isthmus between two good harbours, of the Hauraki Gulf and the Manukau harbour, the fishing and above all the fertile volcanic soils for cultivation, and the hills for defence. No wonder that the area was known to the Maoris as 'Tamaki of a Hundred Lovers' – i.e., desired by many - and that the population increased on the terraced hills. The later fortifications I had detected could be attributed to an incursion of the Ngati Whatua tribes from the Kaipara region farther north at the end of the eighteenth century, when the paramount Chief Kiwi Tamaki of One Tree Hill was defeated on the Manukau, and the isthmus was occupied by the intruders. It is known that the hill-top settlements were deserted by the time Samuel Marsden crossed the isthmus in 1820: their earthwork defences could not stand against imported firearms.

Towards the end of my two years in the museum, in November 1976, I was asked by the director to give a public lecture before I returned to England. I chose to talk about 'Paa of the Auckland Isthmus' with new colour slides, plans and my archaeological analysis and novel deductions.[11] I treated myself to another long blue dress with ethnic trimmings; a large audience of over 400 filled the museum auditorium, including my former university colleagues, and Janet, just returned from Oxford and rather bewildered by the new developments. It went very well; I left the next day, trailing a small 'cloud of glory', and with presents and letters of appreciation from the Museum Council, the staff and the Historic Places Trust. Thus ended my second phase of regular employment.

Chapter Ten

Back to New Zealand
and A Trip to China

1977 – 1983

In my third and last visit to New Zealand, 1977–83, I went back to Auckland as a volunteer, because I felt I had more to contribute to its archaeology, and time on my hands to do it. I became the museum's Honorary Archaeologist: I had a shared room adjoining the library for my slides, books and papers, and help with occasional typing, as well as the right to continue to publish articles in the museum's annual *Records* series and occasional *Bulletin* monographs. The editor was an entomologist – an insect man – who maintained a high standard, but was very pernickety, and I found him rather a trial when it came to proof correcting. I shared the room with Dr Graham Turbott, who had just retired from the directorship; it worked quite well on the 'Box and Cox' principle: I had it two days a week to his three. Graham became much more relaxed when he had time for his special interest in the birds of New Zealand; as director he was rather a martinet, one of those who had to be consulted in advance about what I felt were trivia. With his wife Olwyn, we had some good days on the extensive mudflats on the Manukau harbour, South Auckland, and at Miranda on the Firth of Thames, watching the great flocks of godwits, knots, stilts and wrybill, swirling across the sky and landing on the mud to feed. Graham could always spot the occasional rarity, a party of curlew-sandpipers, a Terek's sandpiper, or a tiny red-necked stint feeding amongst the many wrybill. The wrybill is a strange little New Zealand bird, very like the English dunlin but with a twisted tip to its bill. It breeds only in the South Island, but migrates *en masse* to the North Island estuaries from Christmas onwards. The first time I visited Miranda by myself I had 'beginner's luck' watching a rare white-winged black tern in its striking breeding plumage hawking up and down a streamlet in the marsh: I naively assumed that it was just another strange but common New Zealand bird. All the birds seemed remarkably tame; I remember sitting quite close to a pair of eastern rosella parrots, gaudy recent immigrants from Australia, feeding busily on the buds of a small bush in Northland, whilst the native fantail, looking like a cross between a wagtail and a tit, positively accompanied me in the woodland in search of the flies that were disturbed by my movements. Birdsong too was a new experience; I did not expect to hear a strangely-patterned black and white magpie produce a flute-like gurgling song. There were no nightingales, but the bellbirds contributed a wonderful sequence of liquid notes to the dawn chorus I heard when excavating at Te Awanga in Hawke's Bay. The similar song of the tui I heard more frequently in the woodlands around Auckland, an individual melody broken by gabbling notes from time to time and thus easy to recognise.

With so many new birds to identify and to watch on the coast and in the bush, I did not lack occupation at the weekends, but I did miss my Topsham garden. My kind landlady, Jean Preisler, allowed me to dig up a small shady patch where I planted three camellias which seemed to like the heavy clay, but nothing else thrived. I cast around for someone who needed help, and was introduced to an elderly lady, Miss Gwyneth Richardson, who was going blind: her attractive small garden consequently was becoming overgrown. There I worked away one afternoon each week clearing, pruning and replanting, to our mutual satisfaction. 'How nice to see some fresh brown earth', she exclaimed to me. She had been a talented artist, and when she finally had to go into a residential home, she gave me one of her watercolours, of a vase of full-blown roses, which had the depth and quality of an oil painting.

At the museum I found several jobs to fill my two days there. I took over the sale of publications for the New Zealand Archaeological Association, principally a series of twelve semi-popular monographs, including my own *Prehistoric Maori Fortifications*, which, lacking publicity, had accumulated in store. I circulated members, libraries and particularly overseas archaeological societies and universities; I started a bookstall at the annual meeting and at conferences, and the sales suddenly took off. I also promoted sales of back numbers of the Association's newsletter, and, altogether there was quite a handsome profit. I then convinced the Association that it was time to sponsor a professional journal, and after prolonged discussions by a committee, and making arrangements with Otago University for its printing, the first number of *The New Zealand Journal of Archaeology* appeared in 1979, and has continued annually ever since. The contents cover a wide range of interests relating to the Pacific as a whole, as well as to New Zealand, and include historic as well as prehistoric times. It has undoubtedly added to the prestige of New Zealand archaeologists.

I also embarked on some rescue excavations, not digging but rescuing from oblivion sites which had been dug in the past, but the accounts of which for various reasons had never been published. The first of these was the terraced *paa* on Mount Roskill in Auckland, where an excavation had taken place in 1961 in advance of the construction of a reservoir. The principal excavator, Wilfred Shawcross had moved to Sydney in 1973 and, at the suggestion of Roger Green, was now willing to hand over all his notes and drawings and to agree to the transfer of the finds from the university department to the Auckland museum. From these I discovered the evidence for a double defensive palisade around the crater rim, and, with the help of radio-carbon analyses of four stratified charcoal samples, obtained consistent dates for an occupation within the period AD 1430–1620, a real advance in knowledge of the Auckland volcanic cones.[1]

The next site was a small hill-top settlement at Maioro near the mouth of the Waikato river, South Auckland, excavated by Roger Green in 1965–6. His work showed it to be originally an open settlement dating from the thirteenth century, then fortified by a palisade and scarp in the fifteenth and sixteenth centuries, according to the radio-carbon dates. The layout of the summit platform (*tihi*) with its wooden sleeping house, a cooking shed, three roofed storage pits and an overhead food cupboard (*waka*) was detectable; it was an establishment suitable for a minor chief, here tentatively identifed for the first time.[2]

Finally, Richard Cassels asked me to tackle his 1972–3 excavations of a terraced site among the dunes near Aotea harbour on the west coast of the Waikato, in the North Island. It proved to have been occupied in the late twelfth and early thirteenth centuries, and threw light on the different layouts and domestic arrangements on each of the four terraces that were completely excavated; nothing perhaps of major importance, but this was the first time such a basic site had been thoroughly examined and its economy demonstrated.[3]

It sounds very easy to set out other people's work, but this is not so. Although my friends, the excavators, were available for consultation, it was slow routine work collating their notes, plans and sections, checking and describing the finds, selecting and supplementing the illustrations. It was much easier to write up my own excavations, where the details were stored in my memory as well as in the notebooks. I tried to set out clearly the details of each excavation and then to interpret them in historic and human terms. 'We speak from facts, not theory', as Colt-Hoare once said. The whole exercise was very worthwhile, since it retrieved basic data, and should provide a useful contribution to the writing of New Zealand's prehistory.

As well as this routine work, I had a major piece of research in hand, a pioneer study of carved wooden Maori burial chests. It was Jacquetta Hawkes, on a brief tour of New Zealand in 1976 with her husband, J. B. Priestley, who first drew my attention to the chests in Auckland Museum, saying how dramatic they were and how unlike the rest of the carvings. Thereafter, as I passed the display case on my way to lunch in the museum cafeteria, they caught my eye and took my fancy. Like Celtic decorated metalwork, they incorporated strange images and elaborate patterns, and I felt compelled to study them. Hitherto the chests had been neglected by archaeologists and art historians, partly due to their respect for the Maori people's dread of anything concerning the dead, which was *tapu*, and partly because most were hidden away in museum stores.

My first task was to compile a list and a distribution map, then to obtain good new photographs before proceeding to detailed descriptions and analyses. All told, there were 63 chests extant, mostly concentrated in the north of the North Island, of which 25 had never been published. I made rubbings with soft wax crayons to record details of the patterning and motifs. It was clear at the outset that the chests were not flat coffins, but were designed to stand upright with the disarticulated human bones packed into a cavity at the back of the wooden image and secured by a lid tied on with fibre. They were placed in burial caves, the communal tombs for a Maori tribal group (*hapu*) where, following exposure, the bones of the dead were scraped and washed and then deposited in the cave by the priest (*tohunga*). A description of the Kohekohe cave at Waimamaku, Hokianga, indicated that the six carved chests were set up in a semi-circle against the back wall, an awesome sight confronting two pig-hunters when they entered the cave in 1901.

Naturally I made an effort to locate some of the caves; I had identified a photograph in the Turnbull Library at Wellington, showing chests now in the Auckland Museum being removed from the Tikopiko cave at Waiomio, Bay of Islands, in 1929. I was fortunate to be guided to the same cave by its Maori guardian, the late Mr T. Kawiti; I was very surprised being a woman to be allowed in, as we are generally regarded by the Maoris as inferior (*noa*). The cave was really a fissure in the limestone at the back of the conspicuous rocky eminence (*Tikopiko* means 'bent rock'). The old man and I clambered up with some difficulty the steep thirty feet to the narrow entry. The centre of the cave where the chests had stood was clear, but there were many skulls and long bones in niches at the sides; some had fallen down and Mr Kawiti asked me to pick them up, as he was afraid to touch them. Having handled prehistoric burials many times, I readily did so, but when we returned to his house, I conspicuously asked to wash my hands before partaking of tea and tomato sandwiches; this seemed necessary for personal hygiene as well as conforming to Maori custom, which is thought to remove the *tapu*.

I soon realised that there were five types of chests, the earlier carved with incised patterns, and, later in relief, a stylistic sequence probably extending from the sixteenth to the early nineteenth century.[4] The majority were stylised human figures in a formal frontal pose; some were heads only, and a few were animals, particularly the lizard or monsters associated with death. Their function in the cave was to protect as well as to house the bones of a distinguished individual. I concluded that most images represented tribal ancestors, heroic or semi-divine. In many the sexual organs were prominent, and several showed a small figure on the torso or emerging from the vulva, signifying the importance of fertility and reproduction in the life of the tribe. Some of the terrifying female images probably portrayed the goddess of death, *Hine nui tapu*, who presided over the underworld, or Hina, the moon goddess of the northern people, who is also associated with death. 'The moon', wrote Thomas Kendall, the missionary, in 1823, 'is man's timekeeper and presides over his bones.' I am not aware how anthropologists or Maori writers have reacted to these ideas, which were set out in a fully-illustrated monograph published by the museum in 1983.[5] Certainly this publication had the effect of making Maori people in the north better aware of their heritage, and there has been a strong demand lately for the return of the chests and their contents to the Hokianga. The museum has responded to pressure and has returned the localised human bones to the north, where, rather illogically, they have been ceremonially buried in churchyards. The return of the magnificent carved chests is still under scrutiny; their survival depends on being kept in a controlled atmosphere such as can best be provided in a large museum. Their unique artistic qualities need to be seen to be appreciated, and I have urged the minister to take steps to prevent their destruction or damage by future neglect.

There were two other occasions when I felt in touch with the prehistoric past, as I had done in the Tikopiko burial cave. The first was in Auckland in 1979, when the local water board had to lay a new main from their reservoir on One Tree Hill across the inhabited slopes of the ancient *paa*. A preliminary archaeological investigation was under way when the excavator, Sue Bulmer, uncovered ancient human bones at the back of a terrace. Work ceased immediately, and could not be resumed until the Maori people had carried out the appropriate ceremony, which I watched from a short distance away. A group of three women dressed in black and waving green leafy branches came up the slopes singing and calling loudly to a man standing by the burial, who chanted in reply. The bones were then picked up for burial elsewhere.

Secondly, when Dr Doug Sutton, a university lecturer, was digging in 1983 at Poerua, an important *paa* in the territory of the Ngapuhi, in the Bay of Islands, there was the sudden death of one of the Maori workmen.

It was a hot summer's day, and in the lunch break some young people went for a swim in the nearby lake. One of them disappeared and drowned, presumably due to cramp. All work was stopped and a Maori elder was summoned, an old man wearing a cloak and holding a large staff. He insisted we all followed him up the hillside, where after we had joined him in reciting the Lord's Prayer, he turned and addressed the volcanic mountain, shaking his staff at it. Apparently he tried to propitiate the spirit of the place for the damage done to it by the excavation, and then demanded that it yielded up the missing boy's body. The excavation was closed down for a week; in a few days' time the body duly came to the surface of the lake, and Doug Sutton was amongst many who attended the funeral. No one seemed to find this mixture of pagan and Christian rites incongruous; for my part I felt I had stepped backwards in time into a primitive society. It seemed incredible that such rites and beliefs could exist in the late twentieth century. I did not have the same sensations when I slept in a modern Maori meeting house, only the discomforts inherent in a large mixed dormitory where talking continued far into the night, and on one occasion being bitten by fleas.

The five years I remained in Auckland passed very quickly. My diaries record a succession of events: meetings in Wellington, field work in Hawke's Bay, the annual conference of the New Zealand Archaeological Association, held in different places and so extending my local knowledge; in Auckland lots of concerts, theatres, parties, dinners in small restaurants like 'The Brie' or the fishy 'Pelorus Jack'. I recollect many blissful picnics and swims on remote sandy beaches shared by Richard and Paula Allison and their small daughter Flora, as well as expeditions to investigate yet another Maori *paa* in the north. These were the years in which many firm friendships were built up, based on shared interests and pleasures. My stay was broken by a trip home in the early summer of 1980, when after fifty-five years I revisited Lanslebourg and the Mont Cenis, with my son, George, who shares my interest in Alpine flowers, and then back to England again in 1981 for Christmas, always a time when I felt a little homesick.

Since I was free from routine commitments I could indulge in holidays in the Pacific without a qualm; these included visits to Melbourne, Canberra, Sydney and Perth in Australia, to Rarotonga in the Cook Islands, to Hong Kong and a tour of China in 1982, and, on my final return flight, to Vancouver and Seattle.

The Australian cities did not greatly appeal to me, though the Sydney Opera House, with its cluster of decorative arcs like sails above the harbour, was a fascinating piece of modern architecture. I was fortunate to hear Prokofiev's opera *War and Peace* while I was there. My best memories are of the bird life in the country round Melbourne: the flocks of pink and grey galah parrots; the numerous little blue penguins coming ashore rapidly at dusk, making for their nesting burrows in the dunes; the parties of pelicans swimming on the lakes, four or five abreast, to round up the fish on which they feed; and the incredibly tiny blue wren with brilliant turquoise plumage, were some of the highlights. I was lucky to be taken to the strictly-preserved wooded haunt of the unique lyrebird and to hear its song and see its display, designed to attract the plain brown female, and to warn off other males The bird alighted beside one of its special mounds singing loudly and quivering all over, it lowered its head and raised its magnificent golden tail. Since it was early in the season, it did not reach the climax of the display when the tail is thrust forward to cover the bird's head, but subsided after a prolonged intense loud song.

I had a short holiday in the Cook Islands in 1979 with my friend Duntie Glenny from Te Awanga. Rarotonga is a small tropical volcanic island with a steep wooded interior, and is ringed by a coral reef and a lagoon. It has a good claim to be a place of embarkation by the Maoris on their New Zealand voyages. Despite Duntie's protestations, we clambered through the undergrowth on the steep hillside to find the terraced house sites and the curious stone-faced rectangular platforms and uprights which formed a sacred site, the *marae,* for an early Polynesian community. There is nothing like this in New Zealand, but there are resemblances to others in the Society Islands to the east. Up another valley we found a succession of 'pond fields' made by diverting the stream and terracing where *taro*, an important tropical root crop, had been cultivated. Today cultivation is limited to a narrow coastal plain where the plots are divided by hedges of avocado pears, the despised fruit being fed to the pigs to fatten them, we were told. The Cook Islands are famous for their dancers, lovely graceful dark-haired girls, accompanied by male drummers; we saw them not only in the hotel but dancing for the locals in the village streets.

My most exciting venture was a three-week trip to China in October of 1982. I went with a group of twenty people, from an old-established New Zealand China Friendship Society based in Auckland; we went at a time of transition, when the excesses of the Cultural Revolution were over and Deng Xiaoping had returned to power, but Chairman Mao's life-size image was still a feature of public buildings. There was a move towards new links with the West, but the institutions of the communist state were much in evidence and seemed to be generally approved. Tourism was growing apace and was well-managed. We stayed in new hotels, in twin-bedded rooms with bathroom and loo; we travelled first class on trains with comfortable sleepers, or by air in elderly cramped Russian planes. Our group was given an English-speaking courier, an intelligent university-trained young man who was willing, of an evening, to discuss the political and economic problems of China's modernisation, besides seeing after our luggage and our timetable. He was married, but unhappy in being limited to his one child. Apart from breakfast, all meals were Chinese, a bewildering succession of delicious dishes and titbits placed on the round tables for eight; it was difficult to decide which or how much to eat: a tureen of hot soup indicated that the end of the meal was near. Since there was practically no bread or sweets, I lost seven pounds and I finally mastered the art of eating with chopsticks.

Our itinerary was Hong Kong, Guangzhou (Canton), Beijing, Chengdu and Chongqing in Sichuan province, down the Yangtze river by boat to Wuhan, (Hankow), and then back to Hong Kong by hovercraft from Guangzhou. At each place there was a local guide and we were given excellent coloured brochures in English. I do not want to describe it in detail because I recorded it in my diaries, but will elaborate only on a few places and topics which made a deep impression.

We arrived in Beijing in the dark, after a tiring journey, and my only thought was bed in the luxury Beijing Hotel. Waking early and seeing it was light, I crept to the window, opened a shutter and looked out. There it was, the Forbidden City, its multitude of curved roofs of golden-yellow and red tiles stretching right across the middle distance, but its buildings screened by a thirty-foot-high enclosing wall with its watchtowers. Later, I walked alone to Tiananmen Square. The wide streets were flooded with streams of bicycles, and the pavements were crowded with men and women, all, it seemed, wearing dark blue trousers and white shirts; only the children wore bright colours. There were hardly any cars, and only a few vans or lorries. The great square is a vast rectangle dominated by the main entry to the Imperial Palace and the Forbidden City through the Gate of Heavenly Peace. The square cannot compare with the beauty and architectural subtlety of St Peter's Square in Rome, for example, being surrounded by modern buildings of no great distinction, though restrained and well proportioned, including Mao's mausoleum, the People's Hall and the museum. The walk with a guide through the Imperial Palace was pure visual pleasure, with its succession of separate buildings linked by a central paved roadway, with white marble balustrades across the open courtyards. The buildings were colonnaded, painted red, with double tiered curved roofs of terracotta tiles, and each had a poetic name such as the Hall of Supreme Harmony, the Palaces of Heavenly Purity and of Earthly Tranquillity, not forgetting the more realistic Palace of Military Excellence, or the Palace of Literary Glory, housing the imperial library. The Chinese got their values right, even if they did not live up to their aspirations. The other building that impressed me was the Temple of Heaven, about half a mile away, where the emperor went each spring to fast and to offer sacrifices for a good harvest. It is a small circular building, raised on a white marble tiered base, with an amazing deep blue tiled roof, like a grape hyacinth. Inside there are the four large wooden columns, richly decorated, which with a circle of twelve smaller ones supports the triple-eaved roof, an amazing piece of sixteenth-century engineering.

Our visit to the Great Wall some twenty-five miles north of Beijing was on a bright sunny October day with a piercing cold wind from the north, and a clear view to the blue distance of Inner Mongolia. I was delighted to find that it was a perfectly logical fortification, designed to defend the loess plain of northern China and the Yellow River from raids of the northern nomads. Starting from the eastern seaboard, the stone wall in its final form makes its way for 6,000 kilometres across the tumbled steep-sided hills to end at Jiayuguan on the edge of the Western Desert. It is aligned along the crest or the forward slope of the hills with a commanding view to the north: all its twists and turns are related to the contour and to visual control. Over 7.5 metres high and 6 metres thick, it was an obstacle that no riders could cross. Like Hadrian's Wall, there were gates to the north, presumably for defensive sallies. At the Badaling Pass the Wall has been heavily restored for the benefit of the crowds of tourists. Here I saw the three-storeyed watchtowers on the high points, with two or three interval towers of two storeys in between, presumably to house the patrolling garrison and to signal. With an effort and clinging to the handrail I climbed the stony ramp and steps from the gate to the nearest watchtower, over 600 feet above. The wall-walk here is wide enough for four horsemen to ride abreast, though how they descended the steepest slopes is a mystery. Despite the crowds, I was immensely impressed by the great work and its surroundings and only wished there had been more time to study it and visit some other sections. It is lodged in my memory with other great frontier fortifications, Hadrian's Wall, the German Limes, East Wansdyke and Offa's Dyke.

We flew from Beijing to Chengdu in Western Sichuan, a city not then much visited by tourists. A group of people gathered outside our hotel to watch us enter, and some followed us when we went shopping, and tried to talk to us in their basic English. Chengdu is at the edge of the plains; not far away beyond the Min Jiang river are the great mountains rising to Tibet. We had here the best of our local guides, Mr Liu, cheerful and smiling, very knowledgeable and a delightful storyteller; he even brought his tapes of the local folk music played on flutes, which he relayed to us on the coach.

The settlement pattern in the countryside, through which we drove on our way to see the new irrigation works, was of isolated large farms or hamlets surrounded by a grove of acacia trees and bamboo, and by a series of small fields. The rice harvest was in full swing, with methods unchanged since prehistoric times. The ears had been cut by hand with sickles, the grain was being threshed with wooden flails on a close-woven straw mat at the roadside, and was winnowed by tossing it into the air with a broad wooden shovel and then raked into heaps with a wide-toothed implement. The short straw was being tied into sheaves and taken back to the fields. Some of these were already being ploughed by water buffalo, pulling a wooden-framed plough with an iron share, in preparation for being flooded again and planted with a second crop of rice. When we drove back in the evening, the golden heaps of rice and the straw mats had gone.

The fertility of the Sichuan basin is due to irrigation according to tradition, begun in the mid-second century BC, and much improved by a hydroelectric dam with new spillways in the 1970s. The story in the annals was that the provincial ruler, Li Bing, and his son Er Long had prevented the river Min Jiang from flooding by cutting through a hill to create an artificial island, thus diverting the flow and spreading it to water the land. The ancient cut is still there to see, and its origin was confirmed when a splendid stone statue of Li Bing, carved in 168 BC, was found in the river bed in 1974. It is now exhibited in the elegant little temple dedicated to the two rulers on the hill above, where I inwardly paid tribute at their shrine. It is not often that written history, traditional stories and archaeological discoveries so neatly coincide.

The highlight of our travels was a two-day trip of 100 miles down the Yangtze river east from Chongqing to the new dam at Yichang. The great river, augmented by powerful tributaries from the Sichuan basin, here cuts through the limestone ranges of central China on its way to the coastal plain and the East China Sea and has created a series of three spectacular gorges, each over five miles long. The weather was overcast and whilst bright sunshine was lacking, the soft light and an occasional gleam on the towering rocky hills were magical. It reminded me of the landscape in the early painted Chinese scrolls which I had seen in the Palace Museum at Beijing a few days previously. In the foreground there was the river with its swirling currents; on the bank maybe a small house and some figures, then up to a white waterfall, and beyond to the fantastic shapes of the rocky hilltops masked by wisps of cloud. The river itself was a soft pinky-brown, full of fine silt; the rocks were cream or yellow limestone, weathering black. I saw an osprey, a flight of teal and lots of swallows flying over the water.

The force of the river through the gorges was tremendous; in early times gangs of men had to haul the boats upstream and through the rapids; later there were winches and steel cables, and even now navigation is tricky. At Yichang the third gorge opens out and 'the Dragon river' has been tamed, its power harnessed by an enormous hydroelectric dam. Our boat went into a lock, 64 metres deep, which bypassed the turbines and the generators. The dam,

70 metres high and over 2,500 metres long, is a wonderful achievement; when only two-thirds completed it withstood the floods of 1981 and, according to the illustrated pamphlet, it supplied 14 billion kilowatts per annum.

I saw the remains of three of those remarkable princely burials excavated in the 1970s, though our tour did not take us to Xi'an, where there is the buried army of life-size terracotta warriors surrounding the ruler's tomb. The burials all work on the assumption that 'you can take it with you', and so make provision for feasting, for music, for fine clothing in the hereafter, as well as for servants and weapons for defence. The earliest was at the Wuhan Museum, the tomb of the Marquis Yi of 430 BC. He was buried in a painted wooden coffin placed in a flat-roofed log cabin below ground level. Beside him were the remains of nine women musicians with their instruments, including sets of bells, zithers of five, ten or twenty strings, pan pipes, flutes, rattles and drums. It was fascinating to see and hear the same sort of instruments in use at a concert that evening at Wuhan. Other compartments in the tomb contained sets of silver goblets, bronze bowls, spoons, cauldrons and wine jars, and an armoury of spears, halberds and horsebits.

The next one was a burial of the Han dynasty of the first century AD at Chongqing Museum. The reconstructed model showed a barrel-vaulted stone construction of three chambers entered by a double door of carved slabs opening on pivots. There was a remarkable frieze of terracotta blocks with engraved designs showing the provincial governor and his retinue riding out in chariots, protected by parasols or umbrellas; another showed them at a feast, watching dancers and acrobats. There were also hunting scenes and harvest gatherings, all as vivid and realistic as paintings on a Greek vase.

The famous tomb of the Ming emperor, Shen Zong, is another later example of the same kind with even more lavish contents. Known as Ding Ling, it is one of the thirteen tombs in the vast imperial cemetery, at the foot of the rolling hills north of Beijing and has become a showpiece for crowds of tourists since it was officially excavated in 1956. We entered the cemetery through an elaborate gate with five openings, and walked up the sacred way to the imperial tombs, which is flanked by large stone figures of men and animals, lions, horses, camels and elephants. The tomb itself lies 27 metres below an enormous walled mound, 270 metres across and 10 metres high, and was entered by a ramp – now modernised – leading to a stone slab door. Inside there are three compartments, all stone-built with barrel vaults. The coffins of the emperor and his two successive wives were laid on a stone plinth in the innermost chamber, with chests filled with their possessions, gold, fine jewellery, jade and porcelain. In the central chamber there were three marble thrones, and porcelain lamps and vases. Altogether 3,000 fine objects were recovered from the tomb, which are now in the Palace Museum at Beijing, together with a selection exhibited on the site. Started in AD 1584 the tomb was completed by AD 1590, though the emperor was not buried there until 1620. I reminded myself that the same phenomenon of lavish display and extravagant use of labour can be seen in the pyramids and other tombs in Egypt, at Ur, and, to a lesser extent, in early Celtic graves such as Vix in central France or Hohe Michele, near the Heuneburg in South Germany. All must have provided a stimulus to craftsmen to produce the finest works of art for their patrons and for posterity.

I found some difficulty in getting enough time to study archaeological sites and the material in museums when visiting with the New Zealand group. However, it was soon apparent that most people were interested in shopping, and on occasions I could use that time for a return visit to a museum. Ostensibly our tour was billed with a special interest in arts and crafts, and so it included visits to small factories producing fine silks, ivory carvings, porcelain, cloisonné work and traditional paintings and calligraphy. Almost all were made in dark and noisy workshops and in crowded Dickensian surroundings.

On the lighter side, I was fascinated by the small Chinese children, dressed in bright colours, walking along the street escorted by their teacher in the regulation dark blue. We were taken to a primary school in Wuhan to see a remarkable display of music, mime, singing and dancing by 6–11 year olds. One tot announced the items in a clear shrill voice and the teacher translated for us. One mime, about three chickens in search of a new house was especially attractive: welcomed by ten other chickens and fed by a girl, they all produced eggs for her basket with expressive gestures and humour, to the accompaniment of two accordions. The same sort of talent was displayed in their paintings, which were wonderfully assured and imaginative. These were products of gifted children, selected at an early age by the state authorities, who would eventually be offered suitable jobs in the arts and entertainment world. Our Chinese courier told us that the limitation of families to one, or at most two, children was very unpopular.

All in all, I was glad I went to China at this time, when the stresses of the cultural revolution were over and there were hopes for the future, unfortunately only to be dashed eight years later by the events in Tiananmen Square. State communism seemed to be flourishing, judging by the communal farms we were shown, and there were no strikes or signs of discontent. Tourism was developing fast, helped by the significant contribution of archaeology. The crowds at the Ming tombs and at other Beijing monuments included many overseas visitors, but also plenty of Chinese people enjoying themselves; our guides made it clear that the importance of recent archaeological discoveries was fully appreciated, and this was also evident from their display in the regional museums.

When I got back to Auckland, I reconsidered my future. After ten full and happy years in New Zealand I felt it was now the time to leave. I would be seventy-five in the summer of 1983, and though still very active and healthy, I realised that this was unlikely to continue. At the museum my work was done: the Maori bone chest monograph was in the press, and all my other articles were published, with one exception, a description of Okuratope *paa* in the Bay of Islands visited by Marsden and Nicolas, which was nearing completion.[6] I had many close friends and colleagues, but I would not have wanted to involve them had I suddenly collapsed. None of my three sons was remotely interested in joining me, even if it were possible for them to emigrate. The long air flight and resultant jet lag, as well as the expense, would be a deterrent to frequent visits, which might result in my feeling I belonged to neither England nor New Zealand. I knew I must be committed permanently to one or the other, and the need to be with my family at the end of my life was paramount. So in July 1983 I was on my way back to Devon and my Topsham flat, via Vancouver and Seattle.

My last major engagement was the annual meeting in May of the New Zealand Archaeological Association at Napier in Hawke's Bay, the region with which I had been most closely connected by the Te Awanga *paa* excavation, and by extensive site recording with Mary Jeal. I was asked to give the introductory public lecture, an archaeological survey of Hawke's Bay, a region hitherto little explored, featuring our discoveries.[7] I also led an excursion on a surprisingly cold fine day to a variety of settlement sites and field systems; we ate our picnic lunches huddled together out of the wind in the storage pits of a *paa*.

I realised that at the concluding meeting there would be some formal thanks for my efforts over the years, but I was entirely taken by surprise when I was summoned to the platform by the president and presented with a *Festschrift*, a volume of essays edited by and contributed by my friends. It was entitled *A Lot of Spadework to be Done,* quoting a remark I had made when telling Mary that the Association had accepted my proposal for a New Zealand Journal of Archaeology. It epitomised my wish to get things started and my understanding of the continuing efforts involved. The phrase could also be applied to an excavation, though here a trowel would be the more suitable implement. The 300-page volume contained an introductory appreciation by Janet Davidson, a full bibliography by Nigel Prickett, and twelve articles related to my interests in *paa*, pits, artefacts and regional settlement patterns. I was deeply touched and more than a little flattered by this unexpected parting present.

I could now look back on my ten years' work with some satisfaction. I had come at the right moment, when it was possible to come to terms with

New Zealand prehistory quickly, to read the little that had been written, to find the gaps and so to make a contribution. Now much more has been written, and an up-to-date synthesis, so conspicuously lacking in 1973, is available in Janet Davidson's *The Prehistory of New Zealand* (1984), as well as in the regional studies in Nigel Prickett's *The First Thousand Years* (1982), all based on recent archaeological work. Similarly my *Prehistoric Maori Fortifications* (1976), was the forerunner of other popular works such as *From the Beginning,* ed. John Wilson (1987). There had really been little difficulty in transferring my interest in the past from Britain to the Antipodes, and in coping with a prehistory that started only in the eighth or ninth century AD and continued until the arrival of Captain Cook in 1770, and even until the Treaty of Waitangi in 1840. Dates don't seem to matter, since the aims, principles and methods of archaeology are unchanged. The main difference was in the economies, from those cultures in Britain based on corn-growing and cattle-rearing, to those of the Maoris in New Zealand based on the cultivating of sweet potato (*kumara*) and sea food. Both had used stone tools, but in New Zealand metals were unknown; here wood carving was the substitute for artistic bronze working. The absence of pottery was, however, always puzzling, and I found radio-carbon dating insufficiently precise for the relatively short time-span of New Zealand prehistory.

I enjoyed being a pioneer in the 1970s, just as I had done when I was a newcomer to Devon in the 1950s. How often did I climb a *paa* and sketch its defences, or perceive the significance of humps and hollows on a hillside revealing an open settlement with its storage pits and rectangular house sites, knowing I was the first to record and interpret it. Now, thanks to field surveys organised by the Historic Places Trust and the New Zealand Archaeological Association, the majority of important sites have been recorded and the prehistoric landscape is becoming better known and understood and, hopefully, better protected. There still remains plenty for archaeologists to do.

Another source of satisfaction was that I had been accepted as a working member of the close-knit New Zealand Archaeological Society; I was part of the group and no longer an outsider. Thanks to Roger Green I retained my connection with the anthropology department at Auckland University, giving the occasional lecture, as I also did in the classics department for Professor Pat Lacey. Working as the Honorary Archaeologist in the museum, I developed a very friendly relationship with Nigel Prickett, who had replaced Janet Davidson on her marriage to Foss Leach and her move to Wellington. I had served on the Archaeology Committee of the Historic Places Trust in its formative years, and on the Council of the New Zealand Archaeological Association, becoming its vice-president as well as its active sales manager, as I have recounted.

There is nothing like a committee for getting to know a diversity of people and what makes them tick. In this way over the years I had made many close friends as well as lots of interesting acquaintances. I still struggle to keep up a meaningful correspondence with a few of them, but after a gap of more than five or six years links become fragile. I have always welcomed the succession of visitors, who keep my memories alive. In retrospect, the Pacific remains a real world, not just a blank blue space on a map, and the personality of the two islands of New Zealand and of their people are deeply embedded in my mind. I can summon up pictures of beautiful landscape, of blue water, sandy beaches, flowery gardens, terraced green hillsides and fortified volcanic hills, as well as images of kind, hospitable and congenial people. It had been a wonderful ten years when, although alone, I had been active, happy, creative and successful, for which I am truly thankful.

Chapter Eleven

Return to Exeter
Picking up the Threads

1983

I travelled back home to Devon in July 1983 via Vancouver and Seattle on the Pacific coast of America, where I saw some of the achievements of the west coast Native Americans. I admired the magnificent carvings of their wooden totem poles and houses, displayed in the University of California's open-air museum and on Victoria Island. Their boldness was a contrast to the Maori carvings of New Zealand that I had studied. The dramatic imagery featured their deities, many in animal form.

I stayed with my Bicknell nieces: Sarah in Seattle, who took me to see the fish market, piled with silvery Pacific salmon from the sea and rivers; whilst Catherine, at Pullman University, took me inland to the Snake River where a walk-in aquarium enabled one to see, through a glass wall, the fish struggling upstream to spawn. Pullman is set in rolling countryside, where broad bands of cultivation and grassland follow the contours, creating an unusual and attractive landscape. It demanded to be painted by a modern artist: sadly, I had no time to find out if there was anybody of note working in the area.

Back in my flat in Topsham, welcomed by my family, I had much to renovate after ten years of tenancy, both in house and garden. I rediscovered the delights of living on the Exe estuary, though when I left for New Zealand the motorway had not yet been built. Despite its proximity to The Retreat upstream, the motorway bridge is a handsome structure spanning the river and the reed beds. However, its intrusion, and the loss of the lodge gates at the head of the drive, has done much to destroy the charm and privacy of the property that I bought with such pleasure in 1967. I was soon to find out that the growth of urbanisation throughout Britain, and the unrelenting increase of motor cars on the roads, would make me long for the relative tranquillity of New Zealand.

In fact, that autumn was a difficult period for me, as for all returning exiles. The weather, or the lack of it, is the first thing that rankles. English summers are rarely blessed with cloudless skies or hot sunshine. English winters are another matter: the grey skies, low cloud and lack of light are hard to bear. It often made me restless, and I still today miss the warmth of hot sun on my back.

I was a little circumspect as to how I should get back into the world of archaeology, having made a conscious decision when I retired in 1972 to absent myself, and to let them get on with it. Too many academics having retired still maintain a wish to influence events, only to face rejection by the new generation, who naturally want to do things their own way. Despite a fruitful and enjoyable decade in New Zealand, I really was not ready to retire from it all. Research and interpretation stay in the mind after a lifetime, and I still had energy in abundance. My garden was witness to this, as I struggled to rid it of bindweed and ground elder.

Starting tentatively by rebuilding old friendships, getting back to the Devon Archaeological Society, attending the committee meetings, I began to fill the gaps in my life. Also, I found that my old department at the university, renamed the Department of History and Archaeology, had grown, with two extra lecturers and two draughtsmen in the drawing office. Malcolm Todd was now the professor in charge of archaeology. An old friend, he made me very welcome and generously invited me to use the services of the drawing office if I should need it. There was also Bob Higham, now a senior lecturer, an ex-pupil working on medieval timber castles; Bill Ravenhill, holding the Reardon Smith chair in the geography department; and Joyce Youings, the Tudor historian. These were all good friends, who welcomed me back into the fold of university life and made me believe that I could continue to contribute usefully to the field of archaeology.

Life is never that simple, though, and we are never quite prepared for life's shocks and traumas. That autumn, Charles, my eldest son, had a nasty accident in a train that failed to stop at the buffers at Paddington station. This was a worrying time as he was in pain and had to have an operation. He was in hospital on and off for the next eighteen months, and it finally led to his being invalided out of the Royal Navy, thereby dashing his hopes to make Captain, which he had so long deserved.

I was feeling under the weather, which I put down to homesickness for New Zealand; having missed the summer in England and in New Zealand, which made two winters in a row, was depressing. After Christmas I did not feel much better, and in January 1984 my younger sister Sheila died suddenly. She was three years younger than I, and although she had never been very healthy, it was a dreadful shock. All the family loved Sheila, for she was always kind and took an an active interest in all our children.

I was by now definitely sickening for something and was worried whether I could manage to go to Cambridge for the funeral. Feeling desperately weak and sick, I rang my sister Mari to tell her that I was unable to come. My son George heard that a neighbour was concerned about me, left his work and summoned a doctor. In consequence I was rushed to hospital with a critical case of diabetes, which another doctor had failed to diagnose earlier.

The nurses and doctors were very efficient and were soon to allay my fears about my condition. The treatment of diabetes has improved enormously over the years, and with care and the help of insulin one can live happily for a long time, as is borne out by my present age of 92 years.

With the spring, and with hosts of daffodils on the lawns of The Retreat, I slowly regained confidence and a willingness to get involved with life again. I went to Tenby in April with an old friend, Joan Yeo, my walking companion in Rome. Tenby was in a special way reassuring, for I had so many memories of the place with Cyril and the children in the thirties. There are many photographs in the family album of sand, sea, and children enjoying what was known as the South Sands stretching to Gilter Point. Tenby has a charm still to this day. It was originally a medieval town: parts of the walls are still visible, but it expanded in early Victorian times, like so many seaside resorts.

Wales has always attracted me: even though we had left in 1948, I had kept in touch with friends and colleagues. I was for many years an external examiner for Cardiff University College, travelling up to the examiners' meeting to discuss the degree classifications every June. I usually stayed with Kathleen Ede, who shared my love of music and theatre, so it was always a pleasure to combine work with an opera or a concert. It was a great honour in 1981 to be made an Honorary Fellow of the University College of Cardiff. I thus had a reason to continue to visit Cardiff for the Fellows' Annual Dinner held in July. Kathleen was also a Fellow, so I had a companion; that summer for the first time I went to the annual dinner: Kathleen and I sallied forth in best bib and tucker for the occasion.

1984 was my first summer back in England, and I delighted in the ephemeral nature of blossom and leaf. There are many gardens open to the public in Devon and Cornwall. I visited as many as I could such as Cotehele, Killerton, Lukesland and Trengwainton.

The pattern of the landscape, the field systems with their hedgerows and the villages, were all things I could rediscover with a fresh eye. So too were the towns like Totnes, with their mixture of vernacular and period architecture and twentieth-century additions, all missing in New Zealand.

Further afield, I resumed contact with Maurice and Diana Barley in Nottingham; Peter and Shelly Addyman in York; Gerald and Gwen Collier in Durham; Ann Hamlin in Belfast; and Richard and Paula Allison in Edinburgh. Some I visited and some came down to see me, as would my sister Mari with Peter from Cambridge.

So within a year I had settled into a rhythm of life that was agreeable and varied, but, more importantly, I had through the Devon Archaeological Society created a niche for myself in local archaeology, which was the stimulation I wanted, and which satisfied my need to keep in touch. In the society I developed firm friendships, especially with Henrietta Quinnell.

I had long been associated with the Exeter Civic Society and found it now, under Hazel Harvey and Bill Hallet, continuing with a better relationship with the planning department of the city council, and the views of the society were respected. I was particularly pleased with the development of the quay, and took over from Hallet a campaign for the repair of the Custom House there, and for a limited opening to the public to see the fine seventeenth-century plasterwork.

Susan Pearce, the curator of the museum until 1984, had considerably smartened up archaeology. She was to be followed by John Allan, a man of wide interests, and a pottery expert. There is now an interesting sequence of local British prehistoric and historic displays. Reserve material in the stores has been organised and catalogued for the first time. I mention this as it is important that regional museums should offer the student well-displayed and annotated material.

Most years I went to the Mediterranean in the spring or to the Alps in early summer for the flowers. It was a chance to revisit familiar sites, where so often you return to see them with a different perspective, or to see new ones like the Alhambra or Cyprus. I travelled with my old friend Joyce Youings, or George, who was working in Europe.

The following year, 1985, I returned to Crete, where Knossos seemed ordinary after my excited first impressions on my first visit to Heraklion in the twenties when Evans was making his extraordinary discoveries. I was then on a Henry Lunn Hellenic cruise with my father, beginning to make contact with the ancient world. I should add, though, that the museum in Heraklion today is a testament to scholarship and good display. However, I feel, as Lawrence Durrell did, that the Palace of Phaestos in southern Crete, with its great flight of steps, has retained much more mystery and splendour. In Chania I was able with the help of local archaeologists to examine the remains of the Venetian walled town and the buildings which they used for ship construction. It was really quite remarkable that only recently they were still being used for the same purpose: some five hundred years of continuous use.

The flowers in Crete in early spring are astonishing, especially the extraordinary number of different orchids; how odd it was to find *Aubretia deltoidea* high up in the mountains, instead of in a suburban garden.

I was to see some more of the Venetian empire when I visited Rhodes with Joyce another year. Though the Italian restoration of the walls and the Knights Templars' citadel was rather overdone, it gave one a real feeling of place and style. Rhodes is an unspoilt island, particularly the small mountain, Profitis Elias, its wooded slopes covered with wild blue anemones and small white peonies.

In July 1985 I was delighted to be awarded an honorary degree by Exeter University: suitably clad in scarlet and blue and with a becoming black velvet cap, I paced up the aisle in the Great Hall to the sound of Brahms's *Academic Festival Overture* in the company of Sir Michael Hordern, who confessed to being very nervous. I thought, as we paced, that this made up for the years of struggling to get archaeology recognised in academic circles.

I missed out on Christmas that year, as I had to go into hospital in Bristol for a hysterectomy, performed by Gillian Turner, a skilled surgeon. I soon recovered, and in March flew out to see George, who was living in Provence. We made many excursions, sometimes in the chill of a mistral; before then I had never realised how unpleasant a wind it is. I was expecting warm sunny days, only to find that the weather can be capricious even on the shores of the Mediterranean. The last time I had been in that part of the world was with Leslie Murray-Thriepland, which made me think about lost friends: she had been so close, and we had gone through so much together. I purposefully went back to a site that we had explored together in 1967: the Roman aqueducts of Barbegal, a big pumping station on the southern slopes, between Arles and St Rémy. I have to admit that I did not make much more sense of it than we had twenty years previously.

The towns in Provence still seduce with their sandy stone houses and orange tiles. The large cities are impressive: Avignon, Aix, Arles, Nîmes, and just below the surface you are back in the Roman province of Gallia Narbonensis. It is easy to see the Roman imprint on these towns, indicated by the walls and the grid of streets. However, 300 years earlier the Greeks were colonising and setting up trading posts in Gaul, like Marseilles *(Massilia)* and Ampurias *(Emporiae)* just over the border in Catalonia. They were taking advantage of the natural wealth of grain, oil, wine from the plains, and metals from the hinterland in the Cevennes. They had to contend with the local Celto-Ligurian tribes, who built well-fortified settlements. Above Aix-en-Provence, there is one important site called Entremont, (400 BC) and another outside Béziers, the *oppidum* of Ensérune (600 BC). To see clearly this succession of settlement and evidence of trade is the very stuff of archaeology, and is for me one of the charms of Provence. The only time we got caught out on that trip was when we went to to the Camargue to see the flamingos, but we had not reckoned on the mosquitoes. We were forced to turn back to the car, pursued by a voracious cloud of them, and this was only March.

In 1986 we were to celebrate my sister Mari and Peter's golden wedding, and in 1987 my eightieth birthday. Mari's party was held in the grounds of Finella, on the Backs in Cambridge, previously occupied by Manny Forbes. It was one of those perfect summer days in June, with the roses in full bloom and a slight breeze rippling the trees in the garden.

Part of my eightieth birthday celebrations was to visit the Alps and to explore a region with a rich flora previously unknown to me, around the Col du Lautaret and the Galibier Pass. For two short months the Alps are filled with flowers that have an astonishing brilliance and vivid colour, like the the tiny yellow primula (*Vitaliana primuliflora*) or the bright red saxifrage (*Saxifraga biflora*) in the scree. We were able, with the modern network of roads over the high passes, to see the alpine flowers without having to trudge up through the woods for a couple of hours. What I remember with pleasure was the charming valley, the Val-des-Près, written about so eloquently by Emilie Carles in her book, *A Wild Herb Soup*. Also the *quatorze juillet* celebrations in Monêtier-les-Bains which included folk dancing that had a great intensity, part of the rites of passage for the young in those small alpine communities, isolated for so many months of the year. It was nothing like our English morris dancing!

The birthday party soon afterwards in Exeter was a real celebration, a dinner party for twelve at the White Hart Hotel. Little did I imagine then that I would be alive to enjoy my ninetieth birthday ten years later.

In the sitting room at The Retreat there is a window seat where I often used to perch with my binoculars to see what birds were on the river. From here the channel widens, meandering within half a mile to a broad expanse of water at full tide. Opposite the house downstream there is a large eyot or estuary island, and the curves of the river around it are always pleasing. The daily cycle of low and high water is unchanging, always moving forward by an hour, so when waking you can be caught by the water positively brimming, or by muddy islets surrounded by shrinking pools of iron-coloured water. The tall reeds, changing colour with the seasons, cluster in the river mud and stretch away to water meadows beyond the canal. The estuary is always shot through by the changing moods of light, sometimes obscured by low cloud and slanting rain, or dancing in a bright sparkle of white light on blue water. I have always loved this landscape. In the late summer flocks of starlings whirl and skirl in the evening before diving down into the reeds for the night. In the early morning in January you may catch goldeneye ducks plopping and diving, leaving only traces of bubbles, or a pair of red-breasted mergansers. Over the years the numbers of birds have diminished, but Topsham and Dawlish Warren are not far away, where there are hundreds if not thousands of waders and migrating birds in spring and autumn.

In 1985 the Devon Archaeological Society decided to make a series of archaeological sites more intelligible to the general public by setting up plaques with plans and information, and by producing field guides and pamphlets for sale at modest prices of 30p–50p. I was fully in sympathy with the project, and offered to collaborate. I produced three guides, one for Milber Down, an elaborate hill-slope fort near Newton Abbot; and the others for the Roman fortlets at Martinhoe, and at Old Burrow, Countisbury, on the north Devon coast, dated to the mid first century AD by my excavations with Bill Ravenhill.

Later at the request of Simon Timms, an archaeologist from Devon County Council, I agreed to write a booklet about prehistoric hill-forts in Devon. I already had notebooks with descriptions, and Cyril's plans made in 1949–63, but I needed to revisit most of the sites, assisted by Tony and Rosalind Payton. Illustrated with new diagrams, plans and aerial photographs, with a simple instructive introduction to a list of forty-eight sites, it was published in 1996 by Devon Books.[1] It fulfilled my wish to make archaeological sites appreciated and more widely understood, and to promote their conservation. It is ironic that today we are having to restrict damage by the feet of too many tourists, as at Stonehenge, though it is doubtful that this will ever apply to Devon hill-forts.

During this period two significant articles of mine were published in the Devon Archaeological Society's *Proceedings*. The first was an architectural history of The Retreat, written when I had to leave my flat for nine months owing to the threat of collapse of the building, caused by alterations to the basement flat. This caused much worry and expense at the time. Three hundred years previously, in 1684, the building was a 'Sugar House', a refinery landing supplies of molasses from the West Indies at the quay, until the industry declined. Captain Robert Orme, whose portrait by Joshua Reynolds is in the National Gallery, converted it into a mansion in 1772. He sold it in 1790 to Sir Alec Hamilton, whose descendants lived there until 1929.[2]

The other article was due to a unique find by divers of over forty tin ingots in Bigbury Bay, at the mouth of the Erme estuary in South Devon. Unfortunately there was no dating material with them. I interpreted them as a wreck of a Mediterranean trader, collecting tin from Dartmoor along the south coast in exchange for amphorae of wine or oil in the post-Roman period, probably the fifth or sixth century. Characteristic sherds of the amphorae have been found at nearby Bantham and Mothecombe, as well as at Tintagel on the Cornish coast.[3]

I wrote this autobiography digging deep into my memory with enjoyment, teasing out the facts. I never thought when I travelled back to Exeter in 1983 that I should live for more than fifteen further years. I remained physically active and able to write, up to my ninetieth birthday, even travelling to Rome, having a wonderful time revisiting the Roman sites that had so fashioned my career and influenced me in my youth. George was in Rome, and took me to see one of the treasures that I had missed. It had been worth waiting all those years to see the Ducal Palace at Urbino. Little seems to have changed there since the fifteenth century, from the walls that bind the town, to the maze of medieval streets within the walls, to the great square where the long flank of the palace stands. Inside there is a series of grand rooms on the *piano nobile* that have a harmony and detail that must be some of the finest of the Renaissance period.

Looking back over the years, it has been a good and happy life on balance, with plenty of variety, and with tenacity of purpose once I had discovered archaeology. I had seen great changes from my early years of pampered existence, reliant on Nanny and many servants, to the days of do-it-yourself. I had been a rebel against a wealthy, idle society and its values in the 1920s, until discovering at Cambridge those of scholarship, the importance of getting to the source and of not being satisfied with things at second-hand, whether a poem or a dramatist or, later, an excavation report or a newly-found object in a museum.

I never regretted changing my post-graduate career to archaeology: it led incidentally to a deeply satisfying marriage in which I shared so many interests with Cyril. Our age gap never seemed to matter, though I knew he would predecease me. His loss was to a certain extent made up by my three sons, and by my archaeological writings.

T. S. Eliot in his elegiac poem 'Ash Wednesday' wrote, 'I cannot hope to turn again'; old age and infirmity now make this bitter truth a sad reality for me, as I know I must be nearing the end of the road.

Book List

1952   *Roman Exeter: Excavations in the War-Damaged Areas 1945–47* Manchester UP .

1961   [with Alan Sorrell] *Roman Britain* Lutterworth. (for children).

1964   *South West England* Thames and Hudson.

1973   *South West England 3500 BC–AD 600* 2nd ed. Revised, David and Charles.

1976   *Prehistoric Maori Fortifications in the North Island of New Zealand* Longman Paul.

1978   *Tiromoana Pa, Te Awanga, Hawkes Bay: Excavations 1974–5* New Zealand Archaeological Association. Monograph 8.

1983   *Carved Maori Burial Chests* Bulletin 13 Auckland Institute Museum.

1996   *Prehistoric Hillforts in Devon* Devon Books.

A complete bibliography from 1934 to 1979 is published in *Prehistoric Dartmoor in its Context*, Devon Archaeologocial Society compiled by Valerie A. Maxwell and from 1974 to 1985 in *A Lot of Spadework to be Done* New Zealand Archaeological Association Monograph No 14, Editors Susan E. Bulmer, R. Garry Law, Douglas G. Sutton.

References

Abbreviations:

Archaeol.	Archaeological
J.	Journal
Mus.	Museum
Rec.	Records
Proc.	Proceedings
Soc.	Society
TDA.	Transactions Devonshire Association
UP.	University Press

Contents Page

'To A Friend'
'My special thanks, whose even-balanced soul,
From first youth tested up to extreme old age,
Business could not make dull, nor passion wild;
Who saw life steadily and saw it whole.'

Miriam Allott (ed.) (1979) *The Poems of Matthew Arnold,* 2nd rev. p.
111. New York: Longman Group Ltd.

Chapter 1

1 Spunt, G: *A Place in Time* (1969).
2 Manson-Barr, P: *Life of Patrick Manson.*
3 *Stephenson Harwood 1828–1978*, p. 11.
       (privately-printed brochure).
4 *Bankers' Magazine*, 1899.

Chapter 2

(No notes in Chapter 2.)

Chapter 3

1   Chippindale, C. (1984) : Clarence Bicknell - Science and archaeology in the nineteenth century. *Antiquity* 58, pp. 172–81; and (1998): *A Highway to Heaven.* Univ. Mus. of Archaeology and Anthropology.
2   Anati, E. (1964): *Camonica Valley - A depiction of village life in the Alps from Neolithic times to the birth of Christ as revealed by thousands of newly-found rock carvings* (trans. from French by Linda Asher). London.
3   Burkitt, M. C. (1929): Rock carvings in the Italian Alps, *Antiquity* 3, pp. 155–64.
4   Fox A. and Sorrell. A. (1961): *Roman Britain.* Lutterworth Press.
5   Toynbee, J. M. C. (1962): *Art in Roman Britain.* London. p. 108, pl. 121.
6   Bushe-Fox, J. P. (1932): *[Excavations of the Roman fort at]Richborough, [Kent]* 3. Oxford UP, p. 18, pl. 96; and Cunliffe, B.W. (1968): *[Excavations of the Roman fort at] Richborough, [Kent]* 5. Oxford UP, p. 234.
7   Bushe-Fox, J. P. (1932): *ibid.* pl. 7.

Chapter 4

1   Evans, Joan (1956): *A History of the Society of Antiquaries.* Oxford UP. pp. 288–89.
2   Piggott, Stuart (1965): *Ancient Europe from the beginnings of agriculture to classical antiquity - a survey.* Edinburgh UP.
3   Liddell, D. M. (1930): Report on the excavations at Hembury fort, Devon, 1930. *Proc. Devon Archaeol. and Exploration Soc.* 1 for 1929–32, pl. 9.
4   Fox, A. (1963): Neolithic charcoal from Hembury. *Antiquity* 37, pp. 228–229.
5   Liddell, D. M. (1934): Excavations at Meon Hill. *Proc. Hants Field Club and Archaeol. Soc.* 12, 127–137; and (1936) 13, pp. 7–60.
6   Bersu, G. (1940): Excavations at Little Woodbury, Wiltshire. *Proc. Prehistoric Soc.* 6, pp. 30–111.
7   Hencken, T. Cruso (1938): The excavation of the Iron Age camp on Bredon Hill, Gloucestershire, 1935–7. *Archaeol. J.* 95, pp. 1–111.

Chapter 5

1   Fox, A. (1936): The dual colonisation of east Glamorgan in the Neolithic and Bronze Ages. *Archaeol. Cambrensis.* 91, pp. 100–17.
2   Fox, A. (1939): The siting of some inscribed stones of the Dark Ages in Glamorgan and Breconshire. *Archaeol. Cambrensis.* 94, pp. 30–41.

3 Fox, C. (1936): Caer Dynnaf, Llanblethian: A hillfort of early Iron Age type in the Vale of Glamorgan. *Archaeol. Cambrensis*. 91, pp. 20–4.

4 *Royal Commission Ancient and Historic Monuments Wales, Glamorgan*. 1 (part 2) for 1976. pp. 40–1. Cardiff.

5 Savory, H. N. (1954): The excavation of an early Iron Age fortified settlement on Mynydd Bychan, Llysworney (Glam.), 1949–50: part one. *Archaeol. Cambrensis*. pp. 85–108.

6 Fox, A. and Murray-Threipland, L. (1942): The excavation of two cairn cemeteries near Hirwaun, Glamorgan. *Archaeol. Cambrensis*. 97, pp. 77–92.

7 *Royal Commission Ancient and Historic Monuments Wales, Glamorgan*. 1 (part 2) for 1976. Cardiff pp. 105–20.

8 *Royal Commission Ancient and Historic Monuments Wales, Glamorgan*. 1 (part 3) for 1976. Cardiff pp. 5–11.

9 Fox, C. and Fox, A. (1934): Forts and farms on Margam mountain, Glamorgan. *Antiquity* 8, no. 32. pp. 395–413.

10 Fox, A. (1953): Hillslope forts and related earthworks in south-west England and South Wales. *Archaeol. J.* 109. pp. 1–22.

11 Frere, S. S. (ed.) (1961): *Problems of the Iron Age in southern Britain – Papers given at a conference held at the Institute of Archaeology, December 12--14, 1958*. London. p. 35.

12 Fox, A. (1936): The dual colonisation of East Glamorgan in the Neolithic and Bronze Ages. *Archaeol. Cambrensis*. 91. pp. 100–117.

13 Fox, C. *Archaeologia*. 87. p. 137.

14 Fox, A. (1937): Dinas Noddfa, Gellygaer Common, Glamorgan - excavations in 1936. *Archaeol. Cambrensis*. 92. pp. 247–68.

15 Fox, A. (1939): Early Welsh homesteads on Gelligaer Common, Glamorgan. *Archaeol. Cambrensis*. 94. pp. 163–99.

16 *Royal Commission Ancient and Historic Monuments Wales, Glamorgan*. 3 for 1976. Cardiff. 17; Beresford, M. and Hurst, J. (eds.) (1971): *Deserted medieval villages*. Woking; Robinson, D. M. (1981–2): Medieval vernacular buildings below the ground. *Glamorgan Gwent Archaeol. Trust*. p. 84.

17 Fox, A. (1937): Dinas Noddfa, Gellygaer Common, Glamorgan - excavations in 1936. *Archaeol. Cambrensis*. 92. fig. 4, p. 252.

18 Fox, A. (1940): The legionary fortress at Caerleon, Monmouthshire: Excavations in Myrtle Cottage orchard, 1939. *Archaeol. Cambrensis*. 95. fig. 3, p. 108, pl. 7, p. 124.

19 Wheeler, R. E. M. and Richardson, K. (1957): *Hillforts of northern France*. London.

Chapter 6

1 Kendrick, T. (1940): The Sutton Hoo ship burial. *Antiquity* 14, no. 53.

pp. 6–112.

2   Fox, C. (1943): A Bronze Age barrow (Sutton 268) in Llandow parish, Glamorganshire. *Archaeologia*. pp. 89–126.

3   Fox, C. (1946): *A find of the early Iron Age from Llyn Cerrig Bach Anglesey.* National Museum of Wales. Cardiff.

4   Fox, A. (1944): The place of archaeology in British education. *Antiquity* 18, no. 71. 1944. pp. 153–7.

5   Fox, A. (1946): The school teaching of Roman Britain. *Greece and Rome* 15, no. 44. pp. 42–8.

6   Fox, C. (1940): The re-erection of Maen Madoc, Ystradfellte, Breconshire. *Archaeol. Cambrensis*. 95. p. 211.

7   Fox, A. (1952): *Roman Exeter (Isca Dumnoniorum): Excavations in the war-damaged areas 1945–7* Manchester UP. p. 17.

8   Fox, A. (1968): Excavations at the South Gate, Exeter, 1964–5. *Proc. Devon Archaeol. Soc.* 26. p. 1–20.

9   Bidwell, P. T. (1980): *Roman Exeter: Fortress and Town.* Exeter.

10 Fox, A. (1952): ibid. pl.Xa.

11 Fox, A. (1952): ibid. p. 92.

12 Henderson, C. G. and Bidwell, P. T. (1982): *The Saxon Minster at Exeter*. BAR report, Oxford. p. 45.

13 Fox, C. (1934): Presidential address: *Museums J.*

14 Fox, A. (1955): Some evidence for a Dark Age trading site at Bantham, near Thurlestone, south Devon. *Antiquaries J.* 35. pp. 55–67.

15 Fox, A. (1951): The date of the Orpheus mosaic from The Barton, Cirencester Park. *Trans. Bristol and Gloucestershire Archeaol. Soc.* 70. pp. 51–3.

Chapter 7

1   Fox, A. (1949): Sixteenth report on the early history of Devon. *TDA*. pp. 85–8.

2   Fox, A. (1950): Two Greek silver coins from Holne, south Devon. *Antiquaries J.* 30. pp. 152–5.

3   Fox, A. (1961): An Iron Age bowl from Rose Ash, North Devon. *Antiquaries J.* 41. pp. 186–98.

4   Fox, A. (1955): Some evidence for a Dark Age trading site at Bantham, near Thurlestone, south Devon. *Antiquaries J.* 35. pp. 55–67.

5   Fox, A. (1948): The Broad Down (Farway) necropolis and the Wessex culture in Devon. *Proc. Devon Archaeol. and Explor. Soc.* 4. pp. 1–19.

6   Curwen, E. Cecil, (1927): Prehistoric agriculture in Britain. *Antiquity* 1. pp. 261–89.

7   Fox, A. (1964): *South-West England, 3500 BC to AD 600.* Newton Abbot. fig. 25. p. 101.

8 Fox, A. (1954): Celtic fields and farms on Dartmoor: In the light of recent excavations at Kestor. *Proc. Prehistoric Soc.* 20. pp. 87–102.
9 Fleming, A. (1988): *The Dartmoor reaves: Investigating Prehistoric land divisions*. London.
10 Fox, A. (1957): Excavations on Dean Moor, in the Avon Valley, 1954–56: The late Bronze Age settlement. *TDA.* 89. pp. 18–77.
11 Fox, A. (1958): A Monastic Homestead on Dean Moor. *Med. Arch.* 2.
12 Fox, A. (1969): A continental palstave from the ancient field system on Horridge Common, Dartmoor. *Proc. Prehist. Soc.* 70. pp. 220–8.
13 Clark, A. (1958): The nature of Wansdyke. *Antiquity* 32. pp. 89–96.
14 Fox, A. and Fox, C. (1958): Wansdyke Reconsidered. *Archaeol. J.* 115. p. 4, fig. 2
15 Fox, A. and Fox, C. (1958): ibid. p. 29, fig. 20.
16 Myres, J. N. L. (1965): Wansdyke and the origin of Wessex, in H. R. Trevor-Roper (ed.) *Essays in British History*. London. pp. 1–28.
17 Fox, A. and Fox, C. (1958): *ibid.* p. 160.
18 Fox, C. (1958): Pattern and Purpose. *Nat. Mus. Wales.*
19 Fox, C. (1959): *Life and Death in the Bronze Age.* Routledge.

Chapter 8

1 Fox, A. (1959): The Stoke Hill Roman Signal Station Excavations, *1956–7. TDA,* 91. pp. 71–82.
2 Fox, A. and Ravenhill, W. (1966): Roman Outposts on the North Devon Coast, Old Burrow and Martinoe. *Proc. Dev. Archaeol. Soc.* 24. pp. 3–39.
3 Fox, A. and Ravenhill, W. (1972): The Roman fort at Nanstallon, Cornwall. *Britannia* 3. pp. 56–111.
4 Megaw, J. V. S. (1970): *Art of the European Iron Age: A study of the elusive image*. Bath. p. 212, p. 236.
5 Jouffrey, R. (1954): *Le Tresor de Vix*. Paris; Cunliffe, B. (1988): *Greeks, Romans and Barbarians: Spheres of interaction*. London. pp. 29–32.
6 Bidwell, P. T. (1979): *The legionary bath-house and basilica and forum at Exeter, with a summary account of the legionary fortress.* Exeter; Henderson, C. G. and Bidwell, P. T. (1982): The Saxon minster at Exeter, in S. H. Pearce (ed.) *The early church in western Britain and Ireland*. BAR. report, Oxford. pp. 145–75.
7 Fox, A. and Pollard, S. (1973): A decorated Bronze Age mirror from an Iron Age settlement at Holcombe, near Uplyme, Devon. *Antiquaries J.* 53. pp. 23–4.

Chapter 9

1 Bellwood, P. (1971): Fortifications and economy in prehistoric New Zealand. *Proc. Prehist. Soc.* 37. pp. 56–95.

2   Daniels, J. R. (1970): *A site recording handbook*.
3   Fox, A. (1974): Prehistoric storage pits: problems in interpretation. *J. Polynesian Soc.* 83 (2), pp. 141–154.
4   Fox, A. (1978): Tiromoana Pa, Te Awanga, Hawke's Bay; Excavations 1974–75. *Studies in Prehistoric Anthropology* 2. Otago University.
5   Fox, A. (1976): *Prehistoric Maori fortifications in the North island of New Zealand*. Longman Paul.
6   Fox, A. (1976): Site recording in the Auckland Province, 1975–6. *New Zealand Archaeol. Assoc. Newsletter* 19. pp. 139–41.
7   Prickett, N. (ed.) (1982): *The first thousand years: regional perspectives in New Zealand archaeology*. pp. 62–81.
8   Fox, A. (1976): Pa and other sites in the Parua Bay district, Whangaroa, Northland. *Rec. Auckland Inst. Mus.* 13. pp.13–27.
9   Oliver, A. Murray, (1968): *Augustus Earle in New Zealand*.
10 Spencer, J. H. (1983): in A Lot of Spadework to be done, (ed. S. Bulmer, G. Law, D. Sutton). *N. Z. Arch. Ass.* Monograph 14. p. 77.
11 Fox, A. (1977): Pa of the Auckland Isthmus. *Rec. Auckland Inst. Mus.* 14. pp. 1–24.

Chapter 10
1   Fox, A. (1980): The pa on Mount Roskill, Auckland; 1961 excavations. *Rec. Auckland Inst. Mus.* 16, pp. 45–61.
2   Fox, A. (with R.C. Green), (1982): Excavations at Maioro, South Auckland, 1965–6. *Rec. Auckland Inst. Mus.* 19, pp. 53–80.
3   Fox, A. (with R. Cassels), (1983): Excavations at Aotea, Waikato, 1972–5. *Rec. Auckland Inst. Mus.* 20, pp. 65–106.
4   Fox, A. (1980): A new look at Maori burial chests. *Antiquity* 54. pp. 7–14.
5   Fox, A. (1983): Carved Maori burial chests: a commentary and a catalogue. *Auckland Inst. Mus. Bulletin* 13. pp. 13–27.
6   Fox, A. (1985): Okuratope Pa, Waimate, Bay of Islands. *Rec. Aukland Inst. Mus.* 22: pp. 1–15.
7   Prickett, N. (ed.) (1982): *The first thousand years: regional perspectives in New Zealand archaeology*. pp. 62–81.

Chapter 11
1   Fox, A. (1996): *Prehistoric hillforts in Devon*. Tiverton.
2   Fox, A. (1991): The Retreat, Topsham. *Proc. Devon Archaeol. Soc.* 49. pp. 131–141.
3   Fox, A. (1995): Tin ingots from Bigbury Bay, South Devon. *Proc. Devon Archaeol. Soc.* 53. pp. 11–23.

INDEX

university field trips 132
Dartmouth College 116, 125
Davidson, Janet 153–4, 158, 159, 160, 164, 177–8
Davies, Prof. Arthur 130
Dean Moor, excavations 64, 119–20, 132
Devon
  Bronze Age barrows 114–15, 117
  bronze Iron Age bowl 114
  Dark Age trading sites 107, 114
  Dartmoor 117–20
  Greek coins 113–14
  hill-forts 67–8, 82–3, 114–15, 120, 159, 187
  Martinhoe and Old Burrow fortlets 135–6, 187
  Stoke Hill Roman signal station 135
Devon Archaeological Society 67, 104, 113, 145, 149, 182, 184, 187
Devon County Council, and Archaeological Consultancy 143–4
Devonshire Association 113, 117
Devonshire, Deborah Cavendish, 11th Duchess 129
Dinas Noddfa see Gelligaer Common
Dobson, Dinah 101
Dolomites, and plant collecting 34
Downe House school 27–8, 35, 36
Dunning, Gerald 60
Durrell, Lawrence 184

Eames, John (husband of Penelope Fox) 103
Earle, Augustus 153, 162
Ede, Max & Kathleen 79, 183
Eliot, T. S. 42, 188
Elliott, Clarence 33
Epsom Races 24
Evans, Arthur 60, 184
Exeter
  Civic Society 142, 184
  excavation 102–6, 108, 117, 136, 149
  Museum 112, 114, 117, 129
  St Leonard's Road (house) 109, 115–16, 121, 125, 139–40
Exeter Archaeological Field Unit 105, 144
Exeter University
  AF's Special Lectureship 108–10, 111–13, 126–7, 129–30, 137, 140

AF's teaching methods 98, 111–12
and archaeology department 127, 137–8, 182
and Exeter excavations 144
and field work 132–3
as full university 111, 127, 129–30
halls of residence 111, 134–5
and history department 112, 129–32, 137–8, 182
and honorary degree for AF 78, 134, 185
Readers' and Lecturers' Association 133–4, 137
Staff Club 131, 134

farming, knowledge of 14–15
Farrer, Reginald 31–2
Finella (Cambridge home of Mari Bicknell) 41–2, 186
Firth, Raymond 146
Fleming, Andrew 118, 120
Forbes, Mansfield ('Manny') 41–2, 88, 186
Forster, E. M. 42, 164
Fowler, Charles (architect) 142
Fox, Charles Scott (son of AF) 1, 72, 83–5, 102, 109, 139
  education 90, 93, 103, 116, 125
  and the navy 116, 125, 139, 182
  in New Zealand 162
  Second World War evacuation 96
Fox, Cyril
  archaeology
    archaeological drawings 86, 107, 118, 120, 122–3
    Bronze Age barrows, Glamorgan 85, 95–6, 97
    collaboration with AF 81, 86, 121–2
    field survey of Glamorgan 81–3, 85
    and Llyn Cerrig Bach discovery 97–8
    Offa's Dyke 82, 85, 96–7, 121, 122
    Wansdyke survey 121–2
  as Cambrian Archaeological Association President 78, 84
  as Council for British Archaeology President 101, 106
  daughters 69, 70, 71–2, 84
  death 138–9, 188